"Jesus turned water into wine. Jon turns sand into pearls. From the confessions of a mega-church pastor in Virginia, to the challenges of starting micro-churches in Brussels, Belgium, Jon shows us how to face the sandstorms of our present age. Now, as he works with pioneering artists in Hollywood, the sand is turning into pearls of wisdom. This book will help you see how the church can be set free from restrictive paradigms by engaging in disruptive discipleship, following in the way of Jesus."

—JR WOODWARD, national director, The V3 Movement; author, *Creating a Missional Culture*; co-author, *The Church as Movement*

"*Irritating and inspiring*—that is how Jon Ritner describes the life of the gospel; the great pearl that is formed in the depths of the sea. In the same way, Ritner's book is both an irritating exposé of the cultural blind spots of Christendom religion and a transparent memoir of his own inspiring journey of spiritual transformation. With his wisdom and experience, he offers church leaders an invitation and pathway for their own irritating and inspiring transformation. I believe that in the post-pandemic church, this book will become required reading. It certainly will be for the students I teach and pastors I coach."

—TOD BOLSINGER, Fuller Seminary; author, *Canoeing the Mountains*

"In this age of evangelical crisis, Christian leaders need a clear, practical guide for navigating the murky waters of effective ministry in post-Christian contexts. Ritner's book couples compelling, vulnerable narrative with applicable missional principles and will have you immediately considering ways to put these ideas into practice."

—LISA RODRIGUEZ-WATSON, national director, Missio Alliance

"In *Positively Irritating*, Jon does a masterful job of gleaning from his diverse experiences as a mega-church pastor, a microchurch planter in a European context, and his current role in creating a missionary culture in an existing congregation in Hollywood. He weaves all this together to provide a framework for the church to move toward more fully engaging in God's mission. If you are looking for a guide to help navigate these very uncertain times, this book is an obvious place to start."

—**BRAD BRISCO, director, Bivocational Church Planting, the Send Network; author, *Missional Essentials* co-author, *Next Door as It Is in Heaven***

"Jon has offered us a great gift: insightful, timely, honest reflections on discipleship in this era. The future of the church will depend on us grappling with new ways to engage in our current culture, and this essential and difficult task has been made much easier with this guide!"

—**DANIELLE STRICKLAND, leader, author, speaker**

"The church is being buffeted by rapid and continuous cultural shifts toward secularization. Jon Ritner says either you can complain about how irritating those changes are or you can embrace the challenge of adaptive leadership as we come to the end of the age of cultural Christianity. One feels like sand in your eyes. The other is like sand in an oyster shell. His is an inspiring and challenging message of revitalization and reimagination for the church."

—**MICHAEL FROST, Morling College, Sydney; co-founder, Forge International; author, *Surprise the World* and *The Road to Missional*; co-author, *The Shaping of Things to Come***

"Jon offers Spirit-led innovation and fresh thinking that is crucial in these turbulent times. He also delivers real-life practices that he has actually lived out in a variety of contexts. Bring your staff or fellow church leaders around a table to discuss the ideas in this book, as they will not only stretch you personally, they could transform your church and your entire city!"

—**JON FERGUSON, co-founder, Community Christian Church and NewThing; co-author, *Finding Your Way Back to God***

"In a rapidly changing context, pastors often find themselves disoriented and flummoxed with this unknown missional frontier. With experience in a wide range of ministry contexts, Jon calls the church to embrace her new reality with innovation and faithfulness to God's vision for God's people in God's world. Jon helps church leaders better step into this new reality with practical ideas for churches to more deeply understand their contexts and live into the fullness of their gifts as a healthy expression of God's people on mission."

—TARA BETH LEACH, pastor; author, *Emboldened*

"This book is a primer for the revolution. A perfectly weighted treatment of some of the most pressing and transformative ideas in our time."

—BRIAN SANDERS, founder, the Underground Network; author, *Microchurches* and *Underground Church*

"With a global worldview and grounded in personal practice, Jon Ritner helps us see our current circumstances with the vision of Jesus for the future of the church. When we learn to see differently, we are compelled to live, lead, and love differently. This book helps us see!"

—CHRISTIANA RICE, co-director, the Parish Collective; co-author, *To Alter Your World*

"The model church of the New Testament is Antioch: it was missional, multi-ethnic, and multiplying. So now must the church become in the United States. In *Positively Irritating*, Jon Ritner draws upon his experience in the post-Christian context of Europe to imagine a more inventive, entrepreneurial, and scattered expression of Christ-centered engagement in the community, through which a credible witness of God's love for all people can permeate an increasingly diverse, polarized, and cynical society."

—DR. MARK DEYMAZ, founding pastor/directional leader, Mosaic Church of Central Arkansas; co-founder/ president, Mosaix Global Network; author, *Disruption* and *The Coming Revolution in Church Economics*

"In an incredibly honest and transparent unveiling, Ritner invites us into his journey of unlearning an individualistic, inauthentic, and reductionist gospel that seduces with power and platform in a post-Christendom world. Instead, as he himself describes, he becomes more 'fluent in the gospel.' He is undone by this collectivistic, incarnational, and holistic gospel of Jesus Christ that decenters the lone celebrity pastor and recenters the priesthood of believers. He recaptures the sacred sent-ness of the loving church into the world with a more credible and authentic Christ through its more compassionate and caring Christians. The idols come down. The kingdom rises up. The King is front and center."

—INÉS VELASQUEZ-MCBRYDE, pastor, speaker, reconciler; chaplain, Fuller Theological Seminary

"Jon Ritner has written a deeply personal and powerful story about 'the disorienting sandstorm of post-Christian culture.' His compelling description and diagnosis of navigating post-Christian Europe and America made me nod my head on every other page in knowing familiarity. And his prescriptions for reversing our traditional discipleship pathways are as disruptive as they are necessary to embody a relevant gospel today. I commend this to every planter and pastor as a glimpse into the future."

—LEN TANG, director, Church Planting Initiative, Fuller Seminary

"Jon is a practitioner who understands how to adapt and innovate in one of the most challenging environments in the West. Thought leaders can tell you what to think, but Jon leads an innovative community you should follow. We need more leaders with the vision and boldness Jon has!"

—ALAN BRIGGS, author; leadership coach; founder, Stay Forth Designs

"It is so refreshing to read a book that exemplifies the imagination needed for our cultural moment. Jon Ritner pulls from his breadth of experience to gift the church a framework for approaching a changing world with openness and possibility rather than mistrust or fear. In doing so, he advocates the sort of perpetual innovation that is desperately needed. Jon invites us to join in his journey, not as one arrived, but as one who will keep seeking. Leaders who desire to create a culture of innovation will be equipped and encouraged."

—ONEYA F. OKUWOBI, co-founding elder, 21st Century Church; co-author, *Multiethnic Conversations*

"I'm grateful for the unique cultural perspective Jon offers in *Positively Irritating*, which has arisen from his experience both in the North American and European church. With practical insights and analogies, he shares how to navigate the changing landscape of church and the disruptive terrains of our world during this time of seismic transition."

—DAVE GIBBONS, founder, Newsong Church and Yohaus; author, *Small Cloud Rising*

"Jon Ritner has written a paradigm-shifting book, grounded in the personal account of his journey from megachurch to missionary and then back into leading a church in Hollywood. In compelling form, this book confirms some of our fears but also gives us a road map of redemption and equipping. Jon is a servant leader and an incredible gift to leaders and pastors as they navigate this new world of post-Christendom. Though he is an accomplished communicator, Jon has chosen not to build a church around his own gifts but instead on the equipping and sending of others. His journey and personal sacrifice will minister to you as you serve the church and want to send its people into the world."

—KIM HAMMOND, president, the Forge global board; founder, Forge America; pastor, CityLife Church, Casey, Australia; co-author, *Sentness*

"Through the prism of his personal leadership journey, Jon inspires the reader with a delightful mix of story, Scripture, and the practical how-tos of going with the gospel. If you desire to move from the standard Sunday-centric way of doing church and instead become someone who forms disciplemakers wherever people live, work, play, and create, then this book is a hugely enjoyable and encouraging must-read!"

—**HANNAH ABSALOM, co-founder, Dandelion Resourcing; co-author,** *Hearing the Voice of God*

"Through his own life and experience in post-Christian Europe, Jon shares a gritty portrait of what it can look like for us to incarnate the gospel in a missional context. Using stories of failure and success, Jon shares valuable insights about how we can respond to this cultural moment we find ourselves in. Inspirational, practical, and timely—a must-read for all missional practitioners."

—**TIM CATCHIM, church planter and coach; co-author,** *The Permanent Revolution*

"There is no shortage of people who theorize about the future, but Jon Ritner has journeyed there, scouted the terrain, and has come back to help us. Like a quality guide, he knows how to keenly apply principles and can share deep insights with ease. This book is a must-have resource for those who embrace the journey of the church into the future."

—**JESSIE CRUICKSHANK, Foursquare minister and regional leader; co-author,** *Activating 5Q*

"I'm so grateful that Jon Ritner has come on the scene as one of the next leaders who is helping other to prioritize making disciples. Ritner's long-standing experience, steeped in post-Christian settings, translates well for all contexts. His fresh voice, much-needed in the conversation on making disciples, finally guides readers into the essential frame of intersecting pneumatology and missiology with the art of disciplemaking."

—**NICK WARNES, founder and executive director, Cyclical; co-author,** *Starting Missional Churches*

Positively Irritating

EMBRACING A POST-CHRISTIAN WORLD TO FORM A MORE FAITHFUL & INNOVATIVE CHURCH

JON RITNER

1CM
MOVEMENTS
PUBLISHING

First published in 2020 by 100 Movements Publishing

www.100Mpublishing.com
www.movementleaderscollective.com
www.catalysechange.org

Cover design by Lindy Martin
Pearl logo designed by Addison Ritner
Cover imagery by Shutterstock

For bulk orders, please visit jonritner.com

ISBN: 978-1-7355988-0-2 (paperback)

100 Movements Publishing
An imprint of Movement Leaders Collective
Cody, Wyoming

To my favorite future travelers: Kristyn, Addy, and Jax.
"Let's Go!"

Contents

Foreword

When the famous theologian and missiologist Lesslie Newbigin returned to his English homeland after forty years as a missionary to the people of India, he was given "new eyes" to see his beloved United Kingdom (and by extension, European civilization). He concluded that the continent that considered itself to be *the* bastion of Christianity was in fact a thinly veiled form of paganism; it *appeared* to be Christian on the outside but was largely pagan on the inside. He likened Western culture to a stone that had been in a river for thousands of years. Withdrawn from the river, the stone was well-rounded, coarse, and thoroughly wet on the outside. But if the stone was cracked open, it would be entirely dry on the inside. Newbigin came to the startling conclusion that Western culture had never been truly converted: there was no change from the inside out. And to be true to its missionary calling, Western Christianity needed to once again adopt a missionary stance in relation to its own circumstances … the West needed to be re-evangelized.

In many ways Jon's experience mirrors that of Newbigin. He and his wife, Kristyn, similarly came home from their family's missionary experience in Europe with "new eyes" to see. Jon understands that the North American church must now adopt missional approaches for its own contexts. He likewise discovered that the conceptual maps—that have guided the Western church to this point in our journey—are no longer sufficient to take us forward. And Jon, as a gifted leader, understands that church leaders must learn to ask the questions, "What is not working and why?"

But there are many factors that work against the recovery of authentic missional renewal in our churches. These include, among others:

- ***The huge burden of traditionalist theological baggage.*** How do we sort through what is essential and non-essential? As exiles and pilgrims, how do we travel lighter? Or do we have to lug every theological notion and doctrine into a context that cannot make any sense of them? How do we recover the power of the gospel, which is now buried under the weight of tradition?

- ***The spiritual laziness that the early theologians called acedia.*** This refers to the intellectual sluggishness that arises from relying on answers that were appropriate for entirely different historical and cultural circumstances. The over-reliance on such doctrinal formulations might be deemed virtuous in some circles, but more often than not it masks a sinful unwillingness to think biblically and theologically for ourselves and with our own missional context in mind.

- ***The numbing drug of a ritual religion that dishes out sacraments and salvation to people without the demands of discipleship.*** No wonder Marx called the religion of his day "the opiate of the people."[1] Religion functions like a form of spiritual heroin, a desensitizing institution that in effect keeps the masses from experiencing the radical challenge that the gospel of the kingdom really presents.

- ***The subliminally motivated routines that are lodged deep in the very muscle memory of the Western church.*** We seem to do so many things on auto-pilot, without fully understanding *why* we do them. It doesn't take new pastors long to realize that it is incredibly hard to change even some of the more outmoded and ineffective rituals and practices in the church. The church itself seems to be built on the promise of non-discipleship.

No wonder the church is so hard to change!

But there is always hope. Jon knows that. Because God is *always* involved, Jon knows we can trust that the possibility of renewal *always* exists at the core of the church. The church is still God's chosen instrument ... the sign, symbol, and foretaste of the kingdom of God. That has not changed. We are still sent into the world for God's purposes, and he is still actively present through his Holy Spirit. We can trust that God really wants us to succeed in this mission, and he has done everything to make this possible. But in pursuit of that greater possibility of holiness, we clearly have to do some unlearning in order to learn again.

Coming back to the United States gave Jon "new eyes" to see what he couldn't see before. Following the call of the missionary God, Jon's journey of unlearning and relearning continues to not only unfold in his and his family's lives, but is also at work in the collective life of Ecclesia Hollywood. We were part of this community in Los Angeles for several years and were privileged to see some of this book lived out in the lives of real people! Both Jon and Kristyn are great practitioners, and this is no pie-in-the-sky type of book. It is earthy, practical, and full of learned experience. Armed with many years of working in a mainline American megachurch; tested in the more arid religious secularism of the European environment; strengthened by his involvement in Forge Missional Training Network; and re/formed in the complex multicultural challenges of Hollywood, Jon delivers real insights to leaders struggling to lead the church faithfully into twenty-first-century contexts.

Alan and Debra Hirsch
Authors of numerous books on missional spirituality, leadership, and organization. Founders of Forge Missional Training Network and Movement Leaders Collective.

Introduction

When a grain of sand blows into the human eye, it becomes an irritant. Our body initiates a series of defensive actions to protect us and expel the sand: our eye waters, our lid blinks, and we rub with our hands to eliminate the foreign object. We want to return to the way we were. However, when a similar grain of sand finds its way into an oyster in the ocean, a completely different response takes place. The oyster embraces the sand, coating it repeatedly in a substance called *nacre*. Over time, that coating transforms the irritant into something exquisite: a fresh pearl.* Instead of the oyster seeking to merely return to the way it was before, it allows the new threat to inspire the formation of something prized and beautiful. Only healthy, mature oysters can effect this mystical pearl formation process in a manner which preserves their own health and creates value in the world.

Today, the Western church finds itself in the midst of the disorienting sandstorm of post-Christian culture; secular paradigms threaten to remove any spiritual explanation or purpose to life, and the church as an institution is losing its once privileged place at the center of society. This marginalization brings with it decreased influence and less appeal to those seeking spiritual truth. Every local church is experiencing a torrent of secular sand blowing in its face as it stares into the future. As Christian leaders, it would be easy to view these challenges as grains of sand in our eyes that we seek to eliminate or resist, in an attempt to go back to the way things were. *But there is no going back.* We will never be able to return to the way things were before.

To those open to a new paradigm of church, there lies another possibility: we can embrace the challenges of a post-Christian culture in the same way oysters embrace sand. Instead of trying to expel the sand, we have the opportunity

---

* The pearl-making process can be initiated by a grain of sand or by other irritants, such as a piece of shell or a parasitic organism.

to come around our new normal—not through compromise—but with creativity and new imagination, new thinking, and new practices so that, over time, we allow the imposition to form something precious, without sacrificing our own integrity. Much like the pearl-making process, learning how to form new expressions of church will test our health and maturity and take significant time. But if we are open to adaptation and innovation and willing to persevere, I believe the post-Christian "irritants" we find all around us can catalyze the creation of more robust and Christlike communities.

The church in the West has the opportunity to learn what our brothers and sisters around the globe have known for centuries: if divine dependence is the objective, then weakness and struggle are to our advantage. I say this with great confidence, because I've experienced it first-hand: I lived in our post-Christian future.

This is my story of stepping out of the Christian paradigms that are still prevalent in much of the United States and stepping into the secular context of Brussels, Belgium, capital of the European Union. It's my story of how the unique and unfamiliar elements of post-Christian culture helped me to see what the twenty-first-century church could become if it fully depends on God and embraces the adaptive challenge it faces.

This book spans the last decade of my life: from pastoring in a megachurch in the deeply Christianized culture of Virginia; to planting microchurches contextualized to the irreligious neighborhoods of Europe; and back to the U.S., where I lead a church in Los Angeles, which is undergoing the transformation necessary to thrive in this new world. No personal narrative will connect with everyone; however, I believe the lessons learned along my journey offer something to those who are wondering what is ahead and how to prepare for it.

In my leadership roles within Forge America and Communitas International, I continually hear the same sentiments from church leaders: "I know what we are doing is no longer working; I just don't know what else to do." Leaders are frustrated with aging congregations, dwindling resources, decreased commitment from existing church members, and increased apathy from those outside the church to the activities going on inside the church. Many young people just don't want to come to church anymore; even young families aren't attending as they used to. Pastors are working harder for less impact. The Sunday-centric, program-driven, church-growth-movement paradigms and practices no longer seem to connect.

Denominational leaders in Los Angeles are facing the difficult decision of assessing which congregations are able to adapt to our post-Christian reality. Some churches are simply unable to change, and their leaders accept a role as "hospice pastors," helping the church die with dignity. Some seasoned leaders—those aged fifty-five and older—are reluctant to acknowledge the seismic cultural shifts that are occurring. Those near retirement may believe they should just keep operating their church the same way they always have, in order to keep the doors open and the lights on for a few more years. The temptation is to simply ride out the storm and let the next generation figure out what to do after they leave, even though, deep down, they know the kingdom deserves more.

Many leaders in their 20s and 30s grieve that the prevailing ways of operating as a church are not connecting with their peers. They sense the irrelevance of existing churches for fellow millennials, but lack useful examples of innovative ways to form a church that can make new disciples. In an attempt to reach this generation, some are starting church plants—but in my own city, many of these plants are just the same model of American church, repackaged with fresh branding. Too often what looks like growth is simply existing Christians transferring from their old church to a new one. Leaders share stories with me of this "sheep shifting" taking place all over the country.

COURAGEOUS AND HOLY ENGAGEMENT

While many view the cultural displacement of Christianity and its churches as an irritant to be expelled, this new reality offers tremendous potential for beauty and renewal if we become more creative. Our movement traces back to the people of Israel, who were the smallest of all the peoples in the region,[1] and yet under God's divine leadership they became a source of blessing to the world. Jesus taught of the power of the smallest seed breaking forth from the earth to nourish the birds of the air.[2] Christianity began in first-century Rome in a pluralistic culture, where it flourished on the fringes of society. In that place of marginalization—existing as a minority movement—the gospel spread like wildfire. History tells us that a Spirit-empowered, incarnational faith community on mission does very well in a context of opposition. The expansion of the church in India, Iran, and China reflects that truth today. When the church faces external pressure, it often emerges refined, more Christlike, and more effective at fulfilling its original calling to make disciples and embody the kingdom of God.

In this post-Christian age, God's people will have to resist the temptation to isolate, fearing the influence of secular culture. We must assume a posture of courageous and holy engagement, facing boldly the sandstorm in front of us and acknowledging that potential threats provide the opportunity for future pearls if we embrace the challenge. While culture may seek to push the church to the fringes of society, we cannot fall into the trap of privatizing our faith. Jesus is Lord over every sphere and sector of the world; and, as his followers, we must engage with him there. Our discipleship must deeply inform and impact the way we live. It is essential to embody the alternative Jesus-centered kingdom that challenges the dominion of individualism, materialism, and self-protectionism around us. As theologian and missiologist Darrell L. Guder notes, "The world of the principalities and powers is little challenged by a private and personal, vertical-relationship gospel. And that suits the powers and the principalities fine."[3]

THE FRAMEWORK

I chose to write this book loosely around the framework of my own personal experience. I am privileged to serve Ecclesia, a community of artists and storytellers in Hollywood, California, and together we seek to embody the story of Jesus in the city that tells stories to the world. Over the past five years of reading these storytellers' manuscripts, watching their shows and films, and seeing them perform live, I have been inspired by their courage to present their stories to others. Their tenacity and bravery stirred me to find the discipline to offer my own story and stare down the same potential criticism and rejection. While I recognize my story is merely descriptive of my journey and not prescriptive for others, I find personal narratives possess a compelling ability to spark fresh imagination and inspire others to live differently.

In this first-person format, I must acknowledge my implicit bias. I am writing from a distinctively European American/Caucasian perspective, and it is possible that I may primarily connect with church leaders who are operating in similar environments. I am a white man who grew up in the predominantly white suburbs of New York City and pastored in a majority-white American church, operating in a majority-white community. My exposure to the rich international and cultural diversity of my church in Brussels opened my eyes to new facets of God and his kingdom and the beauty of multi-ethnic communities of faith, for which I am forever grateful. As a board director of an international mission organization, I celebrate that the global church is not in decline; it is merely the forms of church life found in Western Christendom that need significant renewal. I hope my narrow target audience does not minimize the experience of others, but rather helps my own community rethink and reshape our practices.

One last disclaimer before we begin. It is natural for the secular sandstorm to initially feel like an *irritant* before it becomes an *inspiration*. I write about my journey from a place of reorientation, but most of it was experienced amidst disorientation. In the last few months, I reviewed many of the books that impacted me during my first year in Brussels. These texts have since become foundational to my understanding of the nature of God's church, and I hold them in reverence. But what I found in my rereading surprised me. In the margins of those books are the original notes I made. These notes reveal my initial skepticism toward, and even dismissal of, these new ideas rather than acceptance and integration—a tangible reminder that new truths are often rejected before they are considered, accepted, internalized, and eventually embodied.

My journey is marked by confusion and disorientation, and I will do my best to be transparent with those experiences so you might be prepared for similar feelings or reactions. It is easy to hold onto a belief for so long that it *feels* true, when in fact it is not actually true … just familiar. The unlearning curve may be steep. It is incredibly painful and bewildering to have your mental operating systems challenged, torn down, and rebuilt with different source code. Even more so for a leader who is supposed to confidently guide others. But the journey is worth the transformation, if we can find the courage to begin.

I hope this book serves as a primer for those who are just beginning to navigate this post-Christian reality and are looking for resources to guide them along the way. In these pages you won't find a blueprint for change, and I hope I don't imply there is a perfect path or plan to follow. However, I do believe that my journey reveals relevant principles that are valuable for other leaders who are on this same road. My hope is that, as you read my story, you might embrace the opportunities our secular culture offers and that God may shine light on your path and lead you to take the next brave step.

This book follows my personal trajectory as a church leader as I moved through four key phases of this pearl-making process that transforms irritants into gemstones.

Phase One:	Embrace the Irritation
Phase Two:	Experiment With the New Normal
Phase Three:	Create a Culture of Innovation
Phase Four:	Scale and Sustain New Expressions of Church

You may read the book in this order, or you may choose to access the section that relates most to the point where you currently find yourself.

Along the way, I share parts of my personal story that I think connect to the experiences many of us are having, offer principles to guide us forward, suggest ideas for applying those principles in a local-church context, and quote authors who have inspired me and whose excellent books offer deeper dives into each chapter's topic. I close each chapter with a few questions for reflection, to allow you to process what you are learning.

A POST-PANDEMIC WORLD

This book was in its final stages of editing when all of our lives were changed forever by the COVID-19 global pandemic. It is impossible to predict what our world will look like by the time this book is published, but physical distancing requirements, a shattered economy, and the sense of fear and anxiety around the potential harm of large gatherings will continue to impact the life of local churches for years to come. The first wave of the crisis devastated the physical health of many churches and cost the lives of thousands of church congregants and leaders, especially in urban areas around New York City, New Orleans, and Detroit. The second wave of the crisis will continue to be severe, as the economic realities of shuttered businesses, all-time highs in unemployment, and a global recession impacts church funding and sustainability.

The coronavirus has proved to be another eye-and-the-oyster moment. While the negative consequences are profound, it is providing a once-in-a-lifetime opportunity for churches to lean into innovation and experimentation—allowing this pandemic to form something beautiful. It can be extremely challenging for an existing organization to introduce change and innovation without upsetting members, who in turn push back. Therefore, when the world is disrupted by external factors, we must take advantage of it. Many churches around North America are using this disruption to reimagine how they can equip the church to make disciples when they cannot gather for business as usual. I am inspired by the ways so many are embracing the opportunity to innovate—finding new ways to create digital community, engage in contemplative spiritual disciplines, address rising mental health issues (such as anxiety and depression), and serve the overwhelming tangible needs of their local communities.

In the first week of March 2020, a few weeks before COVID-19 was impacting everyday life across America, I attended the annual Exponential Conference in Orlando, Florida—a gathering to equip and support church leaders. After I spoke at the Forge America pre-conference session, several leaders from a megachurch in Texas sat down with me to share the challenges they were facing in their attempts to adapt an existing church to the new-world realities. Their leadership team embraced the paradigms that Forge was teaching and was willing to try different things, but they knew that their older, set-in-their-ways congregation would not be as excited to innovate and change. Finally, the leader of the team looked at me and said, "What we really need is a crisis to shake people up."

The COVID-19 crisis can be leveraged so that when it finally subsides, you will have new paradigms and practices as a church and new rhythms of discipleship that people will consider continuing into the future. While we all pray for a speedy resolution to this global pandemic, I can't help but hope that this book is published before our churches face the temptation to simply "go back to normal." While death and economic devastation are evil, God is giving us a gift in the present—an invitation to let the sand transform us into pearls—a gift that can be used for good long into the future. I pray this book offers guidance for you on that journey.

A bright future lies ahead for the church in the West. A future marked by a more Spirit-filled and Jesus-like disciple ... and a more robust and revolutionary local church.

Let the pearl-making process begin!

Phase One

EMBRACE THE IRRITATION

Any solid object or microorganism that invades an oyster can trigger the pearl-making process. Even a predator, like a crab, or a parasite, like a worm larva, can produce a traumatic event in the oyster that triggers the reaction. The threat just has to enter deep enough to disrupt the cells of the inner mantle. Then something miraculous happens. The oyster not only protects itself; it transforms the crisis into something of great value in the world. It is the traumatic attack of an outside threat that makes the pearl possible.[1]

1

Sunday's Always Coming

Sitting backstage one Sunday morning, a question gnawed away at me: *how did this become the most important hour in the Christian life?*

It seemed that Jesus' dream of a disciplemaking movement, made up of everyday men and women, had somehow been reduced to passive attendance at a once-a-week stage production featuring a few talented professionals. And to make matters worse, I was perpetuating the problem! I invested nearly all of my time and energy as a church leader in this single aspect of church life: the Sunday morning experience.

Based on the axiom "excellence honors God," our staff spent hours in planning meetings throughout the week so that Sunday mornings could be executed flawlessly. Week in, week out—it was always the same: the repetition of multiple services, the concern of ending on time so we could turn over the parking lots for the next crowd, the stress of ensuring this week's slide operators stayed on pace with the song lyrics, and the buttoned-up formality of church in the South with its expectations of a suit and tie and freshly polished shoes.

And the reward of our efforts? Waking up on Monday and imagining how to top it with a better, more creative, and more transcendent worship experience the following Sunday.

As I sat slumped in the pastor's greenroom one particular Sunday in 2010, I knew something had to change. And not just on Sunday.

I had planned, preached, or participated in two to three services a week for ten years. Our team's communal mantra—"Sunday's Coming"—signaled to other church staff members how busy we were preparing for the upcoming weekend. Yet, for all our effort, the pace of life and its abundance of other activities meant the average congregant only attended every other Sunday at best.

It was both demoralizing and futile.

I sometimes found myself checking the weather forecast on Saturday evening, hoping a rare snowstorm would strike Virginia and force us to cancel services the next day.

On paper, everything looked rosy. After all, our church was living the American Dream. We began as a house church, planted by a few families before moving to a school cafeteria. Eventually we procured land to develop our own building and then upgraded it into a state-of-the-art $16 million facility, complete with our own commercial kitchen and café, open daily for lunch. We were "running" 3,000 people for Sunday worship, 4,400 adults on Easter morning, and 8,000 guests for our Christmas concerts. Fifty to sixty people assembled for our all-staff meetings, and our annual ministry budget was a few million and rising. Granted, most of our attendance increase was transfer from other churches or Christians moving into our region who were attracted to the best Bible teaching and music program in town, but I never even thought to question it. We just measured the growth and assumed it was a sign of our health.

Like so many other megachurches in the 1990s, our increase from a few hundred to a few thousand followed a pattern referred to as the "Homogenous Unit Principle" (HUP). A homogenous unit is "a section of society in which all members have some characteristic in common."[2] Many churches at this time either intentionally or unwittingly subscribed to the HUP as a church-growth strategy. Churches targeted a demographic, and crafted programs specific to that group's life experience—without asking them to cross any racial, language, or socioeconomic barriers. Over time, "like attracted like" and churches grew, as more of the same sort of people joined. Churches that addressed the needs felt by middle-class, professional, and predominantly white Americans grew exponentially in suburban settings. Over the sixteen years I attended and pastored in Virginia, our church grew by 600 percent without ever becoming truly representative of the racial and socioeconomic population around us.

And yet, in the midst of all that apparent success, I had fantasies of moving to Las Vegas to become a professional poker player. One day, walking through our office, I caught myself unconsciously humming the lyrics of The Animals' song, "We Gotta Get Out of This Place." I was in such bad shape that, one Sunday when I wasn't preaching, I snuck out halfway through the service so I could watch the NFL pregame shows and set up my fantasy football lineup. Driving home, I thought to myself, *I used to lead a ministry of 250 college kids and never earned a dime for it, and now, if I wasn't in a paid role, I am not sure I would even attend a church like this.*

MY INTERNAL CRISIS; WELL, ACTUALLY THREE

My disillusionment led me into a threefold crisis.[3] First, I was experiencing a *crisis of mission*. My initial pastoral calling was to join God in transforming the lives of people who did not know Jesus. Now, it had devolved into a job maintaining ministries for existing Christians. Over the span of my ten years on staff, I was involved in leading nearly every facet of ministry at one time or another. I planned the annual preaching curriculum and crafted the weekly worship services alongside the music minister. For a season I managed adult discipleship ministries, such as small groups, men's and women's breakfasts, and Sunday school/Adult Bible Fellowships. I led the student ministry department for a year. I headed up short-term mission trips and hosted events for the overseas missionaries when they were in town. One year I officiated seventeen weddings. I felt like a program director on a cruise ship for Christians, dry-docked sixty miles from the Atlantic Ocean.

Deep down, I knew Jesus' church was called to be more than just a vendor of religious goods and services for Christians. At seminary I was inspired by the quote attributed to the late Archbishop of Canterbury, William Temple: "The Church is the only institution that exists primarily for the benefit of those who are not its members." I still believed that; but very little of my time and energy ever went toward investing in the lives of people who weren't part of our community or improving the quality of life in places beyond our own property. I rarely spent time with non-Christians; there just wasn't bandwidth in my life for relationships with those outside the church.

I was not the only one frustrated. As more and more local church leaders seemed only to care for their own Christian community, the younger generation was getting turned off. Our church always connected well with college students at my alma mater, The College of William and Mary, and I held a regular discipleship group with some of them in my home. Back in the 2000s, I was encouraged by a new wave of students who were compelled by the needs of the world around them. A group of young Christians launched sustainable lines of hand-made clothing that provided employment for women in Nicaragua. Others created documentaries that exposed the global sex trade and helped liberate girls from human trafficking. And yet, while they were passionate about their faith, too often they didn't sense the local church shared their concerns about the larger issues of the world. They viewed the mission of churches as simply providing quality programming for existing Christians, and they failed to see its relevance. They longed to impact their world on a much larger scale.

As my friend Brad Brisco once said to me: "Young people who grew up in the church are leaving it because of a crisis of mission that feels to them like a crisis of faith." They feel called to love and serve others, but they don't see the local church carrying that burden with the same intensity as they do. The church I was working for offered the presence of God in a well-scripted Sunday worship service, but the students found him while getting their hands dirty serving the poor and needy and protesting against racism and economic inequality. The Sunday-centric volunteer activities that churches offered them in the name of "ministry" were far too small compared to the causes that broke their hearts.

> "If today's church does not recapture the sacrificial spirit of the early church, it will lose its authenticity, forfeit the loyalty of millions, and be dismissed as an irrelevant social club."[4]—Robert Chao Romero

Second, I was having a *crisis of impact*. I questioned whether our ministry was really equipping the people and places in and around our church to better reflect the totality of Jesus' life and values. For all the effort we put into crafting programs for our community, participation in those activities didn't consistently form robust disciples—people capable of living counter-cultural, Spirit-led lives that flowed over into making more disciples. Often, it felt like the impact only reached as far as people's intellectual beliefs and religious habits. What we did on Sunday didn't seem to carry over to the other six days of the week.

The *Reveal* study—published by Willow Creek Community Church in 2007—sounded a wake-up call to many churches of that era.[5] Willow Creek spent thousands of dollars and hundreds of hours evaluating the effectiveness of their discipleship ministries and eventually concluded that simply adding more church activities to a person's life didn't lead to spiritual maturity. In fact, the study showed that for all the time and effort churches put into teaching and fellowship gatherings, one of the most catalytic spiritual practices in the life of a disciple was extending out to serve others. Willow Creek admitted that their philosophy of ministry was largely a "mistake."[6]

As a young leader, I was inspired by the example of members of our community who led lives of sacrifice and servanthood to the surrounding city. One couple launched a free medical clinic in the under-resourced portion of the county; others discipled graduate students from China studying at William and Mary; another advocated for the adoption of Ukrainian girls aging out of foster care. But these stories felt anomalous rather than characteristic of the normal Christian life. After reading David Platt's book *Radical*, I wanted to grow in personal generosity, so I put twenty dollars in my pocket and asked God to show me someone I could bless.[7] I went four days before I encountered one person who expressed a financial need. My sterile, suburban life—insulated in a bubble of wealth and individualism—prevented me from relating to people with tangible needs.

Many present-day innovators in the church have experienced a similar season where they recognized that a finely-tuned Sunday morning machine didn't necessarily impact the lives of those inside or outside the church. In fact, this Sunday-centric form of church sucked up many of the resources that might have blessed the local community on the other days of the week. Dave Gibbons of Newsong Church in Santa Ana, California, writes, "While spending most of our resources on growing bigger, we had failed to engage our culture and love our neighbors ... . The mystery and danger of God seemed lost in the way we were doing church. I knew something deep had to change."[8] In *Underground Church*, Brian Sanders recounts the story of the Tampa Underground, a city-wide network of microchurches led by everyday people who embody the kingdom and make disciples across all sectors of society.[9] Their network was catalyzed by the frustration of graduating Intervarsity students who felt unable to find a local church that sought to impact the city.

But the third and final straw for me was waking up to the *crisis of leadership* plaguing churches across the nation. By the late 2000s, Christian websites regularly featured reports of high-profile pastors disqualified from ministry for moral violations. Sexual infidelities, alcohol and drug abuse, financial improprieties, and outbursts of anger and abusive treatment of staff wrecked both pastors and their families, one after another. I began to wonder if this model of church in which I was operating was destroying its own leaders. Was it healthy for one senior/lead pastor to be given so much authority and influence? Investing all the church's power in the person at the top of the professional staff hierarchy seemed oppressive to both its leaders and its members. The solo-heroic leadership model—with its focus on platform gifts—seemed to encourage a shadow side of arrogance and abuse that was often overlooked by elder boards and pastoral peers responsible for providing accountability. For several years, I watched from a distance as men I considered role models resigned, or were removed, from their pastoral positions. Megachurch pastors were not finishing well, and I did not want my family to pay the same price.

Sadly, this crisis was about to hit much closer to home. In my own local church, two older pastors—men I greatly admired as mentors on my journey—made a series of unfortunate personal decisions that led to the end of their tenure on our staff. The pain and wounding I experienced led me to examine my own life more closely, and I began to realize that this model of leadership was killing something in me. The pace of life I was keeping was unsustainable. I was out of the house three to four nights a week; and when I was home, I was often too exhausted to meaningfully engage with my wife. One year, she planned our kids' birthday parties with her best friend because I was so rarely present, physically or emotionally. My identity was rooted not in Jesus, but in my professional performance and the approval of others. I wrestled with stress and anxiety that led me to abuse alcohol—a habit I deliberately concealed from others. I was compelled into two years of abstinence after a few nights where my decisions put my family and career in jeopardy.

The status and financial security that came with working in a large church was corrupting my heart, and my motivations for leadership no longer felt pure. My initial call to vocational equipping ministry came in 1997, and I soon began serving as the volunteer huddle leader of the Fellowship of Christian Athletes at William and Mary. To help pay the bills, I worked as a stock manager at a retail store, a substitute teacher, and an assistant coach for a middle school football team—all so I could invest in the lives of college athletes and the campus community. Only by a few instances of divine provision did I emerge from that year debt free. I helped young people dive into the Scriptures on their own, learn how to sense God's presence in prayer, and experience the joy of serving and blessing their friends who did not know Jesus. Through it all I saw Jesus turn their lives upside down: kids escaped addictions, found healing from childhood abuse, and learned to trust Jesus for the first time amidst season-ending sports injuries. My work was unremarkable, unrecognized, and financially uncompensated—but to this day, it was one of the most meaningful seasons of ministry in my life. Those I served alongside are still lifelong friends.

Now I was making a great salary, driving a company car … and yet I was unsatisfied. I remember touring our 1,500-seat worship auditorium while it was under construction and standing in the place that was one day to be the stage. To my great shame, my heart longed for my mentor to turn to me and recreate a Lion King moment: "Someday, son, all of this will be yours; all that the light touches." My heart for God was shrinking, as the craving for personal recognition and external rewards corrupted my soul.

I believe a hierarchical form of church leadership is oppressive to the rest of the church body as well. It is, in essence, a form of "Spiritual Munchausen by Proxy"[11]—the medical term for a condition in which a parent becomes so enmeshed in the care

> "Raising the microphone, I took a deep breath, and the first words out of my mouth were, 'I believe that the day of the single superstar is over!'"[10]—Brenda Salter McNeil

of a sick child that, even as the child's health begins to improve, the parent deliberately keeps the child ill. The parent's sense of value and identity is so closely tied to his or her role as caregiver that he or she "needs to be needed" by the child in order to have purpose in life. I now wonder if I played a part in keeping the majority of the church community malnourished while a select few got to feast on God working through us as professionals. I confess that my enjoyment of being on the platform on Sunday mornings and my personal fulfillment from large-group teaching led me to perpetuate a form of church where some gifts and some disciples were elevated above others. Rather than equipping every person to help others encounter God for themselves in his Word, I encouraged them to invite those people to church to hear our pastors speak. Church members with ideas for new initiatives were often buried in bureaucracy by leaders who needed to approve every step, rather than being encouraged to discern how God was calling them to join his work in the world.

Reflecting back now, ten years later, is it even more apparent what a dangerous place my soul was in. But I wish I had known then what I know now: that I was not alone. All over the Western world, pastors and church leaders were having their own crises and wrestling with their own doubts about the effectiveness of our forms of church in a culture that was rapidly changing. By God's grace, I was on the verge of meeting some of them and finding a new way forward.

Questions for Reflection

1. When you feel frustrated within a local church, what does it make you long for most?

2. Why do you think the Sunday gathering traditionally claims more resources (facilities, money, and staff preparation) than the activity of church in the community the other six days a week?

3. Write down some ways that you can relate to these three crises: drifting from a deeper call to *mission* toward simply maintaining church activities; failing to deeply *impact* those in our church and surrounding community; and ministering in a *leadership* structure that devours its leaders and disempowers the body.

2

From Hero to Zero

In January 2012, I announced an annual theme for our church that was aimed as much at shaking me out of my comfort zone as anyone else. It was to be "The Year of ReachinGOut"—reinforcing the call to GO. My launch sermon examined the rhythm of Jesus' ministry, who told his disciples to "Come to me" (Matthew 11:28) as well as to "Go into the all the world" (Mark 16:15). This pattern of gathering and scattering—coming into the presence of Jesus to rest, learn, and heal, and then going out to the world in the power of Jesus to serve and bless others—provides a spiritual rhythm for life. I compared it to breathing: inhaling life in his presence and exhaling that life into the world around us.

Little did I know how prophetic that series title would be in my own life.

In February, I invited an overseas missionary to share about the work he and his wife were doing in Brussels, Belgium. Carlton and Shannon Deal planted a church and formed a charity, "Serve the City," to mobilize volunteers to meet the tangible needs of the homeless, disabled, elderly, victims of abuse, asylum seekers, and children. Carlton shared with our staff the challenges of pastoring a church in the secular culture of Europe, which rejects the institutional church. They named their church "The Well," describing themselves as a "faith community on mission" that exists to help the city flourish in all facets of life: spiritual, emotional, social, environmental, and economic. Carlton spoke of their decentralized strategy to plant microchurches in various neighborhoods, coming together as a citywide movement once a month to celebrate what God was doing in the everyday spaces of life.

His description of Europe's post-Christian realities, and the optimism and excitement he possessed about these new disruptions stirred something in me. Rather than resisting these cultural conditions that forced the traditional church into obsolescence, he was embracing them and responding with creative innovation and adaptation. They were turning an irritant into an ornament of beauty. In that meeting, I heard God whisper: *What if you could go to Europe and see the cultural future of America and then return to help prepare churches back here for what is coming?*

The Well was experimenting with new ways of being the church in a post-Christian culture, and those lessons would be invaluable for American leaders in the coming years. They were helping an international community of Christians living in Brussels to deconstruct the Western forms of church that had thrived in Christendom and were now experimenting with new ways of expressing the life of Jesus as his body in a secular society. I sensed that the process they were pioneering could be one that American churches could adopt and implement while they still had momentum and resources.

> "In times of drastic change, it is the learners who inherit the future. The learned find themselves equipped to live in a world that no longer exists."[1]—Eric Hoffer

Radical ideas pop into all of our minds from time to time, but this one felt divinely inspired. The previous Christmas, a staff member gave me Clare De Graaf's book, *The 10-Second Rule: Following Jesus Made Simple*.[2] De Graaf recommends acting on God's divine promptings within ten seconds, before your flesh or the devil tries to convince you otherwise. Within ten seconds I determined to meet with Carlton and explore further the prompting I had felt in that meeting. That night, Carlton, my wife, Kristyn, and I went long into the evening, imagining a three-year season in which our family would come alongside The Well and Serve the City.

Fittingly, nine months later almost to the day of that first prompting, Kristyn and I and our kids (at the time aged six and four), boarded a plane for Brussels. In those nine months of gestation and preparation, more than 250 members of our church stepped up to generously provide all of our financial support, and Communitas International accepted us into their amazing tribe of global church planters.

Somewhere amidst the excitement of leaving-parties and the powerful commissioning prayers in our final Sunday worship services, a fellow European missionary did his best to prepare us for the disruption and disorientation that lay ahead. He asked, "Are you ready to go from hero to zero?"

Hero to zero aptly describes the place of the church in the secular landscape of Western Europe. Though shaped by Christian beliefs and practices, the continent cast off that history in favor of a set of beliefs, practices, and values that has come to be known as *post-Christianity*. The term pays homage to the significance and centrality the church used to enjoy, and indicates the U-turn European culture has made away from its former influence.

To fully understand why the local church will not be able to simply resist or wipe away this new cultural worldview, we must fully appreciate how deeply engrained and embedded this change is becoming in society and how it will eventually impact our day-to-day lives across the Western world, if it hasn't already.

A CRASH COURSE IN POST-CHRISTIAN CULTURE

The term *post-Christian* refers to a specific worldview and the change that ensues as society begins to adopt and embody that perspective. Lesslie Newbigin defined a worldview as "what we think of the world when we are not really thinking."[3] It encompasses the largely unconscious assumptions we make about reality, most of which go unquestioned in our day-to-day life. Our worldview sits in our individual subconscious, but it expresses itself in our collective culture. Culture can be defined as

> the learned pattern of beliefs, attitudes, values, customs, and products shared by a people. A culture is sometimes explained, metaphorically, as "the software of the mind" that has been programmed into a given people's shared consciousness through their early socialization.[4]

As members of a society act out the subconscious beliefs of a certain worldview in their public lives, they create a culture that reflects those beliefs. *Collective culture* is an external expression of each individual member's internal perspective.

One of the best ways to understand post-Christian culture is to see how it parallels a more familiar era: *pre-Christianity.* The New Testament describes a world that was not yet influenced by the beliefs, morals, and ethics of Jesus. Values such as humility, grace, sacrificial love, and servanthood were scoffed at in a society ruled by power, greed, tyranny, and oppression. Jesus' first-century ministry emerged in a pluralistic Roman culture that worshipped different gods for the different areas of life: family, economic prosperity, even hedonist pleasures. After the life, death, resurrection, and ascension of Jesus, his followers began to publicly affirm "Jesus is Lord" and sought to integrate all facets of their lives under his lordship and authority. This was in direct opposition to the pluralism of the day, as well as the Roman Empire, which asserted, "Caesar is Lord" (an affirmation of their belief in the royal's own divinity). The early church's claim irked both the Jews, who saw it as heresy, and Romans, who saw it as a threat to their governing authority.

The Book of Acts records the dispersion of the early "Jesus movement," as religious persecution pushed the disciples far beyond the reaches of Jerusalem. The criminalization of Jesus-worship was intended to crush this religious minority, but instead the number of people who claimed to be followers of "The Way" grew from around twenty-five thousand in AD 100 to nearly twenty million in AD 310.[5] This growth occurred even though Christians held no political power or protection, owned no public space in which to gather for worship, operated no training seminaries, and employed no professional pastors besides itinerant missionaries, such as Paul. Christianity was a decentralized movement of ordinary people living in tight-knit communities who scattered out to make disciples in their daily lives and gathered together in secret to worship Jesus as newly formed multi-ethnic families of faith.

Then, in or about AD 312, everything changed. The Roman Emperor Constantine saw a vision of a cross in the sky as he prepared for battle. He claimed to hear the phrase, "In this sign you will conquer" and interpreted it as a message from God that Jesus was, in fact, divine.[6] He began to publicly identify as a worshipper of Jesus, though many historians debate whether this was a genuine conversion or merely a savvy political move in light of the growing numbers of Christians across his empire. In AD 313, Constantine signed the Edict of Milan to decriminalize Christianity and, in effect, make it the *de facto* state religion of Rome. Those who had followed Jesus from the margins of society suddenly found themselves able to operate in the mainstream. Western culture shed its religious pluralism as Christianity rose to a central place of privilege in society. The church went from persecution to prosperity, gaining wealth, status, and influence. What was once a revolutionary, grassroots, minority movement, operating on the fringes of society, became the central religious institution of the day—with formal structures, priesthood, and sacraments.

The rise of Christendom ushered in a new worldview throughout the West. Now the one true God was sovereign over his creation, and his revelation of divine Truth formed the foundation for all of life's beliefs and behaviors. The culture that ensued brought about profound developments in human history that contributed to the growth and flourishing of Western civilization. Hospitals, orphanages, care for the elderly, accessible education for all citizens, strengthened work ethic and accumulation of wealth, rights for the working class, and the political notions of liberty and democracy all emerged from the implementation of Judeo-Christian values. The discoveries that defined the scientific revolution were made possible by a Christian perspective that assumed "certain ideas about how the world must work if it was created by a good, rational God."[7]

We must acknowledge that Western Christianity also cast a dark shadow: abhorrent methods adopted in the global colonization of "pagan" nations under the guise of evangelism; church-sanctioned political corruption; oppression of women and people of color; and highly publicized sexual-abuse scandals within church leadership across the globe. (By God's grace, many of these stains on society were uncovered and abolished by followers of Jesus seeking to reform the practices they knew to be unchristian.)

The growing rejection of Christianity in the West over the last 450 years derives in part from these violations, but also from the philosophical impact of Nominalism, the scientific revolution, the Enlightenment, Darwinism, the romantic movement, modernism, and subsequently, postmodernism. Though these movements all contributed to the fall of Christendom, examining them is beyond the scope of my purposes here.[8] Let me focus instead on how their effects are being felt today.

As the beliefs and assumptions of Christianity are broadly rejected, a new post-Christian way of thinking replaces it. Western society becomes increasingly secular, removing God from every sphere of culture in the name of human progress. "Secularism as an ideology carries with it the express intention of eradicating a religious explanation of the world in which we live,"[9] seeking human progress without having to rely on the divine presence of God.[10]

Here is a short summary of how the philosophical assumptions of secularism propose to answer the ultimate questions of human origin, meaning, morality, and destiny.

Human Origin

When the scientific revolution offered acceptable natural explanations for what were once thought to be supernatural phenomena, the world no longer needed a divine creator and sustainer in its origin story. The universe became an impersonal machine. God was removed from its center and replaced by humanity—not a humanity created to mirror God, but rather an animal species that resulted from the Darwinian evolutionary process. In some current expressions of secularism, the notion of god(s) is now anathema, whereas other streams continue to acknowledge a spiritual dimension to the world ... just not one constrained by the definitions of Christianity. Urban centers are increasingly home to diverse spiritual practices, such as astrology, palm reading, crystals, tarot, or breathwork circles—all aimed at connecting participants with an impersonal life force rather than helping them worship the personal, holy, triune God.

Human Meaning

Historically, humans have derived meaning by finding their place in a transcendent, divine story. The metanarrative of Christianity claims that we are made in the image of God and created with innate worth and dignity. Even though our sin corrupted our original condition, our value was reaffirmed on the cross when God himself offered his life to ransom us from the clutches of evil. We live to bring God glory and join in relationship with him and in his purposes. We are each characters embodying our own personal stories, but we are also part of a divine story that God is enacting before our eyes, infused with the themes of redemption and love, and ending with Jesus returning to claim his own and usher in the final age filled with his glory. For centuries the truth of this cosmic story went unchallenged in Western culture, and it framed how people lived. However, in our post-Christian society, to suggest that there is one universal metanarrative is now seen as "an oppressive, imperialist, and self-serving notion,"[11] a power play to oppress those who do not believe the same story.

Charles Taylor observed that it is now possible for humans to find "significance without transcendence."[12] To believe humanity has inherent value apart from our association with God or the gods is a seismic shift.

> For the first time in history a purely self-sufficient humanism came to be a widely available option. I mean by this a humanism accepting no final goals beyond human flourishing, nor any allegiance to anything else beyond this flourishing. Of no previous society was this true.[13]

Rather than being the receivers of divine meaning, humanity has become the source of our own meaning. We have value because we say so, not because God says so. Meaning and purpose in life are now personally discovered by each individual rather than divinely conferred upon us by God.

> The only meaning that one can derive ... is through a dynamic interaction with or experience of the world. Meaning is therefore entirely a subjective matter and is individual, transitory, particular and never universal.[14]

Meaning can be sourced wherever you wish to locate it—in the materialistic pleasure of possessions, in forming deep associations with a like-minded community, in pursuit of sexual expression, or in social and political activism, to name a few. Social media offers us a window into how the post-Christian generation meets their existential needs, but often obscures the deep anxiety caused by the pressure and responsibility of deriving one's own meaning to life.

Human Morality

"We choose to ignore the lies we've come to accept while using all the numbing agents possible to keep us from reality. Use the death of pop icon Michael Jackson as an example of irony. He died of an overdose of anesthesia. Isn't that a metaphor for our culture?"[15]*—Dr. Mark Weedman*

Without a holy God determining truth and morality, each person is left to determine how to live. The individual has dethroned God as the arbiter of ultimate truth. Truth is no longer an objective reality rooted in the character and revelation of God; instead, truth is a subjective feature of life that each of us must discover personally. Influencers inspire young people to "speak your truth."[16] Contradicting statements of truth are rarely resolved; they just live on their own cable news station. Popular television shows depict characters of varying lifestyles, all expressing unquestioning tolerance of each other's personal moral choices. If there is collective truth, it is determined by majority public opinion and can be changed at the next election cycle.

In this new world, all morality is subjective. Areas of human behavior once governed by biblical revelation are now matters of personal preference. Nowhere is this more apparent than the transition of beliefs about human sexuality away from a matter of divine regulation and toward an individual lifestyle choice. Sexual expression is viewed as an act of autonomy and freedom, an essential part of the process of self-realization. Therefore, acting out one's sexual desires is the highest form of self-expression and self-affirmation. Culture tells us we must not bind anyone by traditional mores that limit the rights of autonomous, freely-chosen personal expression. News reports share that monogamy is on the decline while open marriages are on the rise.[17]

The sentiments of this shift echo across the Western world in phrases like "it's all good" and "you do you." Reason and rational thought have been toppled by the experiential. The most reliable way to discern your personal truth is through your emotions. "It if feels good, do it." The heart rules over the head, and it is impervious to logical argument. One young person swimming in these philosophical waters told me that he rejected the biblical notion of Hell because, "I don't like the way it makes me feel."

Organizations or collectives that seek to control or constrict individual autonomy are subject to attack. Religious institutions are objects of suspicion; distrusted for being repressive and exploitative. This idolization of freedom is turning the West into a post-covenantal culture that no longer honors obligations. Formerly lifelong commitments like marriage are now binding only as long as they are mutually beneficial. I witnessed one couple vow to "be married as long as love shall last." People wait until the last minute before signaling their intention to attend events, reluctant to limit their options. Personal freedom and independence have replaced traditional ethics of fidelity and faithfulness. "The new spirituality then is not one of obedience and faith but rather of breaking boundaries, rejecting definitions, and transgressing limits."[18]

Human Destiny

We now live for goals that can be realized in this life rather than holding out hope that life's deepest desires point to another world that we were meant for one day. As the natural replaces the supernatural, eternity is eclipsed by this present world; it is all we can see to set our hearts upon. The hope is that—through scientific, genetic, and technological progress—we will create a utopia of human flourishing. Ironically, culture seeks to strip out Christ while retaining many of the positive benefits that Christendom introduced to the world, such as social equality, grace, mercy, and human dignity. As Mark Sayers points out, "Post-Christianity is an attempt to have the Kingdom without the King."[19]

And yet, even as society strives toward a technologically and morally superior future, the worlds of art and literature expose our deep fear of what actually might lie ahead. Contemporary novels, TV shows, and films such as *The Handmaid's Tale, The Walking Dead, The Hunger Games, A Quiet Place,* and *Wayward Pines* are filled with depictions of a post-apocalyptic, dystopian future where we are subdued by aliens, artificial intelligence, fascists, or zombies. The films *Outbreak* (released in 1995) and *Contagion* (2011) now seem eerily prescient of the 2020 novel coronavirus and reveal our fears of a global pandemic years before it became a reality. Amidst our external optimism, it seems our subconscious feels the need to create art that expresses our inner sense of hopelessness and despair. Apparently, deep down, people are at least suspicious of the actual impact that secularism is having on the world.

While secularism runs rampant across the West, it leaves in its wake a generation buying into its promises and left with nothing to show for it. Suicide and use of anti-anxiety/anti-depressant drugs are on the rise across the Western world,[20] as the empty pledges of secularism leave its adherents void of any external notion of personal significance or worth. Radical individualism is leaving people desperately lonely and disconnected, and the initially exciting world of social networking has turned out to be an ineffective replacement for genuine and intimate friendship. The political fervor of nationalism that seemed to fade after World War II, is on the rise again.[21] I can't help but think this is partially caused by individuals seeking some form of community bigger than themselves; a place they feel they truly belong, if only by a shared ethnicity.

As followers of Jesus, we know that the allure of dethroning God in order to worship created idols will ultimately prove to be a lie that leaves humanity empty.[22] Secularism is no panacea or utopia, and it should not surprise us that those who go all-in on this philosophy will eventually find themselves still restless. Sentiment-author Julian Barnes poignantly captures this in his remark, "I don't believe in God, but I miss Him."[23]

The empty promises of secularism do not offer a better way to live, but they do demand a new way for the church to function. The fields are ripe for a gospel harvest, but our traditional church methods will not get the job done.

THE IMPLICATIONS FOR THE CHURCH

The West has thrown off the shackles of Christendom and its restrictive norms. It has moved beyond Christianity the way modern-day consumers move beyond an old version of a smartphone. People have upgraded to a more effective worldview with advanced features that improve their quality of life—and they are now post-Christian. Citizens of this emerging strand of Western culture have developed a resistance to Christendom's forms of Christianity; they've experienced just enough of the distorted strains of corrupted, institutional religion to make them immune to contracting the actual life of Jesus Christ. The attitude toward Christianity in Europe is basically "We've been there, done that, and have the empty Cathedrals to prove it." Christianity is passé, and present-day Christians are considered quaint and naïve for not liberating themselves from an obsolete, failed system.

The church herself has gone from hero to zero.

The new culture created by this Western worldview is beginning to impact American churches in ways that are palpable. As God is removed from the public square, the church is feeling the dislocation. Tod Bolsinger puts it this way: "A church bred under the protection of the state is not trained to fend for itself on the streets. So, when state and society withdraw their special favor towards the palace-trained church, it gets a very rude awakening."[24]

> Christian faith and its values no longer dominate the public life of the West. Politics, business, education, and the communication industry all operate on the basis that they need pay no attention at all to Christian ideals and teaching.[25]

When Americans rated professions according to honesty and ethical standards in a 2018 Gallup poll, clergy ranked behind accountants and funeral directors.[26] Christians are no longer seen as a source of good; we are perceived as a force that limits and represses individual expression. In their book, *unChristian*, Gabe Lyons and David Kinnaman share their extensive research into the dominant perceptions Americans hold of Christians:[27]

- Christians are hypocritical: Christians say one thing but live something entirely different.
- Christians are too focused on conversion: Christians are insincere and concerned only with converting others.
- Christians are anti-homosexual: Christians show contempt for the LGBTQ community.
- Christians are sheltered: Christians are boring, unintelligent, old-fashioned, and out of touch with reality.
- Christians are too political: Christians are primarily motivated by a political agenda to promote right-wing politics.

- Christians are judgmental: Christians are prideful and quick to find fault in others.

This reputation partly accounts for the decline not only in church attendance but also in the prominence of Christians in every part of Western society. The concept of a "nominal" or "cultural" Christian is disappearing as the perceived social benefits of publicly identifying with Christianity are removed. The church has lost our home-field advantage. Sunday mornings are no longer sacred times preserved for worship. Now they are filled with youth sports, charity 5K races, and kids' birthday parties. We are espousing one faith among many equal options, including the valid choice of expressing no faith in the supernatural at all. In the last two decades, the rise of the "nones and dones" has been highly documented in books such as *You Lost Me* by David Kinnaman and *Churchless* by George Barna. One generation that is, by and large, "done" with church and no longer practices a communal form of Christianity is rearing the next generation of "nones" who identify as having no religious affiliation at all.[28]

It's not hard to see why many of these shifts can feel like beach sand blowing in our eyes—irritants that, as Christians, we would rather rub away and remove, or respond by simply shutting our eyes in ignorance, hoping it all blows over. I was exposed to the general notion of post-Christianity through books I read in my last years in Virginia, but I was completely unprepared for how much this new worldview and its corresponding societal shifts would affect the way I operated as a local pastor and church planter. As soon as my feet hit the ground in Brussels in 2012, I found myself in a cultural sandstorm that was impossible to avoid. Neither my traditional seminary education nor years of pastoring in the American South prepared me for this cultural moment in which my family now lived.

Questions for Reflection

1. How do you feel when you read the stories in Acts of the early church thriving without property, professionals, or disciplemaking programs and instead as a people-movement on the fringes of society?

2. In your local context, what are some examples of the questions of humanity's *origin, meaning, morality,* and *destiny* being answered by secularism rather than Christianity?

3. What other implications could you add to how post-Christian culture is changing the world's perception of individual Christians or your local church?

Phase Two

EXPERIMENT WITH THE NEW NORMAL

The pearl is the only gemstone that comes from a living creature. While other valuable gemstones, such as emerald or turquoise, crystallize in the earth's crust, the pearl is formed by the deliberate and ongoing activity of the oyster. It is created by the organism's diligent and perpetual response to the new condition created by the outside threat.

3

The End of Industrialized Disciplemaking

When we arrived in Brussels, Carlton told us the cross-cultural transition would hit us in waves, with the two biggest breakers crashing down on us at the six-week and six-month milestones. The six-week mark was hard for the family, as the initial excitement of entry into urban life wore off, and the loneliness of being away from friends and family began to set in. But it was the six-month mark that was hardest for me, as I began to realize that fifteen years of ministry in and around the American church left me ill-equipped for this new world. I found myself unprepared for this new cultural reality, in which my disciplemaking paradigms and practices no longer seemed applicable. It felt as if my previous ministry leadership was all about swinging a hammer to drive nails, and now all the people around me were screws. Doing the same thing I had always done—even harder or more efficiently—was not going to work. I did not have the right equipment in my disciplemaking tool belt for this post-Christian culture, and it triggered feelings of deep inadequacy.

While my frustration was directed at this foreign worldview and its daily secular practices, the real problem was what it revealed in me. If the same sand that infects the human eye produces a pearl in an oyster, then the sand itself is not the issue; the sand merely reveals the existing properties of the host organism. The irritant of post-Christian culture simply revealed what already existed within me: a rigid ecclesiology, and paradigms of disciplemaking that did not allow for adaptation or innovation.

Most local churches launched in the era of Christendom and informed by modernism rely on a strategy for making disciples that resembles an industrial assembly line. As a thought experiment, picture your church as a "Disciplemaking Factory" fitted with a system of steps: an individual, couple, or family moves to town, who are not followers of Jesus, and, over time come into contact with your local church. Now picture those same people ten years later as committed followers of Jesus, embodying everything you would hope for a disciple in terms of character, values, priorities, and behaviors. Assuming the Holy Spirit's active involvement, what structures and systems are operating to engage them, draw them into your disciplemaking process, and form them so they emerge in this Christlike condition? What programs or pathways are in place for them to travel along? Put another way, what exactly is happening behind the walls of this disciplemaking factory?

You might want to take a moment and engage in this activity with your own local church in mind.

Disciplemaking Factory

THE OLD PATHWAY

Most discipleship pathways created for Christendom start with the weekend worship service. Church members are encouraged to meet people in their communities and invite them to attend an upcoming worship service at their church. Sometimes the first invite is to an outreach event like a Super Bowl breakfast, harvest festival, or Easter egg hunt; but in the course of that event attendees are often given a formal invitation to a worship service. When a neighbor accepts the invitation and shows up, a well-trained hospitality team of parking attendants and greeters welcome them as honored guests, offer free coffee, and direct them to safe-and-secure childcare. Inside the sanctuary, professional staff members on stage lead the congregation in music and Bible teaching, sharing the benefits of a relationship with Jesus. They announce all the upcoming opportunities the church offers so that an individual can connect to a smaller community that shares their interests or stage of life—such as a small group, men's or women's breakfast, or a Sunday school class. If the visitor chooses to return and begins to take the next steps to assimilate into the community, they will eventually be invited to serve the church's mission as a volunteer—helping to operate these various activities—as well as to give generously—to fund expansion of the property, support programs, and employ the professionals who lead them.

Ironically, this model is not dissimilar to the sale of timeshares. Williamsburg, Virginia, is a tourist town filled with vacation timeshares, and I often encountered salespeople working the parking lots of the chain restaurants close to the hotel strip. These eager young men and women initiate a conversation the moment you step out of your car and walk with you as you make your way to the Denny's or IHOP. They have just a few seconds to entice you with free tickets to Busch Gardens if you will accept their invitation to visit the resort they represent and take a tour. If you agree, they schedule your visit to the sales center where a friendly host greets you, offers you a drink, and spends some time getting to know your family. After you are softened up, another staff member gives you a tour and describes all the amenities the facility offers those in your specific stage of life. Finally, you meet the professional closer whose responsibility it is to convince you to make a lifetime investment in their community. He or she is always highly motivated to push for the sale; the more units they sell, the larger the business grows. Once you become a timeshare owner, you are incentivized to recruit others to the property and given tools to equip you for this task.

Disciplemaking Factory

This discipleship pathway, common in the church-growth era, moved a person from participation in **_worship_** to **_community_** to **_mission_**. This strategy thrived in a predominantly Christian culture, where the average person you met in your neighborhood held a generally positive view of church and was familiar with the format of a worship service. Large group worship gatherings were so central to the life of the community that they simply became referred to as "Church." If a person seemed hesitant, you could always convince them by sharing that your church was different from other churches they previously experienced: "We are a church for people who don't like church" or "Everyone is welcome; no perfect people allowed" or "We are not like those other churches—we have great coffee, and you don't have to dress up." After developing enough relational credibility, and with a little cajoling, you could convince most neighbors or coworkers to give in and visit your church at least once or twice. Getting people to the church building was the vital step to starting someone on their discipleship journey, because it was key to them accessing our disciplemaking professionals and programs. This centralized worship gathering was the catalyst for spiritual growth.

Church leaders eventually streamlined this discipleship pipeline in order to process as many people as possible, as efficiently as possible. Only a few people in high levels of centralized leadership held power and access to program resources. Church members were trained in a very specific skill set that equipped them to play their part along the discipleship assembly line and allowed them to be quickly replaced if they moved away or dropped out. There was little room for individual creativity or customization of the established programs and, as in any factory, the work all took place on the main property under the leadership of professionals.

This format of church is what I knew—and it still thrives in Christendom.

Then I moved to Europe, where the notion of a church worship service is viewed with the same suspicion and contempt often reserved for a timeshare tour.

THE REALITY OF POST-CHURCH EUROPE

In our first few months in Brussels we met dozens of people: parents at the kids' school, friends at the gym, locals at our corner pub, neighbors in our apartment building. And at the appropriate moment, after creating a genuine friendship, we instinctively invited them to join us for our church service. Most thanked us for the offer, and while not one of them ever said yes, I think we heard all the polite ways people know how to say no.

We learned quickly that, in a post-Christian culture, a church building is not a place people are comfortable visiting, because many have never been in one. Some were not even aware that local churches existed in their city. When we invited one couple to join us "for church," they asked if we met in the enormous cathedral in the center of the city. Cathedrals were often their only understanding of church, and many European cathedrals have no active local congregation, while others are so lifeless they are being "desacralized" by the Vatican and repurposed by local governments as food markets or office spaces. Some smaller sanctuaries now exist as nightclubs or are retrofitted to serve as restaurants. Ceremonies most Americans consider religious are commonly held in secular venues: weddings occur in the local town hall performed by a civil magistrate; one friend attended a funeral in a private reception hall, presided over by a professional emcee. A "worship service" is still assumed to be highly sacred, reserved only for the most holy and devout. One couple turned down our invitation by saying, "Oh, no, I think we are too far gone for church." They viewed the gap between their secular lifestyle and the religious behaviors of a church service to be a chasm too great to cross.

When I mentioned this challenge to a Belgian member of The Well, she was not surprised. "It's not that my friends don't attend church; it's that they cannot imagine a reason they would want to." Church is a four-letter word. People pursuing spirituality in the city do so without the constraints of traditional religious systems. They attend hot yoga sessions, join Reiki energy healing groups, or take mindfulness classes. Neither the Bible nor the institutional church—Protestant, Catholic, or Orthodox—is considered by mainstream European society to be a valid source of spiritual truth. The reputation of Christianity throughout Europe is tarnished by abuses of power, memories of violent Inquisitions and Crusades, and, more recently, leadership scandals similar to those reported in the United States. One night, over beers with some university students I played basketball with, I shared that I was pastor of a local church. Dumbfounded, one of the guys said to me, "But you are so normal! When we think of priests, we think of those old guys who got in trouble for touching little boys." It is easy to see why a generation is not interested in church.

The language, rituals, and practices of Christianity are completely foreign to most of the Europeans in Brussels, who grew up in a post-Christian culture. The thought of crossing over from their secular world into the "sacred space" of a church sparks anxiety, not curiosity. It is hard for a North American Christian who has been part of a church for most of their life to even wrap their minds around this reality. So many of us have spent our whole lives in a culture so steeped in Christian assumptions and influence that we are not even able to identify the elements within our church spaces that are uniquely Christian. We are the proverbial fish who don't even know we're wet, because water is all we've ever known.

THE CROSS-CULTURAL CHALLENGE

Try to imagine it this way. (Forgive the cultural assumptions; just go with it.)

You are a suburban, home-owning, Christian husband and father. One day, new neighbors move in: Joseph, Nadia, and their two little girls. Before you even meet them, you guess by Nadia's attire that they are practicing Muslims. Your family takes them some cookies and welcomes them to the neighborhood, and a natural friendship develops over time. Your kids play with their kids, your wife and Nadia take walks, and you and Joseph chat warmly in the yard. One day Joseph seems to be mustering the courage to ask you something. Awkwardly, he begins to invite you and your family to join his family next Friday for a service at their mosque.

"I really think you'll like it. We have this young imam who teaches every week. He's very funny, and his messages are so relevant to everyday life. In fact, we're doing this teaching series from the Koran on marriage and relationships. You and your wife would really get a lot out of it. And the kids have their own program where they can learn about Allah with other kids. My girls love it, and they always come home with some cool craft they made. Plus, we have this amazing chai tea bar in our lobby. Actually, if you bring this card on Friday, you can turn it in and get a cup for free. And if you look on the other side of the card, you'll see a map that shows where you can park. But don't worry, we have a great team of people in the parking lot who'll help you find the guest parking right up front."

I'm guessing that most of us might politely respond in the moment, "Thanks for the offer; let me think about it." But soon after, a flood of questions would start running through our heads:

"What is it like in a mosque? Will I have to take my shoes off?"

"Can my wife even sit next to me? I think I saw on some TV show that men and women sit in different sections. Will she have to cover her head like Nadia does?"

"What does the Koran actually teach about relationships? I'm not sure I would even believe what it says."

"I don't know if I want my kids learning about Allah; what would they be teaching them?"

"I know there are different types of Muslims, and our neighbors seem normal, but what if this is one of those 'hyper-conservative radical' mosques?"

After waiting a few days to make it seem like we actually considered the offer, I wager most of us would respond politely with, "We are actually kind of busy this weekend, but thanks for asking."

For those of us who grew up in Christian culture, our hesitation likely derives from the fact that Islam is not part of our background. Nor is Islam founded on the basic worldview that makes up most of our existing belief system. Joseph is asking us to cross a huge cultural gap in order to experience his faith. Crossing into another culture is confusing and stressful, even if it is just for an hour. When I visited a few mosques in Turkey years ago as a tourist, it was a tremendously disorienting experience. I was not sure whether to sit or kneel, where to put my hands, or if I was expected to repeat the prayers with everyone else or just listen. The sanctuary was beautifully ornate, and the people around me seemed to be engaging in authentic worship, but I was self-conscious the whole time and constantly aware I was an outsider.[1]

This scenario simulates what it is like for a post-Christian individual to be invited to a Christian worship service in a church sanctuary. Showing up is more likely to trigger anxiety than facilitate a spiritual encounter with the Almighty. They are likely to be asking themselves the same questions, right down to "Is this one of those hyper-conservative, super-evangelical churches?"

As I realized that the "invitation to church" tool on my disciplemaking tool belt was not going to work in post-Christian Brussels, I started to assess whether it might be *theologically* misguided as well. When we ask people who do not identify as Christians to come to our church spaces, we are asking them to cross the cultural divide in order to encounter Jesus. We require them to do the hard translation work of finding meaning in our foreign religious language, symbols, practices, and beliefs. We put the burden on them, when the onus is meant to be on us as Jesus' followers.

Jesus crossed the cultural divide with humanity so that we might encounter God in a form that was familiar to us. God took on human flesh and entered into the world, speaking the language of the local people and living as a member of local society, in order to communicate his character and nature in ways that made sense. Jesus was so effective at becoming fully human that for nearly thirty years nobody around him even recognized him as divine.

Hear me now and believe me later: a time is rapidly approaching when any spiritual formation plan that begins with non-Christians coming to a church building and participating in a worship service will be irrelevant. In many parts of America—major urban centers; the West Coast; the Pacific Northwest; New England; and Hollywood, California, where I now live—that day is already here.

Post-Christian people do not come to church. Full stop.

> "No strategy, tactics, or clever marketing campaign could ever clear away the smokescreen that surrounds Christianity in today's culture."[2]—David Kinnaman and Gabe Lyons

Nothing we do on a Sunday morning will ever bring the next generation back through our doors. They don't care if you serve pour-over coffee, offer free Uber rides from campus, give away fashionable articles of church-branded clothing, or pay world-class musicians to sing beneath massive state-of-the-art digital screens surrounded by fake fog. They don't care how relevant your teaching is or how good your music is. They are not coming to church … because a church worship service is just not part of their culture.

Now, don't misunderstand me: large group worship gatherings have value in the life of a local church body. Corporate worship, Bible teaching, the Lord's Table, and Christian fellowship are all practices commended to God's people. But those activities are of no interest to post-Christians.

It *is* possible to grow the size of your church by spicing up your Sunday mornings, but the people you attract will be Christians who are either bored in another local church or have given up on attending because it didn't meet their needs. In our consumer-driven culture, people are always willing to trade up to something newer, bigger, or better; but I doubt many of us felt called to ministry to simply steal sheep from another flock. Ironically, it breaks my heart to see church plants in post-Christian settings grow quickly; it makes me wonder how many other local churches have fueled that growth, as their people upgrade to the newest model on the church market. I cringe when I hear young church planters in Los Angeles gushing over their preview services and large launches. I wish I could convince them that, by attracting people to a Sunday gathering, they are structuring for future obsolescence from their inception.

BOUNDED SETS AND CENTERED SETS

Social theorists would describe the prevailing form of American church as a *bounded set,* in which a person's *beliefs* and *behaviors* determine their *belonging.* To understand a bounded set, picture a shepherd in a field constructing a large, square fence to keep his sheep together in the pasture, while also keeping out animals that do not belong. Bounded organizations clearly indicate who are *insiders* and who are *outsiders.* They telegraph a standard of accepted behavior and a set of shared beliefs or values that must be met for a person to fully sense that they belong. Bounded sets include country clubs, fraternities and sororities, and the military, to name a few.

In my bounded-set model of church, I taught a membership class in which congregants learned and then affirmed our statement of faith and agreed to a standard of conduct in order to attain voting status. That is classic bounded-set structure: shared belief and shared behavior are necessary for initiation into full belonging. A common bounded-set church sign will read "A place to belong" or "You belong here!" The implication is that if you come join us for our worship service (beliefs) or in our weekly activities (behaviors), you will find belonging. The average post-Christian individual understands there are certain beliefs and behaviors required to participate in church activities, and this creates a mental fence too high for them to scale. In a bounded-set church, they simply see themselves as outsiders who do not belong.

Bounded sets are often created to ensure the community's protection from external danger. Churches organized themselves this way during Christendom because the majority of the culture shared Christian beliefs and behaviors, and the remaining small minority was perceived as an outside threat. However, this structure inadvertently led to the prevailing church mindset of "us vs. them," rather than a mindset that the church exists for the sake of the world.

Working in a bounded-set church, we received calls from parents in our youth ministry with concerns that certain "non-Christian" teenagers, who were reported to be smoking pot or having sex with their partners, were attending our youth group. One parent actually said, "I send my kid to youth group to get him away from those types of kids." They were accusing us of not enforcing our fences to protect their sheep. That is the expectation of the bounded-set member. When a bounded-set church senses a threat from within the community—for example someone believing or teaching erroneous doctrine or violating the accepted behavioral standards—that person can be expelled … either formally, or informally through social rejection. Bounded-set organizations exist to serve and protect insiders and convert outsiders—or else keep them at a distance.

"Church people think about how to get people into the church; kingdom people think about how to get the church into the world. Church people worry that the world might change the church; kingdom people work to see the church change the world."[3]—Kim Hammond

The opposite of a bounded set is a *centered set*—which is soft at the edges, allowing anyone to pass in and out, but firm at the center to preserve an essential DNA. Here *belonging* is offered before a person may decide to even show interest in the *behaviors* or *beliefs* of the core. Picture a centered set as a shepherd digging a well in a large field and then allowing his or her sheep to wander as they choose, knowing that at some point their own thirst will lead them back to the well to drink. The job of the shepherd is to orient the sheep toward the well so that when they are ready to drink, they know where to find water. In a centered set, rather than saying to outsiders "You belong here," the core community seeks to belong to the life of others by going out to their spaces and asking, "May we join you?" Jesus modeled this approach by going to the Decapolis region (Mark 7:31) and entering Samaria (John 4:4) to engage irreligious people where they already lived.

A centered-set expression of church recognizes that everyone shares a common identity as a spiritual being and therefore already possesses some form of relationship to God. Some may be far from Jesus and even have rejected him, while others may feel close to Jesus or be curious about him. Some, who may appear close by their external behavior, may actually be oriented away from him in their hearts. Church youth groups are filled with these sorts of kids who are part of a Christian family and attend church activities, but internally are oriented toward the world, longing to pursue the secular life as soon as they gain their freedom.

A centered-set church has a firm center—often a small leadership team that affirms common beliefs and values and seeks to embody a shared lifestyle, but in a way that does not communicate second-class status to those around them. The leadership of The Well did not refer to people as "non-Christians," because such a term would label them as outsiders. Instead we spoke of people as "not-yet followers of Jesus," reminding us to see what we hoped they would become and to continue to pray for their journey. When I asked Carlton once if a particular individual was a Christian, he said lovingly, "He is trending toward Jesus."

Bounded-Set Bullies and a Centered-Set Savior

These two contrasting systems are apparent in the ministry of the Pharisees and Jesus. The Pharisees constructed a fence of legal restrictions in an attempt to maintain their purity and prevent themselves from being defiled by others (Matthew 23). Jesus, on the other hand, engaged with all sorts of people society deemed far from God—such as the poor (Luke 6:20), the unclean (Luke 8:48), Roman oppressors (Matthew 8:10), and racial enemies (John 4)—in order to orient them toward his Father. In a quintessential moment of contrasting approaches, Jesus enters Matthew's house and shares a meal with his tax-collector friends—both indicators of social belonging in the Ancient Near East. The Pharisees refuse to even enter the house, never mind eat together, for fear of being identified with social reprobates (Matthew 9:9–12). These "sinners" exist outside the Pharisees' religious fence. The tax-collectors would have to change their behavior or beliefs in order for the Pharisees to celebrate common belonging with them. Jesus, on the other hand, sees this shared meal as an opportunity to orient these people to the well of Living Water in their midst. The great paradox is that the Pharisees are perceived to be close to God, when it is the sinners and social outcasts who are in fact drawing near to God's presence in Jesus.

Centered-Set Disciplemaking

I was raised in the bounded-set church. I was taught to convert non-Christians through evangelism strategies and then disciple them. In Brussels, I began to embrace a centered-set mentality. I learned to come alongside those who were not-yet followers of Jesus and disciple them through our community's life in order to help them take the next steps to draw closer to Jesus. As a family, we relinquished a traditional evangelism strategy in favor of a blessing strategy and prayed that our tangible acts of love, offered with no strings attached, might alert people to the divine source of all blessing. We focused more on demonstrating the visible fruit of our faith than arguing intellectual proofs of faith.

"It is said rightly that love is 'the final apologetic,' in the sense that our best argument is our love for the people we talk to."[4]—Os Guinness

Borrowing a phrase from Michael Frost, we tried to "live a questionable life"[5]; a life surprising enough to provoke others to question our motivations. This is the pattern we see in the book of Acts. Many of the proclamations of the gospel recorded in Acts are in response to questions asked by those outside the church.[6] Lesslie Newbigin writes of these stories,

> Something has happened which makes people aware of a new reality, and therefore the question arises: What is this reality? The communication of the gospel is the answering of that question.[7]

The church demonstrates the power and principles of God's kingdom and the character of Jesus until people begin to ask questions to which the gospel is the answer.

A post-Christian context demands that we adopt Jesus' centered-set paradigm that propelled him to go to the people rather than require them to come to him. The future requires us to replace our industrial disciplemaking approach with one that equips individuals to make disciples outside of our factory's four walls. For that, we must restructure our disciplemaking pathway by actually reversing its flow.

Questions for Reflection

1. How does your local church express its discipleship pathway or spiritual formation plan? (Maybe it is written on the walls or at the bottom of the weekly newsletter or bulletin.) Do you see a structure similar to *worship > community > mission*?

2. In what ways can you relate to the decrease in Sunday worship participation by those who are not followers of Jesus? What have you tried in your local church in order to bring people back to worship services by making them more appealing?

3. Does your church primarily operate as a bounded set or centered set? What specific aspects of your church might be outliers to that norm?

4

Reversing Our Disciplemaking Pathways

To make new disciples in a post-Christian culture, churches cannot assume people will attend gatherings on our property led by our professionals. Instead we need to equip disciplemaking people to embody a centered-set approach. A centered-set strategy actually reverses the established disciplemaking pathways. We lead with *mission,* draw people into deeper *community*, and pray the Holy Spirit leads them to *worship* Jesus as Lord.

Much like the pre-Christian context of the first century, the life and activity of the post-Christian local church is to be catalyzed around God's mission. *Missio* is the Latin word meaning "sent," giving rise to the idea of an "emissary"—a person sent out as a representative of another. Scripture reveals God as a sent and sending God. God the Father sent his Son; the Father and the Son sent the Holy Spirit; now the Father, Son, and Spirit are sending the church into the world. Jesus' church is a sent people, a community of faith propelled out into the world by the grace and love of God, to be a blessing to others. "The missional church believes it is God who is on mission and that we are to join him in it. The missional church is made up of missionaries; the people of God partnering with God in his redemptive mission in the world."[1]

The mission of God is his redemptive work to restore all things to the way he created them to be through the transforming power of Jesus. It is God's grand renewal project on earth. God desires to redeem people and places, citizens and systems so that they better reflect his kingdom. "We often wrongly assume that the primary activity of God is in the church. Instead, the primary activity of God is in the world, and the church is an instrument created by God to be sent into the world to participate in what he is already doing."[2]

When we lead with mission, our primary disciplemaking energy goes not into trying to gather the unchurched, but into scattering the existing church to flesh out the life of Jesus wherever they are: his values, his character, his ministry, and his kingdom. The church

"Mission is not just a particular task or activity but a way of life, a participation in what God is doing around the world and across the street."[3]—Kirsteen Kim

then becomes a redemptive presence that points to an alternative kingdom. "We should be sending the people in the church out among the people of the world, rather than attempting to attract the people of the world in among the people in the church."[4] We must stop expecting the world to come to us and instead embrace our "sentness."

Mission is not merely evangelism. Evangelical churches in the past century often confused these two and, as a result, believed that the only goal of serving others or the community was to share the gospel or invite people to church (to hear the gospel presented). When we reduce mission to evangelism, conversion becomes the ulterior motive of our acts of blessing. However, when we define God's mission as the redemption and renewal of all creation through Jesus, the acts of renewal we participate in have value in and of themselves. Such acts are part of God's kingdom work, and they "disciple" others in how the world will one day be when Jesus reigns as king. The rebirth of the people we serve becomes an *ultimate* motive without being an *ulterior* motive. By modeling acts of love and blessing, we disciple those who do not yet follow Christ into the life of Jesus; they see our lives incarnate his passion and priorities. We trust that God was at work in their spirits before we even engaged with them, and we ask the Holy Spirit to help us discern when and how to express the motivations for our actions and invite them to consider the truth of Christ for themselves. When we do this not just as individuals but also as small teams, the love in our relationships and the unity amidst our diversity also models the life of God's kingdom.

> "The role of the church is simply this: to bless the world. In doing this, the people of God reveal God's heart for the world."[5]—Reggie McNeal

One of my favorite illustrations for this approach comes from the French term *amuse-bouche*. The words literally mean "an amusement for the mouth," but practically this phrase refers to the bite-sized *hors d'oeuvres* that restaurants serve to awaken your palette for what is to come. They are presented "compliments of the chef" to prepare the guests for the meal and to offer a glimpse of the chef's approach to the art of cuisine. Our family's favorite Ethiopian restaurant, Kob Kob, offered a small serving of saffron-infused couscous with lemon zest and raisins. When you tasted this single delicious bite, you could barely wait to see what was coming next. You'd think, *If this is what they give away for free, imagine how good the meal we are paying for is going to be!*

The Well sought to be an *amuse-bouche*—a foretaste of the kingdom of God, so that when the world sampled us, they would long to know how they could fully experience God's kingdom. We sought to bless others through tangible acts of service with no strings attached so that our presence became a source of blessing in their lives. We prayed that the story of Jesus at the wedding at Cana would become true again;[6] that when we as servants offered our ordinary acts, Jesus would transform them into extraordinary blessings in the lives of others. We tried to demonstrate the alternative values of God's kingdom, such as selflessness, generosity, forgiveness, and peacemaking, and to juxtapose those against the surrounding kingdom of the world, which rewarded self-centeredness, jealousy, materialism, unforgiveness, as well as racial, ethnic, and class divisions. Through our work in the community, we tried to reflect what we believed would be true in the age to come—an end to poverty, injustice, ugliness, hatred, and fear. We offered a brief taste of these values now, hoping our neighbors would seek Jesus who promises to serve up his fullness later!

RECLAIMING THE CHURCH AS GOD'S PEOPLE

To make disciples in this new context, we must shift how we invest our resources—our money, time, and effort. We can no longer rely on acquiring a bigger property, spotlighting charismatic professionals, or implementing the next prepackaged program. We must reclaim the true meaning of church as God's people sent on God's mission to make disciples and join God in redeeming and renewing all of creation through Jesus.

The disciplemaking tool we need most in this new post-Christian world is *disciplemaking people.*

We must invest more resources in developing God's people so we all know how to effectively make disciples in our day-to-day lives. Those who have rejected institutional church need to see Jesus incarnated in the lives of his people as we flesh out the kingdom in the everyday spaces of life: the places where we live, work, play, and create. We must stop merely inviting the world to church and instead be the church for the world.

Each existing disciple needs to be equipped to embed into the community and participate in the rhythms of life that create common identity with those we encounter every day. We may even partner with people who don't believe what we believe but want what we want on behalf of our neighbors and cities. Those partnerships provide opportunities for God's people to incarnate Jesus in close proximity and affirm the God-given desires in others to make the world a better place.

Imagine if the local church simply began training its members to live as resident missionaries and make disciples in the places where they are already doing life. Imagine small bands of disciples living the missional-incarnational life of Jesus in the mission fields of their own neighborhoods, workplaces, and social spaces, such as cafés, gyms, art studios, and parks. Wherever you are now, wherever you spend the majority of your time—*that* is your mission field.

BLESSING THE LOCAL BAR

Shortly after we arrived in Brussels, a small Irish pub opened just a few blocks from our apartment. The young manager shared with me his heart to make the bar a social center, with live music, pub quizzes, jam sessions, comedy nights, and live football matches. The pub was on the border of two neighborhoods, both of which had Well microchurches. Members of both communities became regulars and did whatever we could do to bless the bar and help the manager achieve his dreams for the place.

Well members watched the Belgian World Cup matches, attended beer tastings and comedy nights, ran pub quizzes, hosted friends' going-away parties, and we even held a staff team-building day in the pub when it was closed to the public from 10–4. When friends came in from out of town, we always took them to the pub for dinner. I even offered my NFL streaming service, so we could host a Super Bowl party, albeit at midnight local time. We posted online reviews and recommended the bar to friends looking for the best burgers in town. We brought in as much business as we could and added as much positive life as possible when we were there. One night it got so crowded that the bartenders were running out of pint glasses and were unable to get around to collect the used ones. I grabbed a tray and bussed a few tabletops around me, delivering the glasses to the sink area, so the staff could keep serving. We did whatever we could to ensure our presence was good news to the staff team.

Over the course of all of those hours, we got to know the people who made the pub special. We met a Romanian bartender and listened to him share his childhood experiences of waiting in line for daily rations in Communist Russia. A young Slovenian woman, living on her own for the first time, told us about a man who tried to push her into a tram one night, and the subsequent fear she felt walking the streets. My family loved it when the head chef would come over to our table before it got busy on a Friday night and bring us some new special menu item he was working on. When the manager was treated for exhaustion at a hospital back in his home country, we texted regularly to see how he was doing and to tell him The Well was praying for his recovery. One of the great honors of my final months in Brussels was being invited to a going-away party for a bartender. When I arrived, I looked around the table to realize I was the only person there who was not a staff member. It was an incredible confirmation that I was part of the community. Don't get me wrong, The Well people were by no means perfect missionaries in that space. Some nights we failed to capitalize on divine opportunities, and other nights we let the culture impact us more than we did it, but our aim was to share life with the community at the pub, hoping to partner with God in his work in their lives.

One night, sitting at the bar waiting for a friend from The Well, I struck up a conversation with a young Brit named Fergus who was just home from lobbying the European Parliament in Strasbourg, France. By the time my Well friend showed up, there was enough affinity that the three of us spent the evening together, sharing stories and connecting on our life as expats in Brussels. I asked Fergus about the spiritual interest in London, where I was preparing to visit, and we talked about my work with The Well and our non-profit, Serve the City. He admitted he had little knowledge of spiritual things. As we went home, we all exchanged business cards and hoped to meet again for a beer.

While we were getting to know Fergus, his girlfriend, Maxine, was in London visiting a few friends who were followers of Jesus. Maxine had spent her childhood around the Catholic Church but was no longer involved in any spiritual practices. However, being with these Christians in London made her long for a community where she might be able to explore faith again. Sadly, her boyfriend showed no interest in spiritual matters, and she knew he would never join her on that journey toward faith. Imagine her shock when she returned to Brussels to find that Fergus had met two Christians at a local bar and wanted to hang out with them again. In that moment she sensed God was real and cared about her.

Kristyn and I spent a few meals with Fergus and Maxine together—and hours alone with Maxine—exploring Jesus. Eventually she expressed interest in attending an 'All Well' spiritual formation retreat. On that weekend, Maxine decided to become a disciple of Jesus, and we baptized her in a nearby stream. With tears in her eyes, she shared with our community how she began the year with a strong sense that she was going to die in the next twelve months and the anxiety that it caused every day. As she was baptized, we celebrated that she was indeed dying to herself and being reborn as a new creation in Christ. It will forever be my most cherished ministry moment in Brussels.

EVERYONE IS A MISSIONARY

"We must plant the seed of the Gospel of the kingdom, and the fruit will be the changed lives living out their faith together, which is church."[7]—Neil Cole

In Christendom, missions was viewed as work done overseas among the people of another culture; but in a post-Christian context, every day offers opportunity for cross-cultural interaction with people who do not hold to a Christian worldview or belief system. Missions is no longer a secondary department in the church; it must be reclaimed as the church's central activity in the world. Living as a missionary no longer requires relocating to a new country; it merely requires adopting a new state of mind that believes we are sent to join God's work in our own neighborhoods and relational networks.

Our lifestyles must evolve to encompass the practices of traditional overseas cross-cultural missionaries. Imagine every member of your local church fulfilling this job description.

A Missionary:

- *Joins a social group.* We identify with others through proximity and shared life routines. We appropriately enter others people's spaces through opportunities, such as common meals and acts of hospitality and are present with them in their lives.
- *Learns the customs, language, and culture.* We refrain from judging but instead take the posture of a learner. As we learn about, and from, others, we listen to God to see where he is already at work.
- *Adds value to the community.* We bless others through tangible acts of love offered with no strings attached. We seek to serve others without recognition and remuneration whenever possible.
- *Displays the kingdom of God in word and deed.* We alert people to the universal reign of God through Christ and discern how to communicate the good news of Jesus through our lives.
- *Helps people learn to live like Jesus.* We disciple people through our relationships, as we model the life of Jesus and articulate the truth of Jesus expressed in God's Word.
- *Establishes communities that care for one another and trains others to live as missionaries themselves.* We form communities that worship God in ways that resonate with the local culture. We study God's Word together, fulfill the New Testament "one another" commands,[8] engage in spiritual disciplines, celebrate our stories of missional incarnational living, and eventually seek to multiply our community to be able to reach new places and new pockets of people.

Notice the *mission* > *community* > *worship* pathway inherent in that description. None of those steps involve getting people to come to a church building, introducing them to a professional pastor, or signing them up for a discipleship program. Each step emerges naturally from the life of a disciplemaking person. To make disciples in this new age, we must equip and deploy the entirety of the church into the totality of the world to join the work God is already doing in every nook and cranny of culture. Everyone has a role to play, not just the professionals or those with Sunday platform gifts.

> In the new post-Christendom era, the church leader will be less a grand orator or star figure who gathers individuals for inspiration and exhortation, and more a convener and equipper of people who together will be transformed as they participate in God's transforming work in the world.[9]

The Protestant Reformation successfully returned the Word of God into the hands of the people of God. Bible translators like John Wycliffe and William Tyndale toiled by candlelight to make the Scriptures accessible to more people in their own language and catalyzed a global revival as a result.[10] But what the Reformation did not effectively do was to return God's *work* into the hands of God's people. The "mercenary model" of ministry still pervades too many churches today. Congregations pay the professionals to do the ministry while they go about their own business. While this arrangement may seem mutually beneficial, I believe it is actually mutually destructive; professionals get crushed under the weight of superhuman expectations, and God's people miss out on the spiritual formation derived from ministry. It is time for those of us who are professional leaders in the local church to be humble enough to de-center ourselves from the life of the church and take up the call to equip every member to operate out of their gifts and calling. Our church members are not meant to generate timeshare leads in the parking lot so that we, as professionals, can close the deal on the main stage; they are invited to get in on the action themselves and utilize their own God-given gifts for his glory. Each follower of Jesus has a divine call to participate in God's kingdom work and to make disciples of Jesus.

"Men and women are not ordained to this ministerial priesthood in order to take priesthood away from the people but in order to nourish and sustain the priesthood of the people."[11]—Lesslie Newbigin

The church's energy must be refocused away from the Sunday platform and into the spiritual formation of disciples for their life in the mission field. Thankfully, this reversed pathway is not only more effective at making new disciples, I believe it is also a more robust form of discipleship and spiritual formation in the lives of those of us who are already believers. Just as the oyster's interaction with the sand activates the pearl-making process, our faith is likewise refined and deepened much more in the context of missional engagement with the world than by sitting in pews or traditional forms of Christian education. And the community life of the church is refined and deepened as we serve hand-in-hand, laboring for the kingdom to come.

To make disciples in a post-Christian world, we must move beyond a Sunday-centric model of church and destroy the debilitating mythology of solo-heroic, platform-driven disciplemaking. We must stop relying on an invitation to "come and see Jesus in our midst" and instead begin deploying people who can "go and be Jesus in their midst." It's time to stop trying to get the world into church and instead get the church into the world, embodying the life of Jesus and embedding that life in the places to which we have already been sent.

Questions for Reflection

1. What emotions do you feel as you consider a church disciplemaking strategy that would not be dependent on property, professionals or programs, but rather on empowering every disciple to make disciples in the everyday spaces of life?

2. Look back at the job description of a missionary. Which of those skills are currently present in the lives of people in your church and which would need to be developed?

3. In what ways do you try to live as an *amuse-bouche* of God's kingdom? When people ask you about those practices and priorities, how can you verbalize your faith in Jesus in a way that is clear but also piques their curiosity?

5

The Good News Gone Bad

Having set aside the church invitation as an irrelevant disciplemaking device, I began to engage in my community as a missionary, leaning on the other tool that served me well in ministry: sharing the gospel. In Virginia, I spent hours in coffee shops, in counseling sessions, and on campus engaging with people who felt far from God and were staring down the consequences of living a life apart from him. I met with men facing bankruptcy caused by their secret gambling habits, students trapped in pornography addictions, women hiding affairs from their husbands. Each person sought me out in the midst of guilt, shame, and failure, looking for hope and absolution. I became adept at sharing the good news of the gospel with people who felt bad about themselves.

My version of the gospel usually sounded something like this:

"God loves you so much that he sent his Son to die on the cross to pay the penalty for your sins so you can have eternal life with him in heaven when you die. The feeling of guilt you have is a consequence of your sin, but if you confess your sin and turn to Jesus, he can take that away and replace it with the joy of his forgiveness."

Some version of that gospel got me through fifteen years of ministry in Christendom, but for some reason it did not seem to be translating into post-Christian Europe. During my first year, I attended a conference where Marcus Fritsch, a Communitas church planter in Gothenburg, Sweden, said, "There is no guilt in Sweden." Marcus explained that one consequence of the post-Christian rejection of absolute truth and universal moral standards is that people generally don't feel guilty. There is no standard to violate, so guilt doesn't come into play. People may admit to poor choices and unfortunate consequences, but they do not sense the weight of transgressing a moral boundary—let alone one set by a holy God.

Returning to Brussels after the conference, it was as if scales had fallen from my eyes, and I began to review some of the encounters that had baffled me. People often amazed me with their openness in sharing parts of their lives that clearly felt immoral to my Judeo-Christian ethic: the couple who spoke about the joys of being "polyamorous" and sharing multiple sexual partners; the father at our kids' school who corrected me when I referred to the woman he had lived with for twenty years as his wife ("Oh no, we're not married; we are just partners"); shopkeepers speaking openly about their strategies for hiding income from the government to avoid paying taxes. I assumed such behaviors would be hidden from the public eye—or at least shared with a hint of remorse. But in a post-Christian society, they were just morally neutral lifestyle choices. Because there was no objective morality to violate, there were no personal feelings of guilt.

In light of this, it dawned on me why I was not encountering opportunities to share the gospel with the people I met in Brussels. My gospel was only good news for people who felt bad about themselves, and nobody around me did. People were not walking around thinking, "What must I do to be saved?" (Acts 16:30). I was keen to share the gospel, but the act of "sharing" implies giving something to someone who wants to receive it. In Europe no one was interested in my version of the gospel.

My first instinct was to figure out how I could convince people of their guilt. Sure, Jesus says it's the Holy Spirit's job to "convict people of sin and righteousness and judgment" (John 16:8 ESV), but maybe he needed a little help. This is the initial impulse I often see in the evangelical church, as the subjective ethics of post-Christian culture sweep across the West. We put on our Junior-Holy-Spirit badges and assume the role of culture's moral police. We look for ethical violations and wag our fingers. The result is that the surrounding culture perceives church people as harbingers of bad news rather than ambassadors of good news. People don't celebrate when they discover a neighbor or coworker is a Christian; they are more likely to roll their eyes and shut their doors. Christians think sharing the bad news about sin will lead to the good news of forgiveness and freedom, but people are not sticking around to hear any of it. They get a whiff of judgment and condemnation and turn away.

RELEARNING THE GOSPEL

I dove back into the Scriptures looking for a better understanding of "the gospel." I started with the embodiment of good news himself, Jesus, to see how he used that term. Jesus regularly used the words *good news* or *gospel* (depending on how each translation rendered the Greek word *euangelion*); but it was not until I reread Luke 9:6—"So [the disciples] set out and went from village to village, proclaiming the good news and healing people everywhere"—that I realized my definition of good news did not align with how Jesus used it.

My definition of the gospel relied on such phrases as "Jesus died on the cross," "paid the penalty for our sin," and "go to heaven when we die." But when Jesus commissioned the disciples in Luke 9, there was no cross, there was no human substitution for sin, and Jesus seemed to be telling people that the kingdom of heaven was already on earth, rather than something that could only be experienced after death. Clearly my presentation of the good news was not what Jesus was sending these twelve men out to share. So what were these disciples telling people as they went out to preach the gospel?

Matthew 9:35 offers an answer: "Jesus went through all the towns and villages, teaching in their synagogues, proclaiming the good news of the kingdom and healing every disease and sickness."

Rather than sharing a system of salvation, Jesus and his disciples declared the good news of the kingdom of God being established on earth. Jesus signaled that the current earthly kingdom, symbolized by the Roman Empire, was being supplanted by a new kingdom that God was establishing. Whereas the old kingdom was marked by tyranny, oppression, and injustice, this new kingdom is marked by justice, peace, compassion, and righteousness. In this new kingdom, captives are set free, the sick are healed, the poor are valued, and the brokenness in the world is set right. This new kingdom is not some future reality; it is being revealed in the present through powerful healings and miracles, and the invitation is for all to enter in through Jesus, the Messiah, the King of Kings himself.

The gospel that Jesus and his disciples shared was a holistic gospel of communal flourishing, described in the Old Testament as God's *shalom*. It impacted individuals but was not limited to the absolution of personal sin. It began to dawn on me that I had settled for a truncated, reductionist version of the gospel. It's not that my gospel was entirely wrong; it was just too small.[2] To use a metaphor appropriate for my time in Brussels, I realized I was not fluent in the gospel.[3]

> *"There is no such thing as McApologetics, though it is significant that the nearest one-size-fits-all approach—the Four Spiritual Laws—was also created at the same time and in the same place as the first flourishing of McDonald's as we know it and the first theme park run by Walt Disney: 1950s California."[1]—Os Guinness*

Belgium has three national languages—French, German, and Flemish (a local dialect of Dutch); but in Brussels, French and English are most common. Our kids attended a French-speaking public school and quickly became proficient for their grade level. However, the ability to speak English in most public settings worked against my ambition to learn French. As a result, I never achieved anything close to fluency. I possessed enough working vocabulary to operate in the city and not embarrass myself, and I could read a newspaper and decipher the general meaning, but I could never express in French the fullness of my life experience or the totality of my identity.

Apparently, even after all my years of pastoral ministry, I was not fluent in the gospel either. I knew some key phrases and mastered a few expressions that I relied on time and time again, but in Brussels I became aware that I was not able to articulate the fullness of God's redemptive experience or the totality of Jesus' work.

Old Testament scholar Walter Brueggemann wrote, "The gospel is thus a truth widely held, but a truth greatly reduced. It is a truth that has been flattened, trivialized, and rendered inane."[4] Let me identify three gospel reductions that permeated both my ministry and my attempts to share the gospel.

"The good news was both about the coming of the Kingdom of God and the character of that Kingdom. It was about what God's Kingdom looked like. It was about what citizenship in God's Kingdom requires. The biblical gospel writers' good news was about the restoration of shalom."[5]—Lisa Sharon Harper

REDUCTION 1: THE GOSPEL REMOVES MY SIN

In my experience, evangelicalism relies heavily on the language of substitutionary atonement as the primary work of the gospel, and the individual as the primary recipient of the gospel. It is true that Jesus became our perfect substitution on the cross and atoned for our sins so that we might take on his righteousness, but that is not the *whole* truth of the gospel. Individual sin is only one aspect of the brokenness in the world, but I had made it the entirety. In my journey to discover a more robust gospel narrative, I returned to the overarching metanarrative of Scripture itself. The Bible tells a four-part story that progresses through the stages of *creation, fall, redemption,* and *restoration.*

At the risk of oversimplifying, let me summarize.

In *creation,* God made a perfect world and formed humanity to bear his image in that world. God commanded humanity to multiply and fill the earth so that the image of God and his presence would permeate every inch of his creation. The King created a kingdom and sent his subjects into every corner of it to bear his likeness and embody his values and character. Divinity and humanity lived in peace and unity amidst the rest of God's perfect creation. And it was good.

The *fall* came when humans chose to violate God's instructions and attempted to elevate ourselves to the position of king. The effects were catastrophic. Expelled from God's presence, we forfeited the things we were meant to experience in our intimacy with God—unconditional love, eternal purpose, a secure identity, communal acceptance, and health and wholeness. Now we seek those things in the created world itself. The effects of the Fall extended to all of the natural creation and, as a result, everything is broken.

God began a work of *redemption* on behalf of his creation. He intervened in the world despite its brokenness and prevented it from experiencing the full effects of its corruption. God's redemptive work is traced throughout the Old Testament and ultimately is fulfilled in the person of Jesus Christ. Jesus' life, death, and resurrection make redemption available for all who believe in him, as well as his creation. Jesus entered into the brokenness of the world in order to restore its original beauty. This redemption is not limited to individuals, but also has social, communal, and even environmental implications. We are now invited into the life of Jesus that brings transformation in us and into the world around us. God sent himself as the Holy Spirit to indwell, sanctify, and empower his redeemed people and as a deposit of the ultimate reward awaiting his people.

Now, in the closing chapter, God is actively bringing about the *restoration* of all things to the way they were originally meant to be. God is renewing the world through Jesus and inviting the present-day body of Jesus to participate in that work empowered by the Holy Spirit. His Spirit is also actively at work within his people to renew the parts and places of our lives that are broken so that we grow into a fuller likeness of Jesus. We are invited into the work of making disciples as a way of multiplying God's image throughout the earth. All of creation longs for the day of Jesus' return when he will complete this restoration, and his kingdom will fully reign on earth as it does in heaven.

The gospel story of God's kingdom centers on Jesus at every phase. Jesus is the agent of *creation*, he experiences personal rejection and suffering as a result of the *fall*, he defeats evil and death to secure *redemption*, and he is at work now and will one day return to bring about the final *restoration* of all things. Jesus is the embodiment of this good news. He is so central to the story that it is fair to say, in effect, the gospel is a Person. Hence salvation is not merely transactional but inherently relational, reconciling us to our Creator and returning us to our original calling.

> When people are saved by God through faith in Christ they are not only being saved from their sins, they are saved in order to resume the tasks mandated at creation, the task of caring for and cultivating a world that honors God and reflects his character and glory.[6]

Moving Out of the Basement

As this more holistic metanarrative saturated my thinking, I realized that the way I presented the gospel only told half of the story. I focused on *fall* and *redemption* without ever articulating the beauty of *creation* or *restoration*. I began with humanity's "badness" and ended with Jesus' forgiveness, but my gospel never included humanity's original goodness or God's ultimate determination to restore things to the way they once were. One day, as I sketched the four parts of God's redemptive story as quadrants within a square, I realized the picture resembled a house. I was only describing the deep, dark basement when there was beauty to be seen from the upper floors.

I was starting my gospel narrative in Genesis 3 rather than Genesis 1. As my friend Deb Hirsch says: "First things must surely come first. We were, after all, created in God's image before we all fell into sin. Genesis 1 comes before Genesis 3. Yes, people are sinners but that is a secondary truth; they are first and foremost image bearers."[7]

> Many Christians have been taught only half the story—that we were born sinners and our focus should be on getting ourselves and others to heaven. To bypass the notion that we were made in God's image or His desire for restoration of the world is to miss crucial parts of His loving story for us....We answer the most elemental questions of life radically differently depending on whether we are living out of half the story or the full story of God's redemption.[8]

I once had a great conversation with a local nightclub owner. He told me he was raised in a Baptist church and even volunteered as a youth group leader, but after coming out of the closet, he had rejected Christianity (or it had rejected him). When he discovered I was a pastor, he said to me, "You know what hymn I never liked? 'Amazing Grace.'"

I was stupefied. "Really? That one is a classic. How could you not like it?"

He responded. "I never liked that phrase 'a wretch like me.' That's not how I think of myself. I don't think anyone should think of himself as a wretch."

He had experienced a toxic version of Christianity, which overemphasized Genesis 3 so much that it caused low self-image. He was looking for a spiritual starting point that affirmed there is some goodness in everyone. In his understanding, he could not find that within the Christian faith.

However, when we look at Jesus' ministry, we see that he begins the majority of his interactions by affirming a person's primary/intrinsic worth rather than condemning his or her secondary/external behaviors. Think of Jesus dining with Zacchaeus,[9] intervening to protect the woman caught in adultery,[10] or asking his Father to forgive his executioners.[11] In each case he could have pronounced judgment over the wrong in their lives, but instead he affirmed the right—that they had inherent value to God. Jesus does not see us merely as we are but as what he imagines we might become by his grace.

This sort of relational optimism brings a prophetic dynamic to the disciple-making of the New Testament. Jesus calls Simon by the name *Peter*, or *Rock*, long before Peter himself exhibits the stability and faithfulness to merit that nickname.[12] Paul calls the people of the church at Corinth *saints*, even though the rest of the letter reveals they were not acting in a very saintly manner.[13] He affirms them as saints by God's redemptive decree before addressing their behavioral imperfections. Just as Jesus called Peter a rock before he became one, we can call out the parts of people's lives that reflect the character of Jesus before they become someone who wants their whole life to reflect him.

A New Appreciative Approach

It is possible to recalibrate the gospel conversation and begin by telling people good news. They are wonderfully made and have tremendous value in the eyes of God who formed them in his own image. We don't need to convince people they are sinners to have spiritual conversations; we can celebrate the parts of their lives that reflect God's character, such as their sacrificial love for their children, the care they bring to tending a garden, or the compassion they show those on the margins of the city.

Imagine when a friend is quick to reconcile with someone who has offended them, communicating to her, "Wow, that was amazing how forgiving you were toward her after what she did to you. That reminds me of Jesus; I want to be more like that in my relationships." Or when an artist captures beauty and shares it with others, encouraging him by offering, "I think God loves how you captured the beauty of his world in that piece." I remember my friend Kim Hammond simply stopping a waitress in the middle of her serving us to say, "You are really good at your job—thank you!" Her face absolutely lit up. These sorts of comments must be genuine; post-Christian culture is riddled with skepticism, so people easily sniff out inauthenticity. However, if our heart is to honestly affirm others as made in God's image and bearing inestimable value and worth, then such comments are a tremendous gift. By calling out what is good and right about people, we celebrate the image of God in the world.

> "The best things about that person are blessings from God. The worst things about that person are arenas for God's redemption. People are hungry for encouragement and love and need help noticing the presence of the divine in their lives."[14]
> —Leonard Sweet

Learning to see people through appreciative lenses was a hard skill for me to develop. I had long approached those who did not know Jesus through a deficit mentality, focusing on what was wrong in their lives and looking for opportunities to correct that through a relationship with Jesus. I saw any goodness in them as an attempt to do good deeds that actually kept them from accepting the full offer of grace. I felt the need to break them down, not build them up. I feared that if I did not help them experience conviction of sin, they would think they were a good person who didn't need God in their life.

However, when I surrendered my Junior-Holy-Spirit badge and began to affirm behaviors and character in others that reflected God, something remarkable often happened; they responded by confessing their imperfections. Their own consciences prompted them to admit their inability to behave well consistently. When I led with a celebration of what was beautiful in their lives, they felt safe enough to share their brokenness! That admission provided an opportunity for me to share my brokenness and the redemption and hope I find in Jesus. In the kingdom, acceptance precedes repentance. I was experiencing first-hand Paul's words to the people of the church in Rome: "the kindness of God leads you to repentance."[15]

> "There is always the possibility of goodness and great beauty in all people. Seeing like this changes everything. Our role becomes to look for God in them, to call forth the image, to fan it into flame, to help them to both see and become like the One they reflect."[16]—Debra Hirsch

As we enrich our disciplemaking relationships with this more appreciative mindset, we embody good news to people. Rather than trying to convince post-Christian people of a need they don't feel, such as forgiveness of sin and alleviation of guilt, we can identify the ways they *are* experiencing the brokenness of this world and seeking to transcend those effects with imperfect solutions.

REDUCTION 2: THE GOSPEL OFFERS FORGIVENESS

A beautiful part of pastoring an international community like The Well was the cultural exposure to people from all over the world. We befriended people from every corner of Europe who were working for the European Parliament; Africans and Persians seeking asylum from religious persecution; Romanians who had grown up under Communism in the U.S.S.R.; Mexicans who showed us incredible hospitality; and university students from China. The more followers of Jesus I met from outside my own white, European-American culture, the more I realized that my understanding of the gospel had been limited by the Western culture in which I was raised and its emphasis on individualism and legality.

A Cultural Gospel

Christians from other cultures worship the same triune God and read the same Scripture, but emphasize very different aspects of the gospel when they speak of the impact of Jesus on their lives.

Jayson Georges' book, *The 3D Gospel: Ministry in Guilt, Shame, and Fear Cultures,*[17] is an excellent resource on the topic, which I discovered in my search to understand the three main global cultures and how they each interpret salvation. Below is his summary of the three cultures as well as Scripture verses that affirm how God's salvation addresses each paradigm's longings.

1. ***Guilt-innocence cultures*** are individualistic societies (mostly Western), where people who break the laws are guilty and seek justice or forgiveness to rectify a wrong. People seek to remain innocent before institutions by obeying the rules and laws, lest they be reckoned guilty.

    "In him we have redemption through his blood, the forgiveness of sins" (Ephesians 1:7a).

"God ... made us alive with Christ even when we were dead in transgressions" (Ephesians 2:4–5).

2. ***Shame-honor cultures*** are collectivistic communities (common in the East), where individuals are shamed for not fulfilling group expectations to restore their honor before the community. People seek to be honorable in the community by respecting the group's expectations and playing the appropriate roles, lest they be shamed.

"God decided in advance to adopt us into his own family by bringing us to himself through Jesus Christ" (Ephesians 1:5 NLT).

"You are no longer foreigners and strangers, but fellow citizens with God's people and also members of his household" (Ephesians 2:19, cf. 2:12–13).

3. ***Fear-power cultures*** refer to animistic contexts (typically tribal or African), where people are afraid of evil and harm, and pursue power over the spirit world through magical rituals. People seek to be powerful in the spiritual realm by observing the proper rituals and techniques, lest they be powerless and vulnerable.

"That power is the same as the mighty strength he exerted when he raised Christ from the dead and seated him at his right hand in the heavenly realms, far above all rule and authority, power and dominion" (Ephesians 1:19–21).

"Be strong in the Lord and in his mighty power. Put on the full armor of God, so that you can take your stand against the devil's schemes" (Ephesians 6:10–11).

"There can never be a culture-free gospel."[18]—Lesslie Newbigin

If you are from a Western cultural background, as I am, but are ministering in an urban center to people from all over the globe, a big part of our gospel fluency is being able to articulate the effects of Jesus' redemptive work in ways that more naturally resonate with different cultural groups. The effects of humanity's sinful condition are just as likely to be felt by people as social alienation, incessant striving, anxiety, and fear of evil spirits as they are to manifest as feelings of guilt. As American communities grow to reflect more of the world's rich cultural diversity, it is imperative that we embrace a broader understanding of God's redemptive work.

New Gospel Narratives

As our thinking breaks free from its Western captivity, our imaginations open to all sorts of different ways to express the gospel of the kingdom. One way to rethink our gospel narratives is to change from asking what is *lost* that the gospel can restore, to instead thinking in terms of what *longing* is present that only the gospel will satisfy. In Christendom, dominant cultural assumptions led those walking in sin to feel guilt for their actions and disconnection from a Holy God. People experienced a sense of *loss*, so our message that "what was lost could be recovered" was good news. In secular post-Christian culture, those who did not grow up in Christendom don't feel that loss, even in their sin. However, without a coherent spiritual narrative in their life, they do often feel a sense of *longing* for something more than this world offers, which we know only God can give.

We begin to identify universal longings by asking God to show us what attributes of his kingdom are lacking in our own lives. As we seek insight into these things, it is helpful to invite others into the process. We can ask those we are discipling what they sense is lacking in their personal lives and in the places around us all. What longings keep them up at night? What do they wish to see in the life of our community? What would good news look and sound like in light of their specific existential hungers?

Let me give you an example. One of my favorite mission fields in Brussels was the basketball court on the campus of the Dutch-speaking National University. I played pick-up games alongside students every Monday afternoon for two years. Even though I was nearly twenty years older than them, my frequent presence eventually made me "one of the guys." Our friendships deepened as we went out for drinks, and I hosted them in our apartment to watch Belgian Red Devil football matches.

Between games one afternoon, I spoke with an upperclassman named Jordan. He was finishing his final semester and had already lined up a job for the fall, assuming he passed his final exams. In the Belgian university system, the final exam score determines the semester's entire grade, and it is not uncommon for students to fail one or two of their four or five courses. Jordan shared his stress and anxiety about passing finals so he could start his job. I asked him about his summer plans, and his response gave me a window into the longings of his heart:

"My friends and I are travelling to South America to go backpacking through the forest. I find that when I am out in nature I feel so relaxed, and all of my anxiety goes away. I hope it helps me get over my exams and rest up before I start my new job."

In that moment I caught a sacred glimpse into Jordan's soul. I sensed this trip was part of his spiritual journey, even if he did not use that language to describe it. I knew his expedition was not just about finding a quiet place to rest for a month from his studies; it was about finding rest from the pressures of a world where our value is tied to our performance and we live in constant fear that we will come up short. Relaxing in nature helped Jordan sense his worth apart from his work; that he is valuable even when he is not being useful. I knew Jordan was not a follower of Jesus, but that Jesus had something to offer him. At the time, however, my lack of gospel fluency kept me from saying much of anything in response.

Fortunately, I knew enough to know what *not* to say:

"Well, Jordan, the reason you feel so anxious and stressed is because you are a sinner who can never measure up to God's holy standard. If you truly want to find peace, you have to accept Jesus as your Lord and Savior."

That would not have resonated with his self-perception.

I wish I had known the language in that moment to respond something like this:

"Jordan, that's amazing! I'm so happy you are going on that trip. I hear you guys talk all the time about how hard you work for your exams. You deserve some rest, for sure. I love that you find rest while outside in nature. I do too. Actually, the origin story of my Christian faith says that after God made the natural world, he took one day to rest in it and enjoy it. Then he commanded his people to rest one day a week from their work. I think rest reminds us that our value isn't based on what we accomplish but that we're valuable simply when we do nothing. I think we struggle with the fact that even when our tasks are finished, the underlying work of proving our worth seems to never end. I hope that as you hike, you feel God's joy over you and sense that you have great value to him."

Now I'm aware that what I just articulated isn't everything there is to say about the gospel. And I'm also aware that if Jordan wanted to become a follower of Jesus, he would eventually have to recognize his sin, repent, turn to Jesus, and accept his finished work on the cross. But by choosing to affirm Jordan's longings as good, and suggesting that those longings have a divine source of fulfillment, I think I might have nudged Jordan forward in his spiritual journey. Imagine the impact if Jordan came back and said he sensed a real peace and joy on his hike and wanted to talk more about how that might be connected to the God I had shared.

All human longings ultimately find their fulfillment in God's presence and his kingdom. The thirst for unconditional acceptance and love, deep healing and wholeness, significance and value, community and connection, all point us to God. Our job as missionaries is to identify the obvious yearnings in the culture around us and help people to find the ultimate fulfillment for those longings in God.

Incredibly, all I did to catch a glimpse of Jordan's longing was to ask a meaningful question and then listen well to his answer. My missiologist friend Alan Hirsch loves to quote the inventor of the stethoscope, René Laennec, who once said, "Listen, listen, listen to your patients; they are telling you

> "All humans have insatiable longings that point to God. The appetite of any living organism shows its function. We must attempt to tell the story of God to people in the language of their longings that already exist."[19]
> —Alan Hirsch and Mark Nelson

the answer." In a post-Christian culture, we need less training on how to *speak* the gospel and more training on how to first *listen* for the gospel longings in those around us. As Leonard Sweet puts it, "Some people need a good listening to."[20] If we listen well for people's insecurities, idols, sources of identity, and ultimate dreams, then we can discern what elements of God's kingdom will sound like good news to them. Os Guinness writes,

Some Christians have won an insufferable reputation for always dispensing answers, even when no one has a question. Raise questions well, and we will be known for the searching questions we raise, to which the good news can be looked to for the only satisfactory answers.[21]

"Being heard is so close to being loved that for the average person they are almost indistinguishable."[22] —David Augsburger

In Appendix 1, I include a list of questions we developed in Hollywood that might help you discern what gospel narratives are likely to best resonate with different individuals.

REDUCTION 3: THE GOSPEL PROMISES HEAVEN WHEN WE DIE

Finally, we must acknowledge the significant "here and now" language Jesus used when referring to the kingdom of heaven. Too often Christendom speaks of the great reward of salvation as the promise of going to heaven when we die, rather than focusing on the many ways God's kingdom is breaking into our present reality on earth and the role we are invited to play in that work. The source of our great eternal hope is not that we will one day go to heaven, but rather that heaven is coming to earth. In John's Revelation, heaven is depicted as descending to earth so that God can fully dwell where his people have spent their lives.

> Then I saw "a new heaven and a new earth," for the first heaven and the first earth had passed away, and there was no longer any sea. I saw the Holy City, the new Jerusalem, coming down out of heaven from God, prepared as a bride beautifully dressed for her husband. And I heard a loud voice from the throne saying, "Look! God's dwelling place is now among the people, and he will dwell with them. They will be his people, and God himself will be with them and be their God.
>
> Revelation 21:1–3

When God wanted to make a perfect world, he didn't make heaven, he made earth.[23] Humanity defiled it, but God is now in the process of remaking earth to reflect his original intentions. We don't leave earth one day to go to Jesus; he is coming back to where we are. We are awaiting his return, here. At that time, God will banish evil, eliminate pain and suffering, and wipe away every tear so that his kingdom reigns on earth as it is in heaven. As N. T. Wright notes, "Jesus' resurrection is the beginning of God's new project, not to snatch people away from earth to heaven, but to colonize earth with the life of heaven. That, after all, is what the Lord's Prayer is about."[24]

Too often heaven is depicted as a distant place that we hope to enter one day. But heaven is only a "place" in that it is where God's good purposes, his rule and reign, are presently stored up and being kept safe until it is time to return them fully to earth.

> "As I overhear God's people talk, Christianity is almost reduced to accepting Christ as your Savior so you can go to heaven when you die … . It is not a version of the Christian faith that has a fair chance of changing the world or its devotees. No ancient martyrs would have been fed to the lions if their faith had been reduced to that."[25]—George G. Hunter

Think of it this way: there is a spot in every family's house where a parent keeps presents hidden from their kids. Maybe it's the top shelf of a closet, or the attic, or a corner of the garage. When the time is finally right, and the birthday or Christmas morning arrives, the gifts are brought out from the place where they were kept safe and are now shared in public. No parent takes the kids into that closet or attic to receive their gift; rather, they bring the gift into the living room where the kids already are. That is the place where the gifts are shared; the closet was just where the good things were being stored up.

When Jesus repeatedly said, "The kingdom of heaven is at hand,"[26] he was announcing the beginning of his work to bring heaven to earth. We are his "advance team," doing whatever he asks us to do in preparation for the ultimate reveal of his kingdom in its full glory. God is redeeming and renewing all of creation. "He is making all things new";[27] that is, remaking everything so that it reflects its original intention when it was made by Jesus in Creation. The kingdom of heaven is all around us—not in its totality, but in increasing measure. If we don't know how to enter heaven before we die, we shouldn't expect to enter it after!

"Heaven is important, but it's not the end of the world."[28]—N. T. Wright

Those of us who embrace this good news are not simply waiting to go to heaven when we die; our eternal life is already underway. We can engage in work that not only makes an impact now, but will remain into eternity.[29] We cannot build God's kingdom on our own, but through the Spirit at work within us we are invited to participate with Jesus in the redemption and renewal of all things. We are the body of Christ through which he is making things new until he returns to complete the project. What God is doing in us and through us is shaping his kingdom for eternity.

As a young church leader who once fell victim to the temptation to think, "Someday all of this will be mine," I now find greater inspiration working alongside God out in the world knowing that "Someday all of this will be his!"

In *Surprised by Hope*, N. T. Wright notes,

> What you do in the present—by painting, preaching, singing, sewing, praying, teaching, building hospitals, digging wells, campaigning for justice, writing poems, caring for the needy, loving your neighbor as yourself—will last into God's future. These activities are not simply ways of making the present life a little less beastly, a little more bearable, until the day when we leave it behind altogether. They are part of what we may call building for God's kingdom.[30]

Evangelism has too often been focused on getting people to heaven when they die. We need to return to an emphasis on discipleship that helps get the kingdom of heaven into people's lives while they are still on earth.

WHY IT MATTERS

If you share my experience around these three gospel reductions, you may also share this observation: often these misunderstandings led us to a transactional evangelism, in which the goal was to help a person acquiesce to a series of spiritual truth statements in order to "get saved" and be assured of heaven after death. Western evangelism sought a *saved soul*, whereas Jesus seemed much more concerned with a *transformed whole*. When we reduce the gospel from the totality of God's kingdom life to mere forgiveness of sins, we lessen the commitment that comes with embracing it. We need to shift from praying that people will "get saved" and instead ask Jesus to become Lord over every dimension of people's lives.

Jesus wants disciples' entire lives to begin to look like his life. As Dallas Willard rightly said, "Jesus teaches you to live your life as he would live your life."[31] He is not only concerned with the ethereal component of our life that is our soul; he is concerned with every aspect of our human existence: body, soul, mind, and strength. Discipleship in the way of Jesus must transform us socially, emotionally, economically, physically, sexually, and intellectually, as well as spiritually. As we disciple people, we may see them beginning to follow Jesus' example in one area of their lives—such as sacrificial generosity or forgiving their enemies—as a sign that they are beginning to explore a full surrender to him in all areas of their life. As one college student I discipled said to me years ago, "You knew I was becoming a Christian even before I did."

Questions for Reflection

1. As your local context becomes more post-Christian, how do you see the cultural notions of sin and guilt changing?

2. Which of these three gospel reductions do you hear most often in your context: an overemphasis on individual sin, forgiveness as the primary effect of redemption, or going to heaven as the only reward of salvation?

3. Can you relate to the hesitation of generously affirming the goodness in people who are not Christians? Who in your current life is not a Jesus follower but expresses a characteristic of God or God's kingdom that you could affirm this week?

6

Mobilizing Disciplemaking People

Those first eighteen months in Brussels were incredibly disorienting. I arrived in Europe, thinking I was a skilled local church leader, only to realize most of what I knew about organizing and operating the existing structures and systems of church was irrelevant in a post-Christian culture. My disciplemaking strategies were all based on outdated paradigms that no longer described this new world. I found it especially hard to assume the posture of a beginner. Much of my identity was wrapped up in my previous success as a leader and my perceived mastery of a skill set that I invested fifteen years in gaining. But there was no mistaking that this new secular world was operating by a set of values and beliefs that, in many ways, made my old skills obsolete.

Once I wrapped my mind around these new paradigms as a leader, I recognized the need for a local church to add on the next layer of innovation. Like an oyster creating layers upon layers of luminescent nacre, local churches who embrace these new paradigms need to cover and concretize them with communal practices that better fit this new reality. If the goal was to mobilize disciplemaking people, then we needed to discover the habits and priorities that would sustain and support that activity—and that process of discovery would require bold imagination and courageous experimentation. Experimentation always involves repeated failure, which I found particularly challenging. Eventually I embraced failure as essential for innovation. I learned that if I was not regularly failing, I was likely not taking any real risks.

Thankfully I was not alone in this season. By the time my family joined The Well, the church had already been experimenting with a centered-set form of church for ten years. And The Well was just one of many of Communitas International's churches across Europe constantly adapting to their local environment, trying out new approaches, while remaining faithful to the biblical patterns of church. Each community prioritized the mobilization of every follower of Jesus to make disciples in the everyday spaces of their lives and then tested ways to equip, support, and sustain their people and those efforts throughout the week.

Reliable experimentation requires some elements of the system to remain constant while other elements become testable variables. For The Well, the constant was faithfulness to the character and calling of Jesus and the nature and strategy of his mission; the tested variable was how to function in a communal rhythm appropriate to the cultural context for each of the various neighborhoods across Brussels.

During my time in Europe I came across a metaphor that helped me imagine how to structure our ongoing efforts of experimentation and contextualization.

FIRM BUT FLEXIBLE

Consider the relationship between our *skeleton* and our *skin*. Rich Robinson, a missional network leader in the United Kingdom and co-leader of Movement Leaders Collective, often uses this language to describe the need for both a firm internal framework of church that is faithful to Jesus' intentions and the Bible's instructions (our skeleton), as well as a flexible external expression of church that relates well to its context (our skin). The skeleton provides a solid structure, while the skin allows for pliable strategies. Ideally, a church is highly accountable to God's Word for its skeletal structure but celebrates a high level of freedom and adaptability in discerning its skin strategies. This physiology provides the local church with the organizational agility essential for the world in which we find ourselves.

In *The Age of the Unthinkable,* Joshua Cooper Ramo explains that we are now in an age of discontinuous and nonlinear social change that is moving at a staggering speed. We have departed from the idea that "our world can be reduced to simple models [and] that the real dynamics of the world make prediction nearly impossible and demand a different way of thinking."[1] He argues that when we experience cultural stability, it is merely "a passing phase, as a pause in a system of incredible—and unmappable—dynamism."[2] In fact, he suggests, "much of what we have to confront will be things that have never occurred to us before."[3] The COVID-19 pandemic has made this point obvious to church leaders around the globe. To thrive as the body of Christ moving forward, we can't simply rely on fossilized or trendy models of church; we need both a solid skeleton and a stretchy skin that allow us to embrace experimentation, start and stop new initiatives, and adapt discipleship pathways to fit the rhythms of our context.

"Today, we live in a postmodern culture of discontinuous and often unpredictable change. When new threats appear on the horizon and new opportunities present themselves, the church needs organizational structures that are flexible and adaptable. Chains of decision-making command and control get in the way in times of rapid change."[4]—Susan Beaumont

OUR CENTRAL SKELETON

Like many European churches, The Well possessed a centered-set skeleton where disciple-making was structured around *mission > community > worship*, and the primary activity was out in the world throughout the week. Another skeletal element was our commitment to facilitate communities of various sizes, knowing that each expression met different human needs. Jesus set this example as he spent time with his inner core of three (Peter, James, and John), his twelve apostles, the broader community of traveling disciples that included women like Mary and Martha, and the crowds in the cities.

Sociologists refer to these groupings as intimate spaces (2–3 people), personal spaces (5–12 people), social spaces (20–50 people) and public spaces (70+). Each space offers a different dynamic essential to human connection; from the security of being known and loved by those closest to you, to the sense of significance that comes from belonging to a movement much bigger than yourself.[5] With skeletal elements like these in place, alongside core convictions from God's Word and following the Spirit's leading, we felt the freedom to experiment and adapt depending on the needs and opportunities within our local contexts.

Even if you accept the elements of this central skeleton that I've laid out, you will need to flesh it out for yourself in a way that reflects the reality of your local community. Your practical strategies will need to remain flexible, be evaluated regularly for their effectiveness, and will likely look different than a similar size church operating in another context. That being said, I will share what the everyday skin of The Well looked like in the hope that it might spark your imagination and experimentation.

OUR EVERYDAY SKIN

Our community primarily existed as a network of microchurches (missional communities) spread across the city, each operating in different neighborhoods of Brussels, known as *communes*. These microchurches ranged in size from 15–40 people—small enough to care for one another in community but large enough to dare together in local mission. Each was responsible for determining how to flesh out the skeleton of mission, community, and worship in a balanced and sustainable rhythm that provided times for intimate-, personal-, and social-space relationships. (More on public spaces in a minute.)

"The way to reach the city is not through programs but by being biblical people. The urban minister must first be able to interpret Scripture, and then must have the tools to interpret the city, so that he can let the Word of God speak to the situation. Theology is God in dialogue with his people in all their thousands of different environments."[6]—Raymond J. Bakke and Jim Hart

Expressions of *mission* varied by community but included activities such as providing a weekly meal for those in situational homelessness, performing small concerts for the elderly constrained to assisted-living homes, after-school tutoring for youth, playing board games and offering manicures at the local asylum center for refugees, hosting pub quizzes and beer tastings to raise money for local charities, and neighborhood cleanups in which our kids could actively participate. Often these activities were done side-by-side with friends who were not-yet followers of Jesus but wanted to help address these common concerns in the city.

If Well members were leading these activities, we usually closed with a time of debriefing to help people process their experience. This also enabled us to sense who might be open to a follow-up spiritual discussion. One standard question we often asked was, "Where did you experience the beauty of our city today?" Then we would ask, "Where did you experience the brokenness of our city?" Finally, we asked, "What are some ongoing ways that our lives might bring beauty into those spaces of brokenness?" We prayed that these questions would awaken people to long for God's redemptive plan to come in them and through them; and we looked for opportunities to share *how* in later conversations.

While each microchurch was responsible for engaging in these regular acts of mission together in small and midsized groups, each individual Well member was expected to spend time developing friendships with those who were not-yet followers of Jesus and to prayerfully discern what aspects of mission God was inviting them to within those intimate-space relationships. This often took the form of acts of blessing, such as giving a gift, or finding tangible ways to serve their needs, such as watching someone's kids or pets for free. Sometimes individuals we were discipling joined our serving activities; other times we met people through serving, who we then continued to disciple throughout the week, outside of the group activity.

We deepened *community* through various gatherings, including hangouts at local pubs; playdates for the children of new moms; shared meals; jam sessions open to local musicians; after-school get-togethers at cafés and parks with local parents; sports-viewing times; and open prayer groups. Through all these activities we sought to fulfill the "one another" commands of the gospel, to offer mutual encouragement, and to benefit from each other's shared gifts and resources. Cities are lonely places, and so, again, many of these activities included friends who did not follow Jesus but were hungry for connection. The Well also helped facilitate prayer trios where two to three members could meet together for deep sharing, support, and mutual prayer.

Local groups came together weekly for *worship* in small rentable spaces they found in their neighborhood, including doctor's offices, back rooms of pubs or cafés, local private schools, and community halls. If there were musicians present, worship included live music; if not, worship might include extended communal prayer or sharing stories of how God was speaking to us or leading us in recent disciplemaking relationships. The Well leadership gathered a teacher from each community to collaborate on a coordinated Bible teaching they would take back to their worship. Communities with children often alternated between including the kids in the time of teaching and allowing them their own space for an age-appropriate discipleship experience.

Each month we created two public-space events, one around mission and one around worship. The mission event was a Saturday serving project that engaged 80–100 volunteers, mostly young professionals and international high school students from all over the city. The event was operated by our partner organization, Serve the City, which was formed to foster relationships with local nonprofits and charities who were less inclined to work with a religious organization. Serve the City operated as an independent entity, which gave them a separate financial structure and a dedicated team that could organize these events and deepen partnerships with local charities in need of volunteers.

Our public-space worship event was known as All Well. One Sunday evening a month, all the neighborhood microchurches—100–150 people—gathered in a central location for a shared meal and a time of intergenerational worship, teaching, and story-sharing. Sacraments, such as Communion and baptism, could be celebrated in either a local worship gathering or monthly All Well. While these gatherings included a liturgy with teaching and worship that might resemble more traditional church services, we also incorporated times of sharing, Bible discussion, and communal prayer, as we sat together around tables.

The goal was to allow each microchurch the freedom to put their own skin on our communal skeleton. Ideally, each local Well community had a rhythm to their week that included shared times of mission, community, and worship while creating intimate, personal, and social spaces. Then our monthly public-space gatherings would sustain the shared vision of the city-wide movement.

This communal rhythm of life was essential in a transient city where many of us lost friends faster than we could forge them. While we may have felt relationally isolated from other Jesus followers in our daily jobs and commute, we knew that there was a cadence to our life that would bring us together at least two to three times a week and bring the whole movement together every month. When The Well was at its best, 50 percent of our time and energy was invested in caring for one another and growing as disciples through activities like prayer groups, shared meals, marriage conferences, and spiritual formation retreats; while the other 50 percent was invested in missional engagement with the city and deepening personal disciplemaking relationships and outwardly-focused soul care.

Often when I describe our way of church, people express concern that with 50 percent of our effort being directed toward the needs of the city, there would not be enough energy left to care for each other and form the deep bonds of Christian community that are usually associated with the American experience of church. In reality, setting aside our preoccupation with our own personal interests and stepping out to work side-by-side for the well-being of others forged deeper community than traditional church "fellowship events." Some churches are resurrecting an ancient term to describe this phenomenon that was experienced by the first-century church: *communitas*—a deep bond of mutual community forged through shared liminal experiences of ordeal or challenge where people must rely on each other to overcome an obstacle or accomplish a mission.[7]

DISCIPLES MAKE DISCIPLES

All of these rhythms I've described were created to mobilize and sustain the disciplemaking of every member of our community. Sometimes our gatherings and events became places where we engaged in making new disciples, as friends from the city joined us, or a group of us joined neighbors in their activities out in the city. However, each Well member was also navigating a series of personal discipling relationships. Take for instance, my wife's relationship with a Muslim neighbor; let's call her, Mina.

Kristyn possesses the StrengthsFinder[8] gifts of Positivity and WOO (winning others over), so she always connects with people quickly. In Belgium, she amassed a diverse group of friends from her interactions at the school, her gym, and with those she met on her daily travels. One day she befriended Mina, a young single mother who rode the same tram with us to school every day. Mina wore a head covering in public, consistent with other Muslim women, and was reserved with me. She and Kristyn grew close through their regular trips to the café after dropping the kids off at school. Eventually Mina shared the pain of her experiences as an adopted child and talked about her spiritual wanderings that had involved dabbling in many different religions. We never invited Mina to our Well events out of respect for her faith practices and because we knew she had deep wounds from past encounters with church. So, it was a great surprise when one day Mina invited Kristyn to join her at a prayer service she was considering attending. The service was held on the grounds of a small monastery chapel that was nestled in a park nearby.

I love hearing Kristyn recount the disorientation of sitting next to a Muslim … in a Catholic monastery prayer service … led entirely in French. It was the quintessential missional experience: coming alongside someone in their spiritual journey in the spaces of their life. Kristyn was the one doing the work of crossing out of her comfort zone into Mina's life and navigating the cultural barriers of language and tradition in order to fit in. They attended those prayer services often and began praying together on other occasions; Kristyn always respectfully praying to Jesus while Mina prayed to Allah.

Throughout that journey, The Well was walking with Kristyn in prayer and support; women regularly asked how Mina was doing, what they could be praying for, and how Kristyn's conversations were going.

"We are trying to empower every kind of person in every kind of context to reach every kind of person in every kind of context."[9]—Brian Sanders

Kristyn used our community as a sounding board for ideas of how she could bless Mina, and she loved sharing updates when we gathered for worship. Our times with The Well for worship, Bible study, spiritual formation, and friendship replenished Kristyn while she was investing in Mina. The larger church body sustained Kristyn in her disciplemaking initiatives and pressed her into intentionality.

One day, on the morning tram ride to school, I noticed Mina was not wearing her head covering. During the next few meetings Kristyn learned that Mina was re-evaluating her belief in Islam and was seeking to know more about Jesus. Over tea one day soon after, Kristyn asked Mina, "Do you still consider yourself Muslim?"

Mina replied, "I respect the prophet, but Jesus is my way now. I believe Jesus is the way toward God."

When we moved from Brussels, we gave Mina and her daughter some of our furniture and thanked her for her great friendship over the years. As we left town, she shared with Kristyn that she was now praying to Jesus as God too.

Disciplemaking in a post-Christian culture requires more prayer, more Holy Spirit discernment, and often more interactions with other Christians, as each of us play a small role in the bigger process. And it takes more time. Just as pearl-making can take half a decade to produce a true treasure, our disciplemaking relationships at The Well took years to develop and deepen, and the conversations about Jesus only came naturally after we had spent hours upon hours in conversations about everyday life. Many relationships seemed never to transcend surface-level pleasantries. It was challenging, arduous work, and it often felt unproductive … even wasted. And no church is perfect. The Well endured turf wars, leaders battled each other's egos, sometimes we cloistered up, becoming preoccupied with ourselves, and we wounded each other like every other family does from time to time. But through it all, God transcended our human efforts for his kingdom purposes.

Over our three years in Brussels, the skin of our church adapted and changed, but our core skeleton remained the same. Sometimes we shed one way of doing things to experiment with something totally different. We tried out all sorts of initiatives looking for the best way to embody God's mission. We created leadership trios in each area to oversee activities, then we tried commissioning ordinary people to serve as neighborhood pastors and provide leadership. We tried doing All Well in the mornings to accommodate families, then tried doing it every week, then we broke out again and tried worshipping by stage of life rather than by neighborhoods. We invested energy in serving local elderly and children in need, and then, as the 2012 refugee crisis began, the community pivoted to meet those immediate needs. God provided amazing opportunities for the church to articulate and proclaim our belief in Jesus and put language to what inspired our kingdom-centered lifestyle. Not everything worked—often things didn't—but we kept on innovating. Along the way I found a sticker I placed on the cover of my journal that read, "Experiment. Fail. Learn. Repeat." Wise words for us all as we pursue innovation within this new paradigm.

Questions for Reflection

1. What are three elements of your local church's unchangeable skeleton? What are three elements of your church's adaptable skin that can change if needed?

2. How much of your church's energy and resources are currently invested in mobilizing individual people to make disciples in the everyday spaces of their lives and how much is invested in centralized programs, on the church property, managed by professionals?

3. How can you encourage experimentation and innovation within your church? What would communicate a bias toward experimentation rather than maintaining existing ways of doing things?

Phase Three

CREATE A CULTURE OF INNOVATION

It takes two to four years for a wild oyster to form a pearl since the process involves secreting layers upon layers of nacre; a substance that is lighter and stronger than concrete. Pearl-making is never a one-time event, but a slow steady progression that builds upon what came before and strengthens the foundation for what lies ahead.

7

The Power of Starting Small

As we begin phase three of this pearl-making process, let's remind ourselves again: the irritants we face in our shifting culture are not the issue; they merely reveal the inner properties of the organism they come into contact with. As the post-Christendom sandstorm blows across the West, each church leadership community is being revealed as either an eye or an oyster—either a body that rejects and repels new cultural environments in an attempt to preserve the status quo or a body that embraces change and adapts and innovates in response. While one leads to infection and blindness, the other causes concretion and beauty. In the face of this new adversity we need a *positively irritated* posture—that is how pearls are formed.

As my time in Brussels was coming to its third and conclusive year, I began to look for an American church that was actively embedded in this post-Christian cultural reality and who held a positive view of these potential irritants, engaging them not as an eye but as an oyster. I was energized by the possibility of sharing what I was learning with a new church family and of leading them through the same process of deconstruction and reconstruction that God was working in me. Together we could experiment and innovate alongside the Holy Spirit to form some fresh pearls in the context around us.

One of the most transformational moments in that final year in Brussels came during a trip to the Netherlands, where I met several authors who had influenced my thinking—in particular, Alan Hirsch. While in Europe I came across a video of Alan telling North American church leaders, "I come from your future." In that moment, I knew I had found a mentor who could relate to my own journey.

Alan and Deb Hirsch served local churches and denominations for many years in Australia, one of the most secular nations in the world. Their engagement with post-Christian culture led them, and fellow Aussie Michael Frost, to develop Forge International, which helps Christians live as cross-cultural missionaries in their own neighborhoods and social networks.

At that event in Amsterdam, I asked Alan what advice he would offer me as I headed back to the U. S. and sought to help a church thrive in these new cultural realities that Western Europe and Australia were already experiencing.

I was eager to jump right into phase three of my journey, creating a church-wide culture that supports innovation. Defaulting to my old paradigms, I suggested maybe a teaching series on Jesus' missional life from the Gospels, or a year-long ministry theme on reclaiming the DNA of the first-century church from Acts. As a capable Bible teacher, I thought for sure I could make the case for a new way of operating as a church. Alan let me finish and then gently said, "If you try to do that, you will blow up your church in your first year."

"Resistance is proportionate to the size and speed of the change, not to whether the change is a favorable or unfavorable one."[1]—George Leonard

Grabbing a whiteboard, he drew a bell curve and explained how organizations successfully implement innovation. Our conversation launched me on a quest to better understand the nature of change.

MANAGING CHANGE WISELY

Let me summarize what I learned that day, and what I continue to discover, that may help us as we seek to become leaders who are able to successfully and repeatedly introduce change and innovation into our churches.

The diagram Alan drew is taken from Everett M. Rogers' book, *Diffusion of Innovations,* and illustrates the various responses individuals have to change.[2] Rogers proposes that within a large social grouping, there are five primary sub-groups that exist in predictable proportions to one another. (For those already familiar with his premise, I invite you to let this serve as a simple review.)

- *Innovators* make up 2.5 percent of a society. They are drawn to taking risks, exploring new frontiers, and pushing the limits. They are likely to feel the need for change before others and often experiment enough to create that change themselves.
- *Early Adopters* make up 13.5 percent of a society. They are willing to try out a new idea for themselves. If and when they adopt it as a new practice, their peers respect them enough to take that idea seriously and explore it for themselves. They are the ones who are most responsible for "sneezing the change" out into the culture so that the "idea virus" ultimately spreads.[3]
- *The Early Majority* make up 34 percent of a society. They are more deliberate in their approach to change. Hesitant to engage too quickly, they need to see the idea put into practice and tested before they are willing to get on board. They are convinced by verifiable evidence, not just ideas.
- *The Late Majority* make up another 34 percent of a society. They are defined by their skepticism to innovation. Change may threaten their sense of identity and security, so they will not change until they find themselves in the majority as it relates to a new practice. They often need leaders to work alongside them rather than just setting an example for them to follow.

- *Laggards* make up 16 percent of a society. They hold to traditions and are extremely apprehensive when it comes to change. They prefer to operate alongside others who share their conservative views. They only acquiesce to new ideas and practices when the benefits of change far outweigh the benefits of maintaining their old ways.

The application for a local church is profound. I was following the pattern of many pastors who seek to leverage their Sunday pulpit to try to effect change in their churches. My plan was to "dump" my ideas on the church community during a sermon series. The danger in that approach is that at least half of the community is naturally wired to resist. They are skeptical and apprehensive of all change, regardless of its potential merits. When confronted with a call to a change in life or lifestyle, they are not evaluating the quality or validity of the proposed change itself, but rather how the change will affect them personally.[4] People don't ask, "Is this change for the better?" as much as they ask, "Will this change make *my life* better?" According to Rogers' research, 50 percent of a community will reject change outright, regardless of how compelling or polished its presentation.

In a church context, that means that even if the ideas are faithful to the biblical text, if they *appear to be new*, the ideas will evoke skepticism and resistance among at least half of the people. That teaching series may excite a few innovators and early adopters who are drawn to new ideas, but it won't be enough to overcome the negative reaction of the broader community who are prone to think it can't be good since it sounds new.

This is just a social-science explanation for what many church leaders come to realize: all organizations have immune systems. When change is proposed within a local church—whether a new form of music, new service times, or a new leadership structure—more often than not, it is initially perceived as a contaminant and a threat to the system. To be fair, it *is* a threat. Change is, by nature, a disruptive attack on any internal system that seeks to maintain homeostasis. For half of the community, the proposed change will upset their sense of well-being and comfort, and they will quickly move to eradicate the threat. The late majority and laggards in any organization often perform the same function as the human eye, flushing out a piece of sand before it can embed itself.

The irony of the pearl-making process is that when a grain of sand finds its way into an oyster, it identifies the sand as a threat to its well-being in the same way the eye does. However, rather than expel the sand, the threat catalyzes the creation of something beautiful. Rather than simply trying to return to the way things were, an oyster both protects itself *and* produces something new.

The same grain of sand can catalyze blindness in an eye, or beauty in an oyster because the sand is not the issue; it merely reveals the true nature of the organism that it encounters. Likewise, the nature of the *body* of Christ—which should operate more as an organism than an organization—is revealed in our response to perceived threats. Sadly, most Western churches are formed around protection (maintaining the status quo and preserving feelings of comfort and safety) rather than procreation (leveraging disruption to grow, multiply, and extend their impact in the world around it). However, no organization is a monolith, and within each church there are individuals who are wired more like an oyster than an eye. For the sake of the whole body, it is essential to identify these innovators and early adopters, and begin by working with them.

SPREADING INNOVATION

You cannot dump change on a group. Instead you must diffuse it through a group in an intentional way.

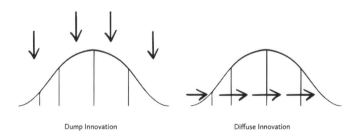

Dump Innovation   Diffuse Innovation

Change is more successful when it is diffused across a group through relationships. Innovators create a new idea and then express their enthusiasm for the idea in a way that causes early adopters to experiment with it. As early adopters become comfortable with the change, they reach out in their social networks and begin to model these new ideas in a way that is intriguing to the larger group that makes up the early majority. Adoption of the change by the early majority tends to calm the skepticism of the late majority, and the late majority in turn convinces the laggards of the inevitability of the impending change.

But notice that each group influences the group that comes along after it on the curve. Hotheaded innovators will not mobilize the conservatives. In fact, they are more likely to drive them deeper into a posture of resistance. As Alan Hirsch and Dave Ferguson point out in *On the Verge*, "The key is to get the radicals to influence the progressives, and then get the progressives to influence the conservatives."[5] The further along the curve you go, the more a person will need repeated exposure to an idea through many interpersonal relationships with advocates for that change.[6] Change happens one person at a time, at the speed of personal relationships.

> "A minority of people working from the margins has the best chance of being a community capable of penetrating the noncommunity."[7]—Eugene Peterson

Eventually, change that is found to be beneficial to the broader collective bleeds across society from one group to another until the new change prevails. This idea was reinforced by more recent books like *The Tipping Point* by Malcolm Gladwell and *Unleashing the Idea Virus* by Seth Godin. According to Rogers, it takes a relatively small percentage of a society—just the 16 percent represented by the first two groups of innovators and early adopters—to buy into a new idea before it hits a tipping point and the change becomes inevitable across all of that society. Other scientific research argues that when as little as "10 percent of the population holds an unshakable belief, their belief will always be adopted by the majority of the society."[8]

DIFFUSION: FROM TEENS TO TECHNOPHOBES

The ministry of Jesus demonstrates this principle. When Jesus attempted to introduce his paradigm-shifting teachings to large groups of people, they were often rejected and dismissed. Recognizing this, Jesus put very little of his ministry resources into the crowds. Instead, Jesus prioritized those on the edges. He invested his best resources in a small group of twelve innovators who were courageous enough to leave their lives and follow him. He then equipped that group to teach and train a broader community of seventy early adopters, who in turn were sent out into the surrounding area to embody and explain the kingdom of God. Eventually, 1 Corinthians 15:6 says that after Jesus' resurrection he appeared to five hundred disciples, who then became the seeds of the early majority. They scattered across the region in the power of the Spirit until his church hit a tipping point. Jesus knew that dumping innovation into a crowd was far less effective than diffusing it across a relational network.

For a more contemporary illustration of this phenomenon, consider the rise of Facebook. In 2004 Mark Zuckerberg and his friends created and released "The Facebook" for university students with a valid .edu e-mail address. Early adopters provided feedback and improved the site, and eventually so many college students were using it that they removed the college e-mail requirement in order to make it available to anyone. When post-college young adults saw the benefits of staying connected with friends through this platform, they too signed up. Eventually, Facebook became the primary place to share life's pictures and stories with others. When Mom or Grandma calls and asks for pictures of the new baby or the kitchen renovation, most of us will say something like, "Just get on Facebook; they are all up on my page." Fifteen years after Facebook was invented to connect college kids to each other, octogenarian technophobes are spending hours a day scrolling through pictures of their grandkids and reposting kitten memes. Of course, by the time the laggards like Grandma are using it, the next generation of innovators and early adopters are years into creating something better. This is often why laggards resist change; they feel like they can never keep up.

Most change diffuses across a particular collective of people. New ideas spread out across networks of personal relationships over a long period of time; just like an oyster coats its pearl with layer upon layer of nacre for several years until it becomes large enough to harvest.

THE CHURCH IN HOLLYWOOD

In August of 2015, my family moved back to the U.S., and I accepted the call to serve as lead pastor of Ecclesia in Hollywood, California. Ecclesia is made up largely of artists and creatives living out the life of Jesus in the entertainment industry. Before our arrival, the church had gone through a time of transition and had declined in both attendance and giving—the traditional metrics of "butts and bucks" that historically we track most closely. However, the core that remained were excited to use this time of pruning to reimagine itself as a church that existed for the sake of the Hollywood community and industry, and not just for its own benefit. They embraced the necessity of reframing their mission around making disciples among the "nones" and "dones" in our post-Christian world.

While the history of Ecclesia is unique, the situation it found itself in is very common across America: dwindling attendance among an aging community, an array of inward-facing ministries that rely on expensive professional leadership, and a growth model dependent on attracting non-Christians to Sunday services that are now seen as irrelevant to an increasing number of post-Christians. I was impressed that the leadership didn't blame the surrounding culture for their decline but rather took responsibility for their own faults and failures and truly desired to reform the church to better serve their local context.

A church of artists and creatives seemed to be the perfect community in which to experiment and innovate new ways of expressing the church. During my interview process, the elders and I connected on a joint vision to reimagine church not merely as a place for Sunday services designed to attract Christians but as a family of faith sent out to live on mission together. We imagined a church that existed primarily to bless the city, not our own people. We dreamed that each person would see himself or herself as participating in God's call to make disciples and to join in Jesus' redemptive mission out in the world. We also recognized that we would need to be patient in order to effect these changes.

EQUIPPING THE NINJAS

For my first year at Ecclesia, I took Alan Hirsch's advice and resisted the urge to use the Sunday sermons as a place to introduce visions for radical change.

Instead I began a search for the innovators within our community. I watched for those who had new ideas for the church and new solutions to problems; people who were bored with church as it was, and who were interested in learning about the way churches were adapting to the changing culture in places like Europe. I prayed God would reveal to me a group of "ninjas," as Alan once called them—missional innovators who could operate on the fringes of the church. This group of pioneers would experiment with how to live as missionaries in the everyday places of life in order to make disciples outside of the existing properties, professionals, and programs of traditional church.

One of the best ways to initiate change without threatening the stability of the broader church is to create a pilot program on the edges that poses no risk to existing

> *"Structures don't change easily through challenge or critique. They change best as people within the organization change and model new approaches."[9]—Hugh Halter*

ministries. Ecclesia's elders gave me approval to launch a local training hub of Forge International that I would lead alongside a fellow church planter, Sam Theophylus. Sam moved from India as a missionary to the U.S. and shared my passion for equipping disciples to make new disciples outside the church walls. Sam and I recruited twelve innovative types into a nine-month learning cohort that Forge calls a *residency*, although the term is a bit of a misnomer, as these men and women do not reside together.

For nine months, the cohort learned new paradigms and engaged in new practices that revolved around the mission of God and the call to embrace our personal sentness to the world around us. The group was comprised of actors and screenwriters, civic leaders, a stay-at-home mom, a lawyer, a musician, and a graphic designer. Only two in the group were ministry professionals, but each embraced the call to view their everyday life as their mission field. Each member identified a specific context in which they would serve as a missionary, such as their apartment building, their neighborhood, their workplace, or a social space they often frequented, like an acting studio or gym. In Forge, we referred to these as first, second, and third places;[10] the places we respectively live, work, and play/study/create. While these were familiar spaces, the group agreed to enter them using unfamiliar practices that would require risk-taking and experimentation.

"Third places are the most significant places for Christian mission to occur because in a third place people are more relaxed, less guarded, more open to meaningful conversation and interaction."[11]—Michael Frost

The group sought to increase the frequency of their interactions in these missional places and to bring intentionality to how they related with the people around them. The goal was not to add a bunch of new "missional activities" into their lives but rather to align their presence in this space with the priority of helping to reveal the reign of God. Engaging more actively in God's work always involves some level of repentance—reviewing and adjusting our cluttered lives and creating space to hear from God—but in a city where most people work two or three jobs to pay rent, it is essential to think in terms of alignment, rather than addition.

LEARNING BY DOING

Forge's structure is designed to create opportunities for "just in time" learning rather than the traditional "just in case" learning environments often found in churches.[12] When someone is actively practicing what they are learning, the lessons often come "just in time" to be applied. When someone learns in a traditional classroom or Sunday school setting, the theoretical knowledge is usually filed away as something to be remembered, "just in case" it is needed one day.

Forge also emphasizes "acting yourself into a new way of thinking" rather than trying to "think yourself into a new way of acting." So, while we read and view videos as part of our paradigm-shifting learning, the real emphasis is on practices that take a value of God's kingdom and turn it into a concrete behavior. The love of Jesus is translated into a daily commitment to bless at least one person through a tangible act with no strings attached. The acceptance and embrace of Jesus toward those on the margins becomes a commitment to share a meal weekly with someone who is on the fringes of your context. The peace of Jesus becomes a commitment to pursue harmony in relationships, and to model grace and forgiveness when others injure us. Group members learn a common set of core practices that they can interpret and apply within their own setting.

As a group, we prayed that God would reveal where he was already at work in the world around us and allow us to join him. We asked the Spirit to facilitate spiritual conversations and empower us to listen well to others so we might discern what part of Jesus' life and kingdom

"We must change our ideas of what it means to develop a disciple, shifting the emphasis from studying Jesus and all things spiritual in an environment protected from the world to following Jesus into the world to join him in his redemptive mission."[13]—Reggie McNeal

would be good news for them—and then to empower us to incarnate that in their midst. We became intentional with meals and hospitality as a way of blessing others and deepening relationships. And we gathered regularly to share stories and celebrate the good, hard, and crazy moments of our experiences. We offered each other feedback on our challenges and reminded each other that failure and mistakes were essential to good learning.

GROWING STRONGER TOGETHER

In one of my favorite memories of that first year, we sat around the dinner table sharing stories from our missional contexts. One member, Kerry, offered a confession to the group. Kerry was a well-respected civic leader who worked to help Hollywood's business districts thrive and flourish. She had recently moved her offices from the safety and comfort of the corner of Hollywood and Vine to the distressed and dilapidated portion of Hollywood Boulevard. During the prior week, a fellow local leader who was impressed by her resolve to serve the city approached her and asked what inspired her to work so tirelessly. Kerry shared with the cohort that she knew it was an opportunity to authentically express her faith in Jesus, but she was suddenly overcome with fear and anxiety. When Kerry became a follower of Jesus, later in life, her only disciplemaking strategy was to invite people to church to hear her pastor talk about Christ. Now she was presented with the chance to speak about Jesus herself, and she froze. She confessed that her response was, "Well … sometimes I knit to center myself." Everyone at the table could relate to that moment of feeling like a failure as a missionary. We did our best to encourage her, and she told us that she was already praying that next time she would have more courage. She said, "From now on, when the answer to somebody's question is Jesus, I am committed to saying it!"

A few cohort dinners later Kerry shared another experience. She was preparing to attend a contentious meeting and knew that her leadership team was going to be attacked, so she asked a friend, Jason, to come and sit in the corner and simply pray for protection over the meeting. Jason is a large, muscular guy who was formerly a nightclub bouncer and security guard for Ecclesia's Sunday gatherings. Even though he merely sat in the corner praying silently during the meeting, his presence and friendship with Kerry drew some attention. A few weeks after the meeting, a board member stopped Kerry on the street and asked, "Who was that guy sitting in the corner at our meeting?" Sensing God was giving her another chance, Kerry replied, "Well, that was my friend Jason. You might not think this makes any sense, but I asked him to come as a sort of spiritual bodyguard. I knew that meeting could become challenging, so I asked Jason to come and pray to Jesus to give us all his peace and protection to get through it." After Kerry recounted her story, the cohort roared in celebration that she took that step of mentioning her faith in the midst of her professional world.

CREATING CULTURED PEARL FARMS

This initial missional-incarnational discipleship cohort functioned rather like a cultured pearl farm where I was *grafting in,* or seeding, innovation into the lives of a few members of our church. Cultured pearls are formed inside farmed oysters that live in artificial oyster beds, under the supervision of caretakers who monitor their progress and care for their health. Rather than try to pioneer with our entire community, this small-batch approach allowed me to cultivate a first generation of innovators who were already embedded within Ecclesia and possessed relational credibility. In fact, most of them had more credibility than I did at that point; I was still the newcomer. The Forge residency includes three one-day intensives, and we opened up those Saturdays to anyone who wanted to attend. The residents began to leverage their relational capital with others and invited other Ecclesians to come and see what they were learning. Those who attended had their curiosity piqued at this new way of living.

One effective way to introduce new paradigms within the broader church community is to focus on personal storytelling rather than logical arguments (even biblical ones). Personal stories have a way of circumventing people's suspicions about change. As the residency drew to a close, I began to invite the residents, one by one, to join me at the end of a Sunday message for a time of personal sharing. I worked to find a connection to the morning's message and then interviewed one of them for ten minutes about how they were living out the mission of God in their daily lives. Each innovator shared a personal story of missional risk-taking and making disciples out in the everyday spaces of life. It was as if we were gently tipping open their shells to reveal their pearls-in-formation, as a way of inspiring others to join this innovation process themselves.

If Hollywood has taught the world anything, it is that stories are powerful tools for cultural change. By introducing themes—such as personal disciple-making, incarnational living, and the sentness of every believer—through stories rather than propositional sermons, I found people receptive and genuinely excited about the pearls that were being created as people's lives were changing. Every time I invited someone up to share, a line of people would form after the service with people wanting to talk to them about their story. And when the line to talk to the "ordinary missionary" was longer than the line to talk to me, the "ordained minister," I knew we were doing something right as a church.

To use Everett Rogers' term, this group became the "champions" of our new way of life. Rogers defines a champion as "a charismatic individual who throws his or her support behind an innovation, thus overcoming the indifference or resistance that the new idea may provoke."[14] Champions are oysters who choose to embrace irritants as a positive force to initiate creativity and innovation. The church-planting catalyst organization, Exponential, refers to this concept as *hero making*—an intentional decision by a church leader to decenter himself or herself in order to spotlight the efforts of others in the church. It requires a significant rewriting of the script in terms of who is doing the actual ministry in a church.

What gets rewarded in a church tends to get repeated. The more we highlight the ways the church is making disciples outside of Sunday mornings, the more people will long to have their own stories to share.

"I find myself trying not to 'lead' the congregation but more importantly to support them and ascertain how I can fan the flames of their leadership. Our staff is the support team. The members are the field team."[15]—Dave Gibbons

"The goal of our missional life is not to grow churches. The goal of church is to grow missionaries."[16]—Hugh Halter

In some ways, creating a Forge residency was like planting a church within a church. As I saw the impact these innovators were having on others who would become the early adopters, the hope that we could actually tip the culture of the church began to swell inside me. One day I wrote "16%" on my office whiteboard and began praying regularly that God would turn the hearts and minds of that small percentage of our church toward this new vision. After a few years, I started keeping a list of that 16 percent by name, dubbing my list "The First Forty." This is the core community in which I invest the largest portion of my time, energy, and resources.

FORMING YOUR OWN PEARL FARM

As I speak to other church leaders around the country, I often find they face the same temptation I did: to bring swift change through large-group vision casting. It seems faster and a more efficient use of energy—but it proves to be ineffective. A better way to implement change is to leave existing services and systems as they are and experiment with something new on the side. You can call it a "pilot program," an "incubator," or simply "an experiment," since not every experiment has to succeed, and experiments often take place for a set period of time before they are stopped and evaluated. By creating an experiment on the edges of the organization, you can experience the benefits of trying something new without threatening existing operations. The best experiments are quarantined off from the old system entirely so that those who are late majority or laggards are unaware they even exist.

Remember, change is often implemented and communicated along relational lines, not through mass communication. It takes longer to diffuse change than to dump it, but it is much more effective in the long run. Don't worry about the masses who gather on Sunday; instead, focus on a small, first-generation group of ninjas who can try things that a large number of people would never attempt. Smaller groups like this are much more likely to innovate and take risks than larger groups, driven by preserving their place and power. Ignore any resistant leaders who get wind of your new idea and respond with skepticism or cynicism. Remember, the best critique of the bad is the practice of something better. In the words of Michelangelo, "Critique by creating."

I've already told you how I looked for innovators (ninjas) at Ecclesia. Here is another key: pray that God will reveal those who seem under-challenged by ministries that simply provide care to those within the community. In a later chapter we will discuss the Ephesians 4 gifts further, but suffice it to say that often "APEs" are the pioneers in the church. "APE" refers to people who are primarily energized by participating in the apostolic, prophetic, and evangelistic ministry of Jesus. Those ministries are the ones that *bridge* the church to the outside culture, whereas the shepherding and teaching functions of the church tend to *build* and stabilize the existing church body. Sadly, APEs are often so misunderstood by churches—or seen as a threat to existing ministries—that they end up leaving to start parachurch ministries or non-profits in the community. I recommend looking around your city for this type of leader who loves Jesus and is meeting community needs in ways consistent with God's kingdom but who may not be involved in a local church. Those who already operate and experiment on the edges will become a great asset to your pioneering group. You might just have to promise them that you won't domesticate their wildness or try to recruit them back into Sunday-centric church activities!

Once you identify a group, invite them into your experiment and commission them to a season of missionary training. You can find great training material from the authors I highlight throughout this book. One of my favorite resources is *Dynamic Adventure: A Guide to Starting and Shaping Missional Churches*, because it includes many team-based activities.[17] Whatever you use, the most important thing is that the group creates the accountability to enact what they are learning in their designated missional context. As Alan Hirsch often says, it is much easier to educate a doer than activate a thinker. When the group gathers, be sure to reinforce that you are all seeking to create a missional discipleship lifestyle that prioritizes experimenting with new practices over a more academic discipleship model that emphasizes merely acquiring new information.

If you are a second-chair leader—such as an associate pastor, or maybe a director of missions or next-gen ministries—don't worry about getting your senior leader into this group. His or her presence will likely cause other members to avoid risks and become more concerned with trying to succeed than trying to experiment and learn. The goal of this group is innovation, not perfection. If you can, try to get at least one other staff member and one elder or well-respected lay leader in that pioneering group. It is important to have champions in these key leadership teams so they can advocate to their peers. Work to find racial, gender, and generational balance as well. You want a group that has a broad range of relational influence.

Innovation and adaptation are necessary to all forms of life. We cannot eradicate change; we must embrace it. Church leaders will always face cultural sandstorms, whether they be as slow and evolutionary as the post-Christian worldview or as rapid and revolutionary as COVID-19. Even if we find a way to hunker down and withstand a sandstorm, the next one will eventually follow in its path. We must find ways to protect our core DNA and mission while also adapting and innovating, so we can thrive under the new conditions.

Questions for Reflection

1. What are some examples from your local church or workplace where large-scale changes were communicated or implemented suddenly and through mass communication and you witnessed significant opposition as a result?

2. Does your church primarily operate discipleship programs that are more academically oriented (right *thinking*) or action oriented (right *living*), and what impact have you seen as a result?

3. Where would you look in your local community to find innovators who would make good members for a pilot program? Who are some of the "ninjas" who immediately come to mind who would be able to lead some experiments on the fringes?

8

Disruptive Disciplemaking

As I worked with my small group of ninja innovators, I began to notice a significant difference between the post-Christian impact in Hollywood in comparison to Western Europe. Because the movement toward secularism began in Europe, its roots have gone much deeper there and are more entrenched in the culture. Many Europeans are so far removed from the paradigms and practices of Christendom that they are unfamiliar with biblical stories, core theological teachings, Christian ethics, and Christian liturgical practices. Often, they have rejected faith in Jesus because of the historical reputation of Christianity, not because of a personal experience with it.

Across most of America, however, those who are not followers of Jesus are often actually *hyper-familiar* with Christianity. Unfortunately though, the forms of Christianity they've been exposed to have often failed to accurately depict either the way of Jesus or a healthy experience of church. The "dones" actually grew up in church before rejecting it; and most of the "nones" who did not grow up in church probably have parents or close friends who did. Consequently, most Americans have a residual understanding of Christian practices, vocabulary, and moral standards, albeit it often a negative and stereotypical one. This situation presents a unique challenge as we try to mobilize disciplemaking people. Discipling people in the way of Jesus today is often less about telling them something they've never heard before, and more about helping them realize they might not understand what they've heard.

How do you teach something new to someone who claims to know enough about the subject to be uninterested in learning anything else about it? As the philosopher Epictetus once said, "It is impossible for a man to learn what he thinks he already knows." This was the challenge Jesus encountered with the Pharisees that led him to say, "Though seeing, they do not see; though hearing, they do not hear or understand" (Matthew 13:13).

> "Post-Christian people assume they know the content of the Christian message and see the Christian faith as offering no potential contribution to their lives."[1]—Martin Robinson

The same is true in our culture today. If we ask others if they want to join us at church, their minds often flood with negative associations such as a repressive morality or an archaic worldview. If we use the term "Christian" to identify ourselves, often the person we are speaking to begins to probe just deeply enough to confirm that we fit their stereotypes. When and if we do, they can write us off as ignorant, irrelevant … or something worse.

We live in an age of information overload, and with that can come a resistance to learning or forming new opinions. We listen just long enough to confirm our preexisting biases, so we can move on. One of my mentors in Virginia, Dick Woodward, used to say, "Five percent of people think; 10 percent think they think; and 85 percent would rather die than think. And the 10 percent who think they're thinking are just rearranging their prejudices!" In an increasingly secular culture, most people are done thinking about the viability of Christianity; they are just rearranging their prejudices about it.

> "The world has seen so much of pop Christian culture that they have a programmed response to us: Ignore, ignore, ignore. What's needed is a change of parameters—something that will alter their emotional response."[2]
> —Hugh Halter and Matt Smay

In *Fool's Talk*, Os Guinness states the postmodern evangelistic challenge this way:

For the early Christian evangelists in the time of the Roman Empire, the challenge was to introduce a message so novel that it was strange to its first hearers, and then to set out what the message meant for the classical age and its sophisticated and assured ways of thinking. For much of the advanced modern world today, in contrast, the challenge is to restate something so familiar that people know it so well that they do not know it, yet at the same time are convinced that they are tired of it.[3]

Most people living in a post-Christian culture are convinced that they are tired of a message they may have never personally truly considered. What are we to do with this paradox?

STRANGER THINGS

One way to facilitate new learning is to disrupt a person's thought patterns, just as a strength coach disrupts the weightlifting pattern of an elite athlete. After a while an athlete's muscles become too accustomed to a repeated regimen. Only by exercising in new ways will he or she be able to break the muscles out of their rut and allow new growth.

In the same way, when sharing our faith, we have to take something that is hyper-familiar and make it seem strange or new. Literary critic Viktor Shklovsky believed this was part of the essential function of an artist: to disrupt a person's perception of an object so he or she can have the fresh experience of seeing it for the first time as it really is. In his 1917 essay, "Art as Technique," Shklovsky calls this process, "defamiliarization."[4] With this strategy, something familiar is made to seem strange. It creates a moment of cognitive dissonance that forces the subject to question their existing assumptions and consider it once again. As contemporary disciplemakers, we must defamiliarize people with a spiritual truth, so they can see it with fresh eyes.

Dr. John Scott Redd, president of Reformed Theological Seminary in Washington D.C., writes,

In literature, objects and situations that are otherwise commonplace are dislodged from their expected settings and re-presented in fresh perspective. The reader cannot rely on preconceived notions or a false sense of familiarity that might serve to disrupt the artistic process, but rather he or she submits to a process of disorientation and therefore must approach the issue anew.[5]

When something is truly unknown, a teacher seeks to make it as simple to understand as possible. But when something is already known yet misunderstood, the teacher seeks to make the familiar concept seem as new and novel as possible, so the existing information can be deconstructed and replaced by truth. The Bible is full of strange-making as a pedagogical device, as God tries to break into the pride and hard hearts of his people who act as if they have mastered a truth they actually have never fully understood.

Dr. Redd adds,

> An idea can be made strange by the use of metaphor, or it can be made strange simply by the use of rare words, foreign words, or other linguistic features such as rhythm, rhyme, accent, and so on. Examples of the former can be found in the biblical parable, vision sequence, or proverb. Examples of the latter can be found in poetic diction, gapping of words, parallel line structures, word postponement, and so on.[6]

SLOW DOWN TO RETHINK

Let me give a concrete example of disruption through strange-making. In Williamsburg I often taught Bible studies and led vesper services at retirement communities and assisted living centers for people whose health prevented them from attending worship services. As I drove onto one of those properties one day, I caught an odd sight out of the corner of my eye. The posted speed limit was 17½ mph. I chuckled out of surprise at that unusual number—but then I looked down to see what my actual speed was and realized I was going too fast ... *so I slowed down.*

That sign is genius. Someone took a common symbol in our culture—the usual speed limit that our hyper-familiarity causes us to overlook—and then defamiliarized it so that people are compelled to think and act in response. If the sign simply posted a 15 mph limit, it would in theory be safer for the community of elderly residents navigating the sidewalks. However, most drivers would pay no attention and simply continue on at a speed that felt appropriate. (That is often what we do as drivers, especially on private property where we assume we are safe from the watchful radar of the police.) By strange-making the number, the property owners captured my attention and prompted me to reconsider my default assumptions about my speed.

"It ain't what you don't know that gets you into trouble. It's what you know for sure that just ain't so."—Anonymous

THE DIVINE DISRUPTOR

As you might imagine, Jesus was a master at disruptive disciplemaking. When he began his ministry, Jewish culture was saturated with misinformation regarding the nature of God and true worship. The Pharisees and teachers of the law reveled in their high place of privilege and power, refused to associate with sinners and tax collectors, and burdened ordinary people with excessive regulations. Jesus entered into that culture and disrupted those norms with his lifestyle and his teachings. He spoke of a new path to greatness that could only be accessed through service and humility; created a new community by sharing space with the social outcasts and rejects; and sought to distill the Law and worship from its complex forms to its true essence. His expression of the life of God was so disruptive that he was considered a drunkard and a glutton, was accused of being possessed by demons, and even his own family questioned his sanity. Just as the fermenting of new wine requires a new wineskin, Jesus' listeners could only receive his kingdom if they possessed a new mindset.[7]

One of the best examples of Jesus' disruptive disciplemaking is his use of parables. A parable is a fictional story or illustration that parallels real life and delivers truth symbolically. Remember that curved line in the "diffusion of innovations" graph? Jesus' parables delivered truth in a similar way. Rather than hit people right between the eyes with propositional truth, he took a roundabout approach to deliver the message. I don't think the point of some of his parables dawned on people until they were walking home wrestling with what he said. Jesus used story as a way of forcing people to rethink and reexamine spiritual truth. (After all, that is what repentance means; to rethink our existing paradigms in order to change how we see and act as a result.)

Consider Jesus' interactions with the Pharisees. Early in his ministry, the religious leaders of that time pegged Jesus as a revolutionary and a threat to their power and place in Judaism. With a few notable exceptions (such as Nicodemus and Joseph of Arimathea), the Pharisees were not interested in learning from Jesus; they were simply trying to trap him with their questions so they could confirm their suspicions and then eliminate his influence. As we noted in the previous chapter, this is often the pattern when those in power are confronted with new ideas.

Jesus knew not to respond to the Pharisees' questions with direct answers. Rather he sought to disrupt their thinking and the thinking of the crowds who were listening in. He often subverted the questioner's agenda by responding with a question of his own or answering with hyperbole or metaphor. Jesus was a master communicator who understood the adage "where predictably is high, impact is low." When he did give a direct answer, he often quoted the Old Testament in order to bring a perspective to the issue that his interrogators could not dispute.[8] This in itself was disruptive, since the crowds assumed the religious leaders were the ultimate authority on scriptural texts.

OUTSIDE-THE-WELL THINKING

In the fourth chapter of John's Gospel, Jesus encounters a woman at a well in Samaria. You can read the entire chapter on your own, but allow me to pull out a few pertinent observations. This is a great text to study with the leaders you are training to live as missionaries in a post-Christian culture, since it is replete with lessons that can be applied to disciplemaking in any cross-cultural context.

- *Jesus went somewhere he was not expected to go and spoke with someone he was not expected to address.* The encounter with this woman only takes place because Jesus went somewhere Jews were not expected to go. Rather than take the well-worn road north that diverted Jewish travelers around a forsaken and almost forbidden region, he went straight through Samaria. When his disciples returned from finding food, they were amazed that he was speaking with a Samaritan woman. Even she is amazed that this Jewish man is willing to speak with her in public. Jesus crossed borders and broke boundaries in order to build relationships.

- ***Jesus led with weakness and not strength.*** By asking the woman to help him—by giving him a drink—he puts her in the position of power. He expresses his need for fresh water and is willing to drink it from her shared container. Doing so creates a sense of commonality between two people Jewish society treated as having nothing in common. He refuses to begin the relationship with any notion of cultural superiority, never mind his divinity. He opens the conversation with a topic that is already of interest to her—water—rather than inserting his agenda into her life.

- ***Jesus acknowledged her lifestyle without condemning her for it.*** Jesus is aware she has been through five failed marriages and was currently living with someone to whom she was not married, but he does not weaponize that information against her.[9] He simply acknowledges her present reality. He affirms the dignity of her humanity rather than pointing out her lifestyle decisions. He sees her through the lens of Genesis 1 rather than Genesis 3.

  Too often we believe we need to be able to affirm all of an individual's moral decisions in order to relate to them. Yet, in this story, a complete stranger, who knows the worst secret this woman has, shows her kindness rather than judgment. What an act of disruption! When as Christians we are invited to an event that we don't completely approve of, we can affirm the dignity of the people involved without agreeing with their choices. Our mere polite presence may disrupt their expectations of a Christian.

- ***Jesus turns a conversation about spiritual forms into one about spiritual essence.*** When the woman pivots the discussion from her failed marriages to the Jewish practice of worship, Jesus interrupts her assumptions by making it clear a day is coming when a person will be able to worship God in any location. When people ask me "Where is your church?" I like to respond, "Oh wow, well, we have people all over L.A." That simple statement helps reorient people from church as *place* to church as *people*. If, as Christians, we can subtly reshape our language, it can alter people's understanding of our faith. Even using language that is less predictable and more winsome might help people reconsider their stereotypes.

- *Jesus saw her as a whole to be restored and not just a soul to be saved.* There is no mention of Jesus assuring this woman that her sins are forgiven because she believes he is the Messiah. There is no invitation to pray the sinner's prayer, and he does not even baptize her, although there is clearly water nearby. Jesus seems more concerned with transforming her whole life than just saving her soul. She is at the well at midday to avoid encountering other women. Her shame has separated her from the life of her community and has made her an outcast. (Remember our discussion of the gospel narrative for honor/shame cultures in chapter five.) For the kingdom to come in her life, her shame must be removed so she can reenter society. By sending her back to her city to report that she has encountered the Messiah, Jesus bestows on her a position of honor. The text says, "Many of the Samaritans from that town believed in [Jesus] because of the woman's testimony" (John 4:39). For generations to come, people credited her as the reason they met the Jewish Messiah. She went from the edges of the society to the center of the city's renewal; from outcast to honor. She is the reason a slice of heaven came to her hometown.

> "When the church lives a radical alternative to the world around them it's a sign and wonder."[10]—Tara Beth Leach

In this story, Jesus sets a great example of how we can join him in discipling someone who is steeped in misconceptions about faith and is convinced that worshiping the one true God is not for someone like them.

God has been disrupting our perceptions of him since the beginning of his relationship with humans, appearing to individuals in ways they didn't expect—to Jacob in a dream, to Moses in a burning bush, to Balaam through a talking donkey.[11] God gets people's attention in unanticipated ways in order to increase the impact of his revelation. Sadly, the church has become predictable to the world; but I find hope in knowing that God is still in the business of disrupting individuals in order to disciple them.

EQUIPPING DISRUPTIVE DISCIPLEMAKERS

If our goal is to mobilize every person to live as a missionary and to make disciples in the same way Jesus did, then we will need to equip them with a skill I refer to as *disruptive disciplemaking*. This is the process of disrupting an individual's preconceived notions of Christianity in order to help them reconsider what Jesus is really like.

To be a disruptive disciplemaker, we must first listen to and learn from our friends and neighbors about what their presuppositions and objections are to faith; then we can demonstrate the Jesus lifestyle in a manner that does not fit in that box. Of course, not every objection to Jesus is incorrect; most notably that he is the only way to salvation. When those objections are raised, we must simply and humbly affirm God's truth. However, many objections to Christianity can be removed if the church will begin to disciple others in the actual way of Jesus and the values of his kingdom. People might pay attention to us if our lives were faithful and our posture humble.

Based on my observations in Europe and Hollywood, let me give a few examples of how we can disrupt assumptions about Christians.

Disruption #1—Lead With Weakness

As we discussed earlier, Christians have gained a reputation for being judgmental and condescending toward others. People perceive the church as acting "holier than thou." One way to disrupt this stereotype is to lead with weakness in our relationships with not-yet followers of Jesus.

Confessing our own inability to adhere to the ethics outlined in our Bible adds veracity to Christianity and gives us opportunities to talk about the grace of Jesus. We can share publicly the ways we struggle with certain parts of our faith, such as why an all-powerful God allows children to be sold into sex slavery. We should be transparent about the challenges of following a God that we cannot see, touch, or directly interact with face-to-face. We must acknowledge that the Bible can be confusing at times, even if a person has studied it for many years.

"The perception of Christians will only change through consistent exposure, over time, to Christ's followers who take seriously their call to proclaim and embody the gospel in everything they do, everywhere they go."[12]*—Gabe Lyons*

We tend to think that these sorts of honest confessions will lead others to discredit our faith; but, in reality, they give credence to our faith practice. Doubts and fears reveal our faith as authentic, and help people identify with us as they wrestle with their own existential fears. We can be honest about the fact that we don't have it all figured out and that we have more in common with them than they think we do. Transparency around our weakness disrupts a culture that is paradoxically both obsessed with image *and* authenticity. A heartfelt apology can be a powerful contradiction to the critique that Christians think they are better than others. Reach out to a neighbor and confess, "You moved in three months ago, and I never welcomed you or introduced myself. I'm sorry, that was rude. Would you like to come over for a drink?" Even a simple gesture like that can help repair and restart a relationship on new terms.

The world assumes Christians think we own the moral high ground, so conceding it to others and humbly asking them to teach us is incredibly disruptive to their notions of a Christian. Look to affirm others for the ways they are flourishing in life. When we see someone who does not follow Jesus living out an exemplary practice, we can comment on it and ask them to share their secret. Encourage a fellow parent at the park and ask how they find the patience to deal with their young children with such kindness. Compliment the integrity of a coworker and ask how they find the strength to not cut corners on the job. Ask a couple who have been together longer than you have with your partner or spouse what they have discovered as the secret to a lasting relationship. I am continually working on this practice of searching for the image of God in others and calling it out as beautiful as I confess my weaknesses in those same areas.

Disruption #2—Talk About Spiritual Things in a Natural Way

Too often Christians discuss spiritual things with such a heavy church accent that people can't even understand us. As cross-cultural missionaries, we need to work at speaking the language of local people. It takes some practice and courage, but simply trying to infuse spirituality into everyday life and talking naturally about spiritual things can have a big impact.

A great mentor for me in this is Dave Gibbons, who is able to translate spiritual truths into the language of the marketplace in a way that is free of religious baggage. He will quote an "ancient proverb from a wise sage" and then offer the biblical truth from the book of Proverbs. Or say, "Everyone has somewhere they go to find truth; my truth source is the Bible." He helps people discern their "design and destiny" as a way of leading people to understand that they have a transcendent purpose. This helps open them up to the possibility of considering a sovereign God who created them in his image and called them to join his work in the world.

One of my favorite "natural" ways to identify that God is working in someone's life is by saying, "I think God is trying to make friends with you." Sometimes I describe the mission of God by saying, "I believe Jesus came to change everything that is wrong with the world." And I often begin discussions of the Bible by saying, "In the origin story of my faith tradition it says ...."

In my own missionary engagement within Hollywood, I rarely identify as a Christian or use that label in any context other than within the church. If someone asks if I am a Christian, I usually say, "Oh no, I am just

"We need to violate people's expectations. We need to be counterintuitive .... We can engage people's curiosity over a long period of time by systematically 'opening gaps' in their knowledge—and then filling those gaps."[13]—Chip and Dan Heath

a follower of Jesus."[14] Or to use the pervasive language of Hollywood, I say, "I am spiritual but not religious, and I follow the way of Jesus." As many others have noted before, people are more open to Jesus than they are to Christianity, so any time I can reframe the conversation around the person of Jesus, I try to do so. When I sense that a person doesn't believe in God and has a negative perception of Christianity, I might ask them, "Would you tell me what you think the God of Christianity is like?" Often their perceptions are based on bad experiences with Christians and not on biblical truth. If they offer a cultural misconception of God that is not consistent with Scripture, I like to reply with, "I don't believe *that* God exists either, so I guess we have that in common."

If people find out we are part of a church, they may ask us, "What kind of church is it?" Rather than rattle off an official mission statement or describe our church polity, we can use their question as an opportunity to disrupt their likely stereotypes. We could answer by saying, "We want to see our city look more like heaven." My favorite answer is, "We are a church of people who want to live more like Jesus and less like Christians." That almost always gets a laugh and "I like that," to which I respond, "See! You're one of us!"

When people ask me about my faith, I prayerfully try to discern the intent behind the question—to determine whether they are asking more in the vein of a tax collector or of a Pharisee. That is, is it a genuine search for truth, or is it an attempt to confirm biases so they can categorize me and then dismiss what I believe? If the question is genuine, then we are wise to do our best to honor the intent of the questioner and answer according to the invitation they offer. But if we discern the question is merely a trap laid for us, then I suggest we change the trajectory of the conversation and seek to give a more disruptive response. This is just a contemporary application of Jesus' instruction to "be wise as serpents and innocent as doves."[15]

Disruption #3—Be Curious Rather Than Convincing

In a culture that values tolerance of all spiritual beliefs, Christians' claims to universal truth are viewed as condescending toward those who don't agree. Often the most disruptive approach is to simply ask people about their spiritual beliefs or their guiding values in life rather than trying to share our own. In an attention-deficit culture, genuine and compassionate curiosity directed toward another person becomes an expression of generosity. Sometimes people articulate values that are inherently Judeo-Christian; they just don't recognize them as such. When someone says they believe love is the greatest value or that they try to treat all people equally with respect and dignity, I reply, "That's great; that's a foundational teaching of Jesus that I follow as well." That usually messes with the heads of those who think they have rejected Christianity. It can create a curiosity in the minds of people who long since stopped wanting to know about the Christian faith.

BE PREPARED

These sorts of disruptive conversations take some practice and certainly take some courage. Only Jesus was wise enough to respond to trick questions with on-the-spot retorts like "Whose image is [on this coin]? ... . Give back to Caesar what is Caesar's and to God what is God's."[16] I suggest anticipating the sorts of questions not-yet followers of Jesus might ask, and scripting out disruptive answers that might pique curiosity and prevent the person from stereotyping you and dismissing your faith.

The goal in creating these disruptive moments is to plant a "splinter in the mind"[17] that a person can't seem to get rid of after the conversation ends. Something that makes them think, *Maybe I don't know as much as I think I know. Maybe I need to reconsider my assumptions, and maybe this is the person who could help me do that.* Strange-making is not a direct path to knowing the truth but rather a path to unknowing what one thinks they know so that true knowing can take place. Once a person realizes they don't know what they thought they knew about Jesus, our discipling takes on a more traditional approach of presenting the teachings of Jesus in ways that are understandable and applicable.

LIVING IT OUT

Disruption is more than just the *words* we use about Jesus. It must permeate our daily practices so that our lives are incarnating the life of Jesus. When Jesus chose to wash his disciples' feet, he was disrupting the assumed hierarchy of social standing.[18] Jesus was revealing God's true nature to the world by taking on the form of a servant. Sadly, present-day Christianity is more associated with domination and power than sacrifice and servanthood. The most effective tools we have in discipling those who do not share our faith are the towel and the basin. Acts of radical service in a self-centered culture are extraordinarily disruptive.

In his book *The Next Christians*, Gabe Lyons identifies the postures today's disciples are adopting to disrupt the reputation of Christianity, all of which are marked by love and service:[20]

> "The church must not come with the sort of judgment or with any other weapon of domination. It must come instead with the basin of water and the simple towel to address the tears of a culture and crisis."[19]—Martin Robinson

- *Provoked,* not offended: The next generation of disciples are provoked to take positive action for change rather than put off by the world's corruption.
- *Creators,* not critics: The next generation of disciples are creators of culture that reflect God's beauty and goodness, not sideline critics of the ungodly culture around them.
- *Called,* not employed: The next generation of disciples see themselves as joining God's call to participate in his mission in the marketplace, not merely earning a paycheck so they can return to their religious spaces.
- *Countercultural,* not "relevant": The next generation of disciples seeks to live as salt and light, preserving agents in a decaying world, not just to mimic culture to be seen as relevant.

Our lives need to be filled with small creative acts of disruption—regular practices that counter the accepted patterns of the world—not bizarre acts that draw attention to ourselves. We don't need street-corner preaching or pithy Christian t-shirts; we need the sorts of winsome and wonderful acts of service and love that offer life to the people and places around us. Michael Frost invites us to "keep Christianity weird":

> Today, the church in America seems to have traded in its mandate to be eccentric and aimed instead at an unconscious conventionality .... When I call on you to keep Christianity weird, I'm asking you to reject materialism, foster community, promote diversity, share resources, protect the environment, start ethical businesses, feed the hungry, play beautiful music, bring peace and joy and life back to our cities.[21]

When was the last time you or your faith community did something so lavish and generous that no one understood why you were doing it? What have we done recently that demonstrated *remarkable* joy or *remarkable* generosity to the point where it actually caused someone else to *remark* on it?

The more genuine the act, the more powerful it can be. In the 1862 novel *Les Misérables,* Jean Valjean is convicted for stealing bread and, upon release from prison, is offered the hospitality of a local bishop who invites him to share a meal and spend the night. Valjean awakens in the middle of the night to steal all the silver from the home before leaving. The next day, the police arrest him and return him to the bishop to confirm that the silver was in fact stolen. In that encounter, Valjean assumes the bishop will act according to God's justice and have him punished for this crime. Instead, the bishop disrupts his expectation and tells the police that the silver was freely given as a gift. He goes so far as to chastise Valjean for forgetting to take a pair of valuable candlesticks with him when he left. The police are stunned, quickly apologize for the misunderstanding, release the prisoner, and depart. As the bishop adds the candlesticks to Valjean's bag of silver, he looks him in the eye and says, "Jean Valjean, my brother, you no longer belong to evil, but to good. It is your soul that I buy from you; I withdraw it from black thoughts and the spirit of perdition, and I give it to God."[22] A single disruptive act of grace and service by God's ambassador changes the direction of Valjean's life.

Daily life presents us with regular opportunities to serve others if we simply begin to live with this level of intentionality. Not every act of disruption will be as noteworthy as giving away your silver to a stranger. Often the opportunities present themselves in the normal course of everyday routines. Jeff, one of our first Forge residents, was on staff at a local acting school. He decided to put away his cell phone during the class breaks in order to be available to engage with the students on a personal level. He was amazed at how many great conversations emerged with students eager to connect with a more successful artist who expressed genuine interest in their lives. One night after class, a student was about to arrange for an Uber home. Knowing how cash-strapped starving artists can be, Jeff offered a free ride instead. That simple act of service subverted the implied hierarchy of successful teacher and aspiring student and was a disruptive act in the competitive and self-centered Hollywood culture.

Questions for Reflection

1. Find five instances of strange-making or defamiliarization in advertising or communication around you. How did they disrupt your thought pattern in order to get your attention?

2. What questions do you get asked about your faith from those outside the church? How can you leverage those questions to articulate the nature of Jesus or his church in a way that might pique curiosity?

3. As you consider the four postures from Gabe Lyons book *The Next Christians,* which one is your church thriving in and which needs improvement? What other postures would you add to this list to create a new experience of Christianity in your community?

9

Enough of the Same Old Ship

Dr. Crawford Loritts once told my seminary class on urban leadership, "As a leader, you will overestimate what you can do in one year and underestimate what you can do in five years." I drew great comfort from those words in my first few years leading a church in Hollywood. There were days when the work we were doing as a few pioneers on the fringes of our ministry seemed insignificant compared to how I sensed God calling the entire church to change and adapt. However, the momentum needed to create lasting change in an organization begins with a series of small wins, just as a pearl is created by the slow and steady coating of one layer of nacre upon another. As long as God kept us winning in the areas that mattered most, I trusted that a kingdom movement of missionaries would be the result.

Slowly, the enthusiasm of our first group of innovators was spreading. As the ability to identify and accept the challenges arising from a post-Christian culture became less irritating and more inspiring to the community, something beautiful was forming. Early adopters were catching the vision and beginning to align themselves around the call to live as personal missionaries making disciples rather than as sales persons for a Sunday service. Our staff and elders were learning new paradigms, experimenting together with new practices, and selecting new staff and elders who were excited to head in this direction. As our commitment grew to serve those outside our church family, some people chose to move on to other local churches that were primarily oriented toward meeting needs within their community. But while some moved on, even more began to step up to the challenge and embrace this new others-centered life. As positive change seeped into the community from the edges, we needed to think more systemically about changing the broader culture of the church.

"If you want to change how the world thinks you first have to change how they imagine. That is why today artists are our apologists."[1]—James K. A. Smith

In order to change the paradigms of an existing church we need to spark people's imaginations so they think differently. Creatives know that art is conceived in the artist's mind and soul before it is externalized as a tangible piece that can be enjoyed by others. If we as leaders cannot break free from our existing paradigms and structures to imagine something new, we will never be able to help our church embody that new reality.

One of the best ways to free people from old ways of thinking is to change our metaphors. We use metaphors to structure how we think; they provide a conceptual framework that shapes and gives meaning to our experiences, perceptions, and thoughts. When we change a metaphor, we often change the meaning we associate with it. Even referring to your church as a "community of missionaries" rather than as a "congregation of members" will help people view their primary orientation as outward and not inward.

SAILING IN NEW CULTURAL SEAS

One helpful metaphor is imagining church as a ship. Our goal as the crew is to keep God as True North and navigate our vessel and the souls on board in the direction of our biblically mandated mission: to make disciples who participate in God's redemptive work in the world. For many generations in the West, our church ships floated in waters that moved in the same direction we were heading. The natural current of culture, steeped in Christian values and a Christian worldview, carried us along and allowed us to go further and faster than our own efforts merited. However, the tide has changed. To remain faithful to our True North, we must now orient ourselves against the directional flow of an increasingly secular culture. The surrounding waters are choppier and more threatening, and forward movement is harder to achieve. In the same way the eye rubs away irritants to protect itself, the temptation can be to batten down the hatches and try to ride out the storm, as if we are an ark whose only purpose is to protect those already inside.

I suggest the better option is to adapt the nature of our vessel so that it is more suited to these waters, and to have the courage to make this change while our boats are still out at sea.

A famous philosophical thought experiment often presented to university students is entitled *The Ship of Theseus*. This hypothetical scenario was first posed by the Greek historian Plutarch regarding a ship captained by King Theseus, one of the rulers of ancient Greece, and the man credited with founding Athens. The scenario describes King Theseus as a captain sailing a single ship throughout his life; a ship that carries him to victory in numerous battles. At the end of his life, his ship is moved out of the harbor and into a museum to be preserved. As the years go by, a few of the wooden planks begin to rot. Curators at the museum pull the rotting planks and carefully replace them with new planks made of the same type of wood. This process of changing out rotted planks continues for many years until, a century later, all of the original parts have been replaced by newer ones that serve the same function.

Here is the question asked of the students: does the museum still have the right to call this Theseus' Ship, or is it now a new ship that must be considered a replica? If you consider it a new ship, when did it become a new ship—after the first plank was replaced, after the last was replaced, or somewhere in the middle? As a follow-up, the students are asked to imagine that the exchanged rotting planks have been stored away until, one day, new scientific discoveries are used to restore their health, and the ship is put back together with the original planks. At this point, are there two of Theseus' ships ... or just one?

I offer that story not to speculate on a philosophical quandary but as a metaphor for the challenge we face as local churches. For our purposes, let's change one important element of the scenario: let's make King Theseus himself the one who identifies the rotting planks and replaces them one by one while the ship is still afloat. This is a better metaphor to describe the situation most church leaders find themselves in; identifying and replacing outdated planks in our churches while keeping the boat afloat and all passengers alive. The challenge

"Transitioning traditional churches to missional ones is a non-linear process of deconstruction and reconstruction."[2]—JR Rozko

of creatively destroying and remaking our churches for this new world feels like an overwhelming task. It might seem easier to just let this ship sink and begin building new ones based on improved blueprints and better raw materials. But those of us whom God has called to steward these vessels and the souls on board know that is not a viable option.

CULTURE-MAKING

Each plank on our church-ship represents a part of our culture: the stories, habits, traditions, language, symbols, and ceremonies that determine how we operate. Remember, culture is rooted in a worldview that offers a set of values and ideas, but it is expressed as external activity (behaviors, practices, liturgy, and language) as well as tangible items that we can see or touch. Andy Crouch, a leading expert on culture-making, calls the tangible goods of culture its "artifacts."[3] In the same way we look at ancient artifacts in a museum and gain a sense of the culture of that previous civilization, the artifacts of our church culture tell a story and shape people's behaviors.

When I began working with Ecclesia, I found in my office desk an assortment of items, such as magnets, pens, and even slap bracelets, all branded with the Ecclesia logo. I examined these as artifacts of the prior culture and considered their implications. They were, in effect, corporate promotional materials; free swag given away to members to help spread the word about Ecclesia. They revealed a church culture that called on its members to help create a buzz about Sunday gatherings with products that members could give away or use in the presence of others. These were not tools to equip them to personally make disciples, or resources for their spiritual formation; these were just objects to promote Ecclesia as a trendy place where you could come on Sundays. Their mere existence informed me of the values inherent in the previous culture.

We must begin to identify the activities and artifacts of our culture that were built for a different set of nautical conditions and replace them with tangible expressions of a new culture that is designed for the post-Christian seas. It is not enough to simply remove the old; each plank must be replaced with new elements of culture that tell new stories and embody new values. As Crouch suggests, "The best way to change culture is to create more of it."[4] We must decide what planks to pull and what new ones we will put in their place in order to preserve the core essence of the organization while also stimulating change and innovation.

As we consider what cultural changes to make, it is also important to consider the timing and tempo at which we make these changes. In seasons of significant cultural disruption, such as COVID-19, we may be

> *"Growth, whether personal or within an organizational structure, can only happen as a result of embracing chaos."[5]—Danielle Strickland*

required to make changes quickly. However, in times of greater stability, rapid and frequent change is likely to invite resistance. We would be wise to learn from a sector of society that deals in introducing change: the world of product design.

Commercial designers face the challenge of creating products that strike "just the right balance between the well-known present, on one hand, and a new and innovative future on the other hand."[6] If a new product is too futuristic, such as Google glasses, it will be rejected; but if the change is not innovative enough, it fails to create momentum. Imagine an iPhone launch that doesn't promise enough new features to entice owners to upgrade. Designers managing that tension apply what is known as the MAYA Principle: "Most advanced yet acceptable." Raymond Loewy, who first coined the phrase, "believed that consumers are torn between two opposing forces: neophilia, a curiosity about new things; and neophobia, a fear of anything too new. As a result, they gravitate to products that are bold, but instantly comprehensible."[7]

Here are a few MAYA design principles, applied to the challenge of making cultural changes within your local church.

- *Make your changes gradually over time*: Calendar out the introduction of new elements over the year, so the pace of change does not feel threatening or disorienting. Stay away from changes at times when people are experiencing anxiety—holidays, for example—and instead try seasons where people expect change—like January or the start of the school year.

- **Include familiar patterns in the new change**: People tend to more readily embrace change when it contains some element of the familiar. Root structural or programmatic changes in language, imagery, or leadership that is remaining the same, or vice-versa.

- **Draw on your user's present skills and mindset**: Build on the community's preexisting knowledge base to explain something new. Think of the launch of Airbnb, which was first described as "eBay for homes" or how TaskRabbit was described by friends as "Uber for errands." Using existing knowledge to explain new things helps mitigate the sense of unfamiliarity.

LEADERSHIP LAPSES

There are three key mistakes leaders might make as we begin to shift culture. Each can derail the process before any lasting change can be accomplished. Let's identify them and consider how we can correct them.

A Failure to Let Go

First, leaders often fail to admit how personally committed we are to preserving our existing culture. It takes incredible courage to allow elements of our culture to be replaced, knowing that we once spent months, if not years, establishing them. Too often, our value as people becomes enmeshed with our contributions in ministry, and the thought of cultural innovation threatens our sense of worth.

I remember a young leader taking over a ministry I formerly led and changing the ministry name in order to help it connect with the next generation. Even that simple change made me feel a sense of loss and separation from something in which I had once invested so much of my life. We would be wise to seek the Holy Spirit for the strength and security to objectify these changes and understand they are not reflections on us personally.

To best serve the church we must consider how to leverage our influence to set up the generation before us for future success. Every leader over the age of forty would be wise to cultivate a discipleship group of leaders in their twenties and thirties, not only to offer them what you know but also to create a team that can offer fresh perspective on the church through the eyes of a new generation. We can give them permission to speak the truth in love to us about our church culture and celebrate that feedback as a gift, not a threat. Ask them, "What three changes would you make if you took over my job tomorrow?" or "If you were planting a new church in this town, what would you do differently?" Give them permission to lead experiments on the fringes of the church and share what they are learning, so you can implement successful ideas throughout the broader community. Building meaningful relationships with the next generation creates a sense of partnership that will help us celebrate alongside them when we see them championing and effecting change.

Some of you reading this book may be younger leaders. You may be encountering a generation above you that is struggling to implement change or is unwilling to pay the personal price to rebuild at this stage in their careers. These leaders may want to keep sailing the ship as it is, knowing it will remain seaworthy throughout their tenure. It may take great tact and discernment to engage them in important conversations without threatening their identity and security. As you approach these conversations, be sure to appreciate and acknowledge the investment previous leaders have made and frame your innovative ideas as ways to preserve and expand their legacy. I write this book with young leaders in mind, and I pray it is a resource you could read with older leaders to inspire cooperation that will help the church change now and flourish well into the future.

An Inability to See Our Blindness

Second, leaders are often blind to the elements of our culture that are in need of change. Those of us who have been in one church context or one denomination for a long time can find it hard to recognize our own cultural distinctives, since we are likely blind to them. We already spoke about how to disrupt those outside the church who are hyper-familiar with Christianity; many of us will need our hyper-familiarity with our own local church disrupted as well.

One of the best ways to get a fresh perspective on your church culture is to get away from it for a while on a sabbatical or extended vacation. Stepping away for a season is a good process of strange-making, and it will enable fresh observations and learning. The COVID-19 pandemic gave many leaders new perspective on which activities were actually essential to the health of their churches and forced us all into atypical rhythms of life that caused us to innovate.

Another strategy we can employ to gain a fresh perspective on our own culture is to enter into a foreign environment where we are forced to surrender our role as an expert. This place is often referred to as liminal space, from the Latin word *limens,* meaning "threshold." It is the place of discomfort where you have left the old world but are not yet fully comfortable in the new one.

> [A liminality] is composed of any or a combination of danger, marginality, disorientation, or ordeal and tends to create a space that is neither here nor there, a transitional stage between what was and what is to come.[8]

Liminal spaces are places where all fictional characters experience their most significant transformation. Think of Frodo Baggins on the road to Mount Doom in Mordor; Simba when he is exiled from the Pride Lands; or Harry Potter away at Hogwarts. Crossing out of our own comfort zone and over the threshold into a new place puts us back in the position of a learner and forces us to see things with new eyes. Often those new eyes are then able to look back on our own culture afresh.

My experience in Brussels put me in a place of liminality. I found my first year personally challenging, as I faced down a swirl of new irritants in this culture around me, and unfortunately that made me pretty irritable around the team! I had an established way I had "done church" for ten years, and I had to unlearn it all in order to experiment with something new. This process caused internal anxiety and frustration that at times expressed itself as an argumentative and critical spirit; but that struggle was an essential part of the learning process. My wife and I refer to that season of liminality in Brussels as the best of times and the worst of times. We now look back on it as the most transformational time in our lives.

If you look at many of the pastors in America who are pioneering new ways of expressing church, you will find they share in common a season of life where they too crossed over into liminal space and changed their perspective on how they were operating "back home." Examples include Dave Gibbons of Newsong in Santa Ana, California, who travelled to Thailand; Brian Sanders, who launched Tampa Underground after spending nine months with his team in the Philippines; and Francis Chan, who spent time in China before starting a house church movement in San Francisco and who is now based in Hong Kong. Each of these leaders has written of their journey, and there is much to be gleaned in their respective books. There are also some excellent biographies of midcentury activists, such as Aimee Semple McPherson and Dorothy Day, who crossed over gender and social divides and pushed local churches to do the same.[9]

If you are not currently able to enter into a season of liminality and experience the benefits of crossing cultures, you may have to invite another culture to cross over and bless you with their insights. You may want to ask friends, relatives, or neighbors

> *"God got Israel out of Egypt in a month or so, but it took another 40 years to get Egypt out of Israel."*[10]—JR Rozko

who are not part of your church community to serve you by attending a service, visiting your website, reading through your printed materials, or participating in some activities and sharing their perceptions. As much as I hate the consumerist connotation, you are inviting them to be a "secret shopper" in order to give fresh perspective on something you are too familiar with to evaluate. Here are some things you could ask them to identify:

- What do you think matters most to our church?
- Why do you think our church exists?
- How do you think our church measures success?
- What did you sense we want people to do as part of their commitment to the church?

Be sure to ask them what specific activities and artifacts in your culture (behaviors, language, symbols, materials, signage, etc.) indicated to them the answers to these questions. You would be wise to recruit people who express the diversity represented in your community—in age, ethnicity, socio-economic background, and maturity in their faith in Jesus. As a way of valuing their time,

I suggest you give them a small gift of thanks or offer to buy them lunch to hear their responses.

An Undue Emphasis on Words Over Actions

The third mistake leaders make is to rewrite the vision/mission statement as the first plank we try to replace. We get fooled into thinking that a new vision/mission statement will successfully launch a new strategy, even though most of us intuitively know the truth of the axiom "culture eats strategy for lunch." It is better to first understand the existing culture, begin to slowly reshape it, and *then* summarize those changes in a new vision/mission statement. Clearly the leadership team needs to agree upon the shared values that are guiding cultural shifts, but it is better to present those to the broader community by slowly introducing new activities and artifacts rather than getting well-crafted words on a wall.

Remember our "diffusion of innovations" discussion in chapter seven? Those who are resistant to change need to see it modeled as a benefit to the lives of others around them before they will consider any modifications for themselves. Only the first 16 percent of a community buys into change based on the presentation of new ideas. The overwhelming majority will not buy into an innovation until it is fleshed out in new practices modelled and measured as an improvement on the past. They won't embrace the call to innovate until they can see and behold some visible pearls that were made through that process. If we lead with church-wide rebranding efforts, more than half our community will begin this journey resistant to the idea of change before they ever have a chance to experience it. Well-crafted mission statements are far better received when the church body reads them and thinks, *Well of course that's what we are, and we've been that for a while. I'm glad we found a better way to express it in words.*

AN AUDIENCE OF ONE

Along the way, I realized that the external process of changing a church culture also required an internal process for me as a leader. I often observe local church leaders who sense the value of a more missional-incarnational approach but don't want to do the hard and painful work of deconstructing their paradigms and slowly reconstructing from the inside out. That process risks personal rejection at the hands of their existing congregation. Leaders can easily fall victim to what Forge America leaders refer to as the temptation to "slap a coat of missional paint on it"—a cheap substitute for true change. Jewelry stores are filled with imitation pearls that are easily manufactured by simply dipping a glass bead into a solution of luminescent fish scales. The coating is thin and eventually wears off, leaving the owner with something worthless. Are we forming new pearls or simply slapping a coat of fish scales on our existing programs?

A true test of whether we're authentically pearl-making is how we measure success. For the decade in which I pastored a megachurch, success was measured by our quantitative growth in attendance, resources, property size, and influence among other local churches. Even our qualitative discipleship metrics were input-based (such as attendance at programs, financial giving, or hours invested at church by volunteers) rather than output-based metrics (such as disciples who can make disciples, or local schools and communities transformed by our engagement). More often than not, input-based metrics soothe the ego of the leader—creating a pathway to bigger stages, larger audiences, and often heftier salaries. As I shared in chapter one, the dangerous allure of this temptation is part of what drove me to run from this form of church.

As Ecclesia became more decentralized, open sourced, and empowering of every believer to make disciples in their everyday context, it took me a while to rewire my sense of professional success. Even though I knew Sunday attendance was not our goal, it was hard not to compare our community to others in town with whom Ecclesia was once a peer in both size and attractional appeal, never mind comparing myself to Hollywood's celebrity pastors. As we sought to turn toward equipping disciples more than entertaining Christians, we began to see a drop in those attractional metrics, and it was difficult not to become discouraged. I could no longer find my significance in previous leadership metrics of success. Instead, the journey became about obedience to God's call, and a commitment to the quality of our "seven day a week" disciples, over the quantity of Sunday morning attendees.

It takes new levels of humility and trust in the Holy Spirit to move away from professional and public affirmation for our sense of success. I found comfort in remembering that Jesus' call to follow him was ultimately rejected by nearly everyone around him, but he was faithful and obedient in the eyes of the One who mattered most.

Many in the crowds around Jesus viewed the cost of discipleship as sand in their eyes; an irritant to brush away and turn from. Yet, those who embraced the discomfort became, themselves, objects of great value in the new kingdom.

I was also encouraged that this approach allowed the rest of the church to experience fruit that was once reserved for a few professionals. This calling to equip every disciple to make disciples and join God's redemptive mission in their everyday lives is a much higher bar—not only for leaders but also for church members. No matter how slowly and strategically you diffuse your attempts at innovation, if you move in this direction people will leave, and those losses will feel personal and painful. Cultural change will lead to a population pruning, and, as leaders, we have to trust that God is able do mighty work through a faithful minority, just as he did with Gideon's 300, the Jews in Exile, or Jesus' twelve core disciples.[11] Mark DeYmaz recently encouraged me to remember that although one person may leave because they don't buy into the vision, the one who stays becomes more committed and has a greater chance of discipling one more because of their passion. "So, in the end," he says, "you're trading one for two." I like to remind our leaders and staff that if we are successful as an equipping team, the fruit of our work will grow in other people's trees.

A FEW EXAMPLES

Changing culture requires changing artifacts. But which ones? For the sake of simplicity, let's look at three key elements most contemporary churches share in common: an *online presence, large-group gatherings,* and the *Sunday sermon.* Within these culture-shaping activities, I'll comment on a few cultural artifacts such as language, stories, and images—and will offer some examples from my experiences and from other churches. (In chapter ten, I will discuss some ways you might consider changing the culture of your community life, or small groups, as a local church as well.)

Online Presence

For our purposes, let's combine websites, blogs, social media, and e-newsletters—any digital media that you use not for transactional communication but for inspirational communication to those inside and outside the community. Let's look at what these current artifacts of culture are communicating and how we can replace them to create something better suited for the times ahead.

Websites are great tools to articulate church vision, but regardless of a well-crafted mission statement about impacting the world, too often the rest of the language used online actually centers on activity within the community for the benefit of the community. This language positions the church as a vendor of religious goods and services operating to meet the needs of existing Christians. Links help people contribute resources to the church, such as financial donations or registering to volunteer. Social media is often used to remind everyone to come to church because "You won't want to miss out," followed by reminders to listen to the message if you did miss it. Midweek communication might be limited to encouragement to come back for other ministries or to persevere in the midst of a long week in the secular world until next Sunday's fix.

The stories we tell online reveal which people we choose to celebrate. Often the spotlight is placed on the lead pastor and other platform personalities, and their stories are curated in a compelling format to keep them authentic and re-latable. The website's "church history" page usually revolves around the story of a few courageous professionals who planted the church.

Online images perpetuate the Sunday-centric paradigm of church. Scroll through the social media and websites of a handful of local churches and notice how many photos depict church property, church professionals, or church programs. Rarely are there equal, if not more, pictures of everyday church people engaging in God's kingdom work. Often the images portray faith as perpetually joyful, exciting, and inspiring; as if the Christian life is a party filled with shiny, happy people.

Let's imagine replacing those cultural planks with some new ones.

Our online language is a great way to put Sunday in its proper place as one part of the life of the church, and not the core around which everything rotates.

Imagine communicating a church structure that does not relegate God's mission to a "department" but rather expresses it as every part of the church joining God's mission in different ways. How about replacing the catch phrase "You belong here!"—placed atop a picture of the Sunday gathering, with one that says, "God is at work out here!"—placed atop pictures of your city. Is there space to share resources to equip the larger body for their daily ministry work, not just to solicit resources for the work of the professionals and programs?

Think about starting your church's origin story not with the history of the pastor(s) or founder(s), but by first celebrating how God has always been at work in the city and what specific part of that work he called your church to join. What if you used these platforms to tell stories of God's rule and reign breaking through into every sphere and sector of the world? Imagine telling stories that celebrate how other churches or even secular organizations are contributing to the common good and making your city a better place to live. Or a narrative that reveals how the church cares about redeeming the whole world around us and not merely saving souls. Feature as many stories of everyday people living on mission in the world around them as you have bios for pastors who engage in vocational equipping ministry within the organization. Use online video testimonies to highlight how people are seeing God at work, transforming not just individual behaviors but also communal systems of injustice.

Choose images that highlight the beauty of God's people joining God's work rather than the beauty of your campus property and its buildings. Include shots that express a full representation of your neighborhood or city so that a person, whatever their demographic, might see someone online that looks like them. Of course, this cannot be mere tokenism; it must be a genuine reflection of your community. You will have to have a community that represents this before you can capture it in appropriate photographs!

All of this said, let me state my personal bias on the matter of online communication. I don't think the post-Christian world has any interest in church social media or websites; they are not looking to join a church, so it is foolish to target them with these platforms. I think the best use of these resources is, first, to shape the culture of your community and to express it to Christians who are looking for a church home—hopefully because they moved to town or are motivated to find an expression of a disciplemaking church and not because they are simply church shopping. Second, use these tools to reiterate vision and values and to communicate news and events to those who are part of your church family. If you are planting a more missional/incarnational form of church that seeks to grow by making new disciples, I suggest not even having an online presence initially. It merely attracts existing Christians who may dilute your DNA with their own expectations of traditional expressions of church.

Large-Group Gatherings

For the majority of churches, the weekend worship service has been the center of life—to the point that, in our language, it is synonymous with church. We say to one another, "See you at church." A staff member stands on stage and says, "Good morning; welcome to Crosswalk," implying that this church, Crosswalk, is a place you come to. When guests or visitors attend a service, we often invite them to a newcomers reception to hear about how they can connect with us, recognizing them as people who have come to church to learn about us. The newcomers reception often begins an assimilation process that moves someone along a journey toward membership. I am not opposed to church membership; but remember that membership is a powerful bounded-set metaphor that assumes insiders and outsiders and privileged status for some. (Just think of how many rewards-club memberships we are all part of, for the sole purpose of receiving special benefits.)

When stories are told during worship services, they often consist of professions of faith (aka testimonies); ministry highlights that are used to help recruit volunteers to our programs; or missions teams sharing about their travel experiences. Each of these categories of stories powerfully reinforces assumptions about the purpose of the church and the role of each person in it. There are implicit messages, such as: the initial decision of salvation is our goal, not ongoing marks of transformation; God's gifts are best used inside the church walls; and mission is something a few people go do "over there," not something we're all engaged in right here in our daily lives.

The church's most powerful images are often found on the platform. Lights, staging, maybe even flowers all frame a few people who exercise their specialized gifts, such as music and teaching. Vast resources and intentionality go into cultivating a certain atmosphere in the worship room, creating an experience that can never be replicated in the life of a disciple throughout the week. As a result, Sunday is seen as the center of the church life—not because people are closer to God or finding deep fellowship with one another, but because our senses are powerfully stimulated with professional teaching and live music in a magnificent environment.

Imagine replacing those cultural planks with some new ones.

Think about greeting those who join the large-group gatherings with language like, "Good morning, Church" or "Good morning, Crosswalk; it is great to have the church gathered together today." Imagine referring to the worship time as our weekly large-group gathering and not as "church" or as a "service," which has consumer implications. This communicates the church not as a place or a program but as *people*. Use the welcome to remind the church that "We are a community of Jesus' followers who are scattered all over the city during the week to join the mission of God, and then on this day we gather back together to celebrate how we have seen God work and to worship him together." I love how Tampa Underground refers to their large-group gatherings as a "weekly conference for missionaries in the city." Reinforce the idea of breathing in and breathing out the life of Jesus as we gather and scatter each week. Consider inviting guests to a "new collaborators" lunch where they can "share how God is calling you to make a difference in the city." From the start, this positions the gathering event as equipping for everyday missional activity. Consider referring to the pastoral staff as an *equipping team* or *support team*; this communicates that the professionals are not hired to do the ministry for the people, but to equip all people to participate in God's mission.

Imagine using stories to decenter Sunday as the focal point of the church's ministry and instead put the emphasis on how we are joining God's work in the world. Invite different people to share how they encountered God during the week or how they made disciples in the everyday spaces of life. One friend, Jonathan Wu, who heads up the Los Angeles pastors' network Made to Flourish, told me that during his local-church gathering, people are invited to share their "TTT" reflections—what they will be doing "this time tomorrow." After a person shares, a pastor prays for them. This celebrates the individual's professional work in that public space as central to their disciplemaking call and as part of their personal worship. Whenever we baptize someone in our Ecclesia gatherings, we close our time together by bringing the individual back up to share their first, second, and third places in life. Then we commission them as God's missionary to those places, since every summons to Jesus is also a sending to his world.

Consider how the images in the large-group gathering could shape culture. When someone is baptized, would it be possible for the person who discipled them to be the one to baptize them, rather than a professional? Think of how powerful a picture this would be—for an ordinary disciple to baptize the disciple he or she made through the power of Jesus at work in them! Are there ways to create art that reinforces new values? After an Ecclesia teaching series that focused on every disciple making a disciple, the community had the opportunity to place a piece of sea glass in a jar to indicate that they were discipling at least one other person. A local artist in the community then turned those pieces into a mosaic that now sits in our lobby with a sign that indicates what each stone represents.

Sunday Sermon

Within the large group gathering, the sermon is probably one of the most powerful cultural elements to adapt but is also potentially the most controversial. In many churches, the spoken message has ascended to a place of prominence that far exceeds its value. Don't misunderstand me; God's Word is essential in the life of a disciple, and the church has a biblical mandate to proclaim it as part of our corporate worship. But we are equally responsible to equip and encourage God's people to study it for themselves and to be able to teach it to others. I fear the charismatic manner in which our professionals preach implicitly communicates to the average person that they are incapable of understanding God's Word and unworthy to teach it to others in their own disciplemaking.

This emphasis on the professionally delivered sermon is reinforced by comments exchanged in church lobbies, such as "I came to church to get fed from God's Word" or "I didn't get anything out of the message today." This passive language reiterates the expectation that the professional pastor is responsible for spiritually feeding and nourishing the community rather than to equip them to learn to feed themselves from God's Word.

The images of a Bible teacher standing center stage or behind an ornate pulpit lifted above the community were initially meant to signify honor for God's Word. However, over time such visual cues simply support the notion that the professional teacher has special insight into God's Word that the average congregant cannot possibly access in their own study. Too often, the net result is that our disciples are not confident enough to help those whom they disciple learn to read the Word for themselves, electing instead to merely invite people to a service so they can hear the message delivered by a professional.

We must also acknowledge that the contemporary brain is no longer wired to acquire information through long-winded oral presentations.[12] For most adults, the weekly sermon may be the only time they listen to someone speak uninterrupted, with the exception of podcasts—which are commonly consumed while doing other activities, and are often conversations among several participants. In a postmodern culture—which leans more toward images and stories—propositional monologues are an increasingly ineffective form of communication. Perhaps this might partially explain why there has been so little transformation in the character of the Western church even after years upon years of biblically faithful sermons.

Consider alternative ways to use the sermon time in your weekly gatherings to disrupt people's thinking patterns and to facilitate deeper spiritual formation. How could the traditional sermon time—even periodically—be used for another spiritual formation activity that is more engaging and participatory? How could we make the sermon a new cultural artifact that reinforces the idea that God speaks to all his people as a collective—after all, we often learn more when a community studies *together.*

I am privileged to be Ecclesia's lead teacher in a city filled with creative people who take artistic risks for a living, so I am able to experiment more widely and at a more accelerated pace than most. Here are a few ways we periodically replace the sermon plank in our culture with more engaging activities.

- ***Flip the model***: Like many churches, our community groups sometimes process the material from Sunday's messages when they meet later in the week. In one series, inspired by the "flipped classroom" movement,[13] our groups studied the passage *first* and then submitted insights and questions to the teaching team. We allowed their input to give direction to the messages so that we were speaking to real issues in people's minds. We put direct quotes on the screen from e-mails and texts we received and celebrated the person or the group who offered that contribution.

- *Dialogue during the sermon*: During one series we informed everyone that the teacher would be stopping at points during the message and asking the community to interact with him or her by responding to a question. The questions were provided on a handout, so people could consider them in advance, and moderators walked the aisles with microphones so everyone could hear one another's responses.

- *Contemplation and community*: In one series, we shortened the sermon time by fifteen minutes and then offered people a choice as to how to spend that time. They could either remain in the worship room where they were led through a simple contemplation activity, such as *Lectio Divina*, to help them encounter God in a different way, or they could step out into the lobby to connect with other Ecclesians in small groups of three or four and discuss a single question related to the message. We did this for several weeks, and people relished the opportunity to choose which environment they wanted to join.

- *End-of-year sharing*: The last week in December, Ecclesia's elders always give all of our volunteers and staff the week off and hold a much more informal family gathering. Rather than offering a sermon, the elders facilitate an open-mic time where people can take up to five minutes to share how Jesus worked in and through their lives to bless others the prior year. (Just don't let your facilitator wander too far from the microphone. We all have stories of open-mic sharing gone awry!)

- *Conference format*: For a nine-week series on relationships, we decided to follow a conference format with large-group speakers and topical breakout sessions. On weeks one, four, and seven, we remained in the worship room, and pastors taught on a biblical text that had application across a broad range of relationships. On the in-between weeks, at the point in the service where we traditionally would have the message, everyone had the choice to attend one of three breakout rooms where members of our community led more interactive presentations on topics related to relationships. We sought out people in our community with personal experience in an area, or with professional training, such as marriage and family therapists or counselors, and then built the topics around the speakers. We held each breakout twice over the six weeks to limit how many teachers we needed and to ensure everyone could attend.

- **Prayer stations**: We concluded a series on prayer by using the sermon time to allow everyone to move around the room and engage in activities that represented the six forms of prayer we studied. Each station included a tangible activity that facilitated that specific type of prayer, such as lament, adoration, intercession, and thanksgiving.

- **Kingdom come**: Our boldest experiment was to eliminate the sermon altogether for an entire four-week series on the kingdom of God. Each week, after a time of corporate worship, we broke the community into groups and sent them to other spaces in the building to participate in an activity that would help them experience a facet of God's kingdom. The "kingdom rest" week included a guided meditation in a peaceful room. "Kingdom beauty" involved watching a film on the artistry of origami. "Kingdom creativity" involved a communal craft project and a discussion on the spirituality inherent in our own acts of creation. Each activity had a debriefing time that allowed people to engage with each other and helped build deeper community.

"Sunday is about telling a story, praying prayers, and worshipping as a family. The rest of the week is about getting that story, prayers, and worship into the particulars of individual people."[14]—Eugene Peterson

Let me add that, with the approval of my elders, I now only teach around thirty Sundays a year. When I am scheduled to speak, I try to limit my sermon preparation time to ten to twelve hours weekly. This creates more time to invest in people and prevents me from becoming overly polished and pedantic in the pulpit. I also think that less preparation has made me more Holy Spirit dependent in my delivery.

Reducing my frequency of teaching has also given opportunity for other pastoral staff and elders to teach, and four to five times a year we also invite members from our community or another local church to come and share how they are seeking to incarnate "Good News for L.A." They choose a passage from God's Word that inspires their work, and we read it aloud as our scriptural liturgy, but the speaker is not expected to exegete that passage. Instead they share how God's Living Word is working in them and through them to fulfill God's redemptive mission in the world. We have heard from a civil rights lawyer, a social worker caring for teenage runaways, a crisis pregnancy care director, and a civic leader seeking to solve homelessness, just to name a few.

PLANK BY PLANK

Every decision we make, every service we lead, and every object that takes up space in our church property is creating culture. To change our culture, we must evaluate these activities and artifacts and begin to replace them, plank by plank, at a pace that our community can absorb.

Questions for Reflection

1. What personal factors are keeping you and your church from being more innovative and open to change? How might you seek out a season of liminality to change your dominant assumptions about church?

2. What "cultural planks" do you think need to be replaced in your local church with ones that are more appropriate for operating in a post-Christian context?

3. What concrete "artifacts" (language, symbols, rituals, activities, measurements) could you create to express these new elements of culture?

10

Getting the Body in Shape

Creating a culture of innovation requires reclaiming the expansive, pioneering, and revolutionary spirit of Jesus. Operating in the waters of Christendom for nearly two millennia has warped the Western church; we overemphasize the inward-facing functions of community care and theological formation and neglect the outward-facing functions of culture care, kingdom expansion, and missional engagement.

Jesus modeled five primary ministries that structure the mission of God, and we must understand these if we are going to accurately evaluate whether we are truly forming Jesus-shaped disciples and guiding Jesus-shaped churches. Spiritual formation plans within a church often seek to form people into the *character* of Christ with an emphasis on the fruits of God's Spirit: love, joy, peace, patience, kindness, goodness, faithfulness, gentleness, and self-control (Galatians 5:22–23, NLT). Rarely do we spend as much time focusing on the *competencies* of Christ—the aptitudes and skills that defined his ministry on earth. Thankfully, there is a growing awareness that we need to reclaim the functions of Christ's ministry and actively participate in them if we are going to represent Jesus' fullness on earth.

The movement to recover these functions has been catalyzed by the excellent resource from Alan Hirsch, *5Q: Reactivating the Original Intelligence and Capacity of the Body of Christ.*[1] Hirsch presents a comprehensive exegesis of

Ephesians 4, as well as a depiction of how Jesus embodied the five gifts listed there. For our purposes, I will merely summarize these functions and explore the implications of reclaiming all five in our church leadership.

ONE BODY, DIFFERENT GIFTS

In Ephesians 4, Paul makes a comprehensive case that to be the body of Christ we must incarnate the original gifts, or ministry functions, sourced in Jesus himself, who is our head. Paul expresses these gifts in personified terms: "So, Christ himself gave the apostles, the prophets, the evangelists, the pastors and teachers" (v. 11). Another way to understand this list is to say, "Jesus gives to members of his body the apostolic gift, the prophetic gift, the evangelistic gift, the shepherding gift, and the teaching gift." (These five gifts are often referred to by their acronym, APEST.) Christ gave these gifts in the form of people who fulfill their function and express it in the world. The people *are* the gifts. Imagine saying to a colleague, "You are such a gift to our team. Thank you for your dedication and passion!" In one sense, dedication and passion are the character gifts that she possesses, but as she lives them out and personifies them to the team, we say, "*You* are a gift!" Paul is reminding the church that each one of us is God's gift to the world! By referring to the gifts as people, Paul also reinforces that these gifts are core to our identity as a community. We are a collective body consisting of these five different types of gifted people, and we must work together to fulfill each of these functions in order to represent the fullness of Jesus.

In expressing these gifts, Paul borrows from the common cultural language of the day. In fact, in the first century, each of the five gifts was actually an occupation. An apostle was a person sent off on a mission as a representative of another, akin to a modern-day emissary or diplomat. We are familiar with Old Testament prophets, of course, but there were also other prophets who travelled around as itinerant oracles, offering to speak on behalf of various gods. An evangelist was the one responsible for publicly declaring the good news of a new emperor, similar to a modern-day reporter or TV anchor. Shepherds and teachers both still exist today and still perform similar functions: overseeing the health and safety of animals and imparting wisdom and knowledge into the next generation. Paul is taking vocational language and turning it into functional language.

In some contemporary Christian streams, these terms have unfortunately been used to confer power and privilege; but these were not intended to be titles or offices. Paul is not advocating for a capital "A" Apostle who now has authority over others, nor is he advocating for a capital P "Pastor" who gains privileges others lack.[2]

> *"Individually, these gifts reflect parts of a whole that, when seen together, manifest the full image of God and the full measure of Jesus Christ."[3]—Neil Cole*

These gifts are given for use in service of others. They are the functional roles that God's people play in his work in the world.

JESUS: THE ULTIMATE GIFT AND GIFT GIVER

Jesus is the perfect embodiment of the five APEST gifts that constitute his ministry. Imagine Jesus as the source of white light shining toward a prism. The prism serves to disperse that unified light into its separate, distinct colors, which were previously indistinguishable to the naked eye. The prism allows us to examine and study the qualities of each of the colors separately.

Paul has placed a prism in front of the life and ministry of Jesus and is now describing the five separate functions that exist as the apostolic function, the prophetic function, the evangelistic function, the shepherding function, and the teaching function. None of them are complete on their own; rather, they must exist in unity for the world to experience the fullness of Jesus. These gifts are the five modes of Christ's presence in the world today, and they are hardwired into the body of Christ. They are the five redemptive priorities expressed through Jesus' life. His church now must embody these functions so that the world can thrive and flourish as God intended.

The diagram below shows how these five functions relate to each other in the life of the church. The circle represents the church, and each aspect of Jesus' ministry is positioned in a place that symbolizes the role it plays within the community.

I will describe the gifts in reverse order (TSEPA) to allow us to begin with roles that we are most familiar with in the present-day church. (I encourage leaders to introduce them this way in their churches as well.)

The *teaching* function serves to keep the church rooted and grounded in the truth of God's Word and its faithful application. It provides consistency, stability, and protects against heresy that might lead a church to fly off the rails. It regulates the church according to divine wisdom and knowledge. It helps perpetuate traditions and liturgy, relates stories, and passes on biblical doctrine to the next generation. The teaching function operates the organizational systems and structures that maintain repeatable processes, and provides resources for the other gifts.

The *shepherding* function exists at the center of the body and serves to promote health and wholeness with the church. It cares deeply about creating bonds of community and nurturing expressions of love. It promotes honest communication between members, promotes unity, and is willing to fight for reconciliation when divisions arise. This function cares for the wounded and protects the weak. It monitors the health of the body and calls out for help when it senses dysfunction, injury, or fatigue.

The *evangelistic* function exists on the edge and seeks to build bridges to the world and invite others into the body. It desires to make the circle wider. It thrives on the fringes of the church where it can keep an ear tuned to the culture to know how to share the gospel story with outsiders in a way that is contextually relevant. It recruits others to the kingdom cause, often with strong charisma, infectious enthusiasm, and bold calls to action. When it operates within the church body, it creates points of connection between members and catalyzes people to action.

The *prophetic* function maintains the church's alignment with the heart and holiness of God. This function keeps the church attuned to God's spirit and sensitive to God's leading. It plays the role of truth-teller and reformer and brings correction to the body when needed. This function thrives at connecting with God in prayer through both speaking and listening. The prophetic can be expressed vertically, as a call to get right with God (to tear down idols, repent of sin, and raise the standards for obedience to God); and it can be expressed horizontally, as a call to get right with others (to eliminate injustice, fight for the oppressed, and seek fair and ethical treatment of all people).

The *apostolic* function exists on the leading edge of the body to pioneer the church into new places and confront new challenges. It extends and expands the impact of the body and serves as guardian of the core DNA as the body grows. It thrives on taking new hills, breaking new ground, and leading the kingdom movement into new places. As it moves the body forward, it creates the map for others to follow and establishes the networks needed to thrive in new places. The apostolic function mobilizes the church and multiplies Jesus' DNA into the next generation.

Note in the circle diagram that the shepherding and teaching (ST) functions serve to *build the core of the church* by providing a strong foundation and healthy community. The apostolic, prophetic, and evangelistic (APE) functions serve to *bridge the church* to the outside world by operating on the outward-facing edge and engaging actively with the culture outside the church.

It is critical for the maturing of the body of Christ that *all* capacities of APEST find an expression in every local church organization. When all five gifts are deployed, a faith community will extend the mission of God into every sphere of culture (A), deepen our abiding in and obedience to God (P), proclaim the gospel of Jesus in word and deed (E), cultivate a healthy community of unconditional love (S), and seek to live the truth of God's Word (T). That is a community full of Christ.

"Jesus' Church is made of Dream Awakeners (A), Heart Revealers (P), Story Tellers (E), Soul Healers (S) and Light Givers (T)."[4]—JR Woodward

Let's differentiate again between *individual giftings* and *communal functions.* Jesus bestowed these five *giftings* upon individuals so that they can embody and practice them in a local church community to allow the church to live all five corporate *functions* of Jesus' life and mission. It is best to initially emphasize APEST as the communal functions that Jesus fulfilled and then bestowed upon the church. In a hyper-individualistic Western culture—and since the Ephesians 4 language is personified—the APEST discussion often devolves immediately into a categorization of people by their primary giftings and a celebration of "my individual gifts." If it becomes first and foremost another "personality test" along the lines of StrengthsFinder, Myers-Briggs, or the Enneagram, it will quickly lose its true value as a metric for broader community health.

That being said, when an individual is acting according to his or her gifting, it seems almost second nature—as if he or she is just wired that way. Sometimes it can be challenging to understand why others are not more like us—or worse, more like Jesus in the way we feel we are like Jesus. Yes, each one of us is supernaturally capable in one or two of these ways, but we are merely stewards of our gifts, and it would be foolish to take credit for them ourselves. We must resist any temptation toward superiority. We must also ensure we don't limit our participation in Jesus' ministry to just the area of our primary giftings. As Jesus dwells within us through his Spirit, we have the capacity to live out each of the giftings. While we steward and develop our primary gifts in the community, we can also learn from others, and from Jesus himself, how to better express the gifts that require more effort and intentionality.

THE TEAM IN ACTION

To understand this distinction between functions and gifts, let me offer a quick illustration from my experience as a high school basketball coach. Each of the five players on a court often has a primary area of gifting in one of the game's fundamentals, such as dribbling, shooting, rebounding, passing, or defending. A coach is responsible to put players on the floor who can fulfill all five of these *functions* as a team. He or she selects a player with an innate ball-handling *gifting* to be the primary dribbler—often the point guard; an innate rebounder—usually someone gifted with tenacity and considerable height—to play close to the basket as a forward; and so on. You get the picture. Regardless of where the person usually plays, every team member practices dribbling, shooting, rebounding, passing, and defending, because times arise in each game when every player must exhibit the different skills. A point guard will quickly prove themselves a liability on the floor and end up on the bench if they refuse to rebound or shoot simply because that is not their gift. No coach expects the 5' 9" point guard to grab as many rebounds as the 6' 9" center; however, s/he must be prepared to make an effort when the opportunity arises. A successful team is formed when each player makes the most of their innate gifts to serve the team, each member is willing to fulfill any of the roles when the opportunity presents itself, and the team plays with cohesive unity amidst a diversity of talents.

In Ephesians 4, Paul makes a rather convincing argument for the importance of these five gifts operating together as a team. He claims that when these five gifts are present in the life of the church:

- The body of Christ will be equipped to serve others (v. 12).
- The body of Christ will be built up and strengthened (v. 12).
- The body of Christ will grow into maturity (v. 13, 15).
- The body of Christ will reflect the fullness of Christ (v. 13).
- The body of Christ will be protected from outside deception (v. 14).
- The body of Christ will grow up in love to be more like our Head, Jesus (v. 16).

I don't know any pastor who doesn't long for these marks to characterize his or her church. This is the original design for every church—to participate in these five gifts so that we might reflect the whole measure of the fullness of Christ. "Fullness of Christ" means that the church will be overflowing with Jesus. As each person increasingly lives out their gifts as an expression of the life of Jesus, there is increasingly more of Jesus in the body. Paul says these five gifts are for equipping the church; or, to say it another way, these five aspects enable the church to manifest Jesus in our world. They are essential to our calling as the body of Christ.

A HOLY CHURCH IS A WHOLE CHURCH

The collective church's growth and health is dependent on each part doing his or her work. In the same way a basketball team won't succeed with only two competent guards and no one contributing from the front court, you cannot grow as a church by only one or two parts doing all the work. However, that is exactly what many Western churches are attempting to do, primarily because this seemed to be a successful strategy in our old cultural waters.

In Christendom, external society already reflected many of the values and priorities of the church, so churches were able to put their energy into internal functions, such as care and training. As a result, most churches now pour nearly all of their resources into the shepherding and teaching functions. Many of the cultural planks we explored in the previous chapter need replacing because they are rooted in a shepherd-teacher paradigm. Professional pastors spend the majority of their time crafting Sunday morning teachings and shepherding the congregation. The church properties we've built are constructed to accommodate large-group gatherings, classroom teaching, and community fellowship. The weekly calendar is filled with Bible studies, community care small groups, pastoral care ministries, and stage-of-life fellowship activities.

To innovate within our churches so that they can once again make new disciples and serve our more secular society, we need to reclaim the forgotten outward-facing functions. Unfortunately, as churches experience decline they often do the exact opposite—doubling down on teaching and fellowship activities. But more of the same does not produce different results. Instead, ST-dominated churches need to lean into the functions of Jesus they are neglecting. The APE is nearly extinct in most North American churches, and when those functions are exercised, it is often for the purposes of a one-time event, such as an evangelistic crusade or concert, a night of prayer, or a conference. Nearly all of our volunteer hours, money, leadership, and energy are going into the ST areas of church life, whose primary purpose is to build up those who are already in church. More than any other single factor, I believe this is why the church is in drastic decline—not just in attendance, but also in our influence in the world. All five functions must be operating together at full strength and in balance for Jesus' church to operate as he intended.

In our increasingly secular world, there is a great need for APE activity by the church to bring about kingdom-centered reform. We need crusaders championing biblical causes, such as protecting God's creation; empowering the

"No major denomination in the United States regards apostolic ministry to card-carrying, secular, pre-Christian outsiders as its priority or even as normal ministry."[5]—George Hunter, III

voice of women and marginalized ethnic groups as equal citizens in God's kingdom; advocating for the plight of the poor and homeless; defending the value of human life in all its stages; and fighting to end institutional and individual expressions of racism. Within evangelicalism especially, the overemphasis on ST functions and a focus on "my personal relationship with Jesus" has created an unhealthy skepticism toward these sorts of culture-care efforts. They are seen as secondary priorities and distractions from the church's true work. I greatly lament that the prophetic #MeToo movement catalyzed the parallel #ChurchToo movement, and not vice versa.[6] As a church leader, I feel ashamed that those who do not follow Jesus had more courage to hold powerful men accountable for engaging in sexual harassment than the body of Christ did.

REPOPULATING THE APES

Ephesians 4 promises that God has given the church everything we need if we celebrate each function as equally important. It may be easy to assume that disciples with the APE gifts are not as prevalent as those with ST giftings, but the truth is they exist; they likely just don't feel valued in many of our churches. The preference for shepherding and teaching activities drove these followers of Jesus to practice their APE gifts out in the world. However, those APE-gifted people are the catalysts we need in order to innovate and become a church more faithful to Jesus' entire mission. As leaders, we need to ask God to reveal these people to us, and we may have to look outside our current pool of church leaders to find them.

When I moved to Hollywood, I spent my first few years investigating what kingdom work was happening in the city outside the walls of the church. I knew that APEs "thrive in the wild," so I researched and visited with leaders of local non-profit charities, parachurch ministries, film studios telling redemptive stories, and social-enterprise businesses promoting ethical and fair trade. Time and time again I found that the leaders were followers of Jesus who saw their organization as fulfilling Jesus' calling to make disciples and participate in God's mission to redeem and renew the city. While they were worshipping members of local churches, they rarely expressed their leadership gifts in those communities, preferring to pioneer out in the culture. Knowing their tremendous value in the kingdom, I invited them to share their stories in our large-group gatherings to help spark and catalyze APE imagination in our people. I also recruit volunteer leaders from within my church community to join them in their activities out in the city.

IMPLICATIONS FOR THE LOCAL CHURCH

There is much by way of application of APEST that we could discuss for the local church. We can assess our current ministries and our resource allocations to see how balanced they are across all the APEST functions. It may be wise to allow some of our ST ministries to cease as they naturally lose momentum, in order to create margin for new APE-focused ones. We can forge partnerships with ministries in the city that are exercising the APE functions and offer them our resources—volunteer hours, finances, or free use of our space—in exchange for exposing our community to their activities. The potential is endless.

But let me dive deep into two cultural practices that might need replacing in our churches.

The first is *how we recruit leaders*. We need to actively recruit disciples with the APE gifts into leadership. It will take some convincing to bring these people onto our leadership teams, elder boards, or pastoral staff, because their experience in churches has taught them that what they offer is not valued. ST leaders will need to resist the urge to domesticate APEs and force them to fit within existing systems and structures or burden them with too much church-centric activity. Once our teams are built, we need to push for the diversity of all five gifts operating together in maturity and unity.

Leadership teams need to fight to create a better balance between:

- The ST reluctance to change, and the APE instinct to be restless without change.
- The ST desire to manage long-standing ministries and keep them operating, and the APE impulse to eliminate ineffective ministries and put resources into starting new things.
- The ST call to serve those within the church, and the APE call to serve and reach those outside of the church.

- The ST bent to be cautious and move slowly, and the APE impulse to take risks and move too fast.
- The ST desire for safety and preservation, and the APE desire for risk-taking and expansion.

"Contained within APEST are competing values and interests. Therefore, left to their own impulses, each of the ministries will seek to delegitimize the others. They will seek to alleviate tension by eliminating its perceived source or isolating themselves from the others."[7]—Alan Hirsch and Tim Catchim

---

Only when our church leadership teams begin to acknowledge and value the APE gifts will the other APEs who lie dormant in the church begin to feel comfortable and step forward to exercise their gifts. Now, five years into my time with Ecclesia, our leadership is organized around all five functions. When it is time to select new elders, we inventory the gifts of those members rotating off and seek to replace those gifts in our new members. The balance is never perfect, but even the process reminds the team that we are responsible to lead in a way that values and embodies all five functions. We have also promoted and recruited outside pastors to the staff so that we have a five-person pastoral team where each person possesses a different primary gifting. Each one oversees a direct area of responsibility within the church—such as kids and youth, or operations—but each one is also expected to provide leadership to the community in the area of their gifting.

When we created time for contemplation in the worship service, as I mentioned in the last chapter, the pastor with a prophetic gifting stepped up to guide our people to connect deeply with God. When we hosted a conference on relationships, the pastor with shepherding gifts provided leadership all day. Even in our staff meetings, we often invite each pastor to speak into an issue through the perspective of his or her gift. My giftings as an apostle and evangelist are wisely balanced with those who move more slowly and deliberately and who regularly remind me to consider the needs of our existing community as well as those we seek to serve in the city.[8]

The second cultural practice we might need to replace as our APEST understanding grows relates to our *sermons* and *Bible teaching*.

As the lead pastor, I create the annual teaching calendar and select the texts and topics we will study. Alongside ensuring a balance of different sections of Scripture and discipleship themes, I have also started selecting one of the APEST functions to guide the tone of each series. For example, when we taught on forms of prayer from the Psalms, I wanted the tone each week to be consistent with the prophetic function. So I tried to slow my delivery while also speaking boldly, I left space for God to speak to the community directly by ending the message with a period of silent reflection, and I invited our prophetic-gifted pastor to teach in the series, knowing she would add insights I might miss. This has revolutionized my weekly approach to preparation. Without even being aware of it, I had tended to turn every sermon series into an apostolic/evangelistic challenge. Six weeks focused on prayer can easily become a call to launch a city-wide prayer movement with weekly applications about praying for lost people to meet Jesus. I see the Scripture through an AE lens; it's my natural bent. But my bias toward those functions can quickly burn out the community with calls to risk-taking and evangelistic activity if they are not balanced by the other gifts.

By rotating through the five functions, the community experiences the totality of Jesus' ministry through God's Word, not just the parts that align with my gifts. As hard as it is for me, I know that I will only get one series a year with an apostolic tone, calling the church to take risks, cross out of our comfort zone, and live sent lives of blessing. While the apostles come alive in that series, by week six the teachers begin to send me e-mails pushing back! However, the next series may resonate more with their gifting. I have found a healthy rhythm to be A-S-E-P-T, because it feels like *inhaling self-care* and then *exhaling fresh life for the world*. By rotating like this, you remind the church of our responsibility to participate in the full ministry of Jesus.

This idea of using APEST in a set rhythm can guide your staff devotional times, structure community group studies, and give direction to prayer meetings. If you plan out these events in an APEST rotation, you will do a better job of meeting the disparate needs in your community and activating their diverse giftings. APEST is also a good metric to use when you assess your weekly worship liturgy to make sure that you honor and emphasize all five functions.

THE PROBLEM WITH BEING OUT OF SHAPE

When a church assumes that only a few functions are valid expressions of Jesus and then ignores or marginalizes the other functions, it tears people down rather than building them up. This can occur either because a majority of the leaders express the same gifting or because all of the ministry activities reinforce the same function. Here are some examples:[9]

A church culture dominated by the *apostolic* function/gifting can become:
- Too *task*-oriented, leading to *wounded* people
- Too *future* oriented, leading to *confused* people
- Too *speed*-oriented, leading to *burned-out* people

A church culture dominated by the *prophetic* function/gifting can become:
- Too *issue*-oriented, leading to *divided* people
- Too *spirit*-oriented, leading to *disembodied* people
- Too *action*-oriented, leading to *simplistic* people

A church culture dominated by the *evangelistic* function/gifting can become:
- Too *transaction*-oriented, leading to *disenchanted* people
- Too *positivity*-oriented, leading to *frustrated* people
- Too *inspiration*-orientation, leading to *disorganized* people

A church culture dominated by the *shepherding* function/gifting can become:
- Too *needs*-oriented, leading to *co-dependent* people
- Too *safety*-oriented, leading to *fearful* people
- Too *harmony*-oriented, leading to *conflict-avoidant* people

A church culture dominated by the *teaching* function/gifting can become:
- Too *information*-oriented, leading to *prideful, puffed-up* people
- Too *consistency*-oriented, leading to *rigid* people
- Too *repetition*-oriented, leading to *complacent* people

As leaders, we need to equip people to mature in their areas of gifting and to grow in the other giftings. Here are some ways you can encourage individuals to deepen and develop their personal giftings within your community:

- Find someone who expresses a certain gift in a mature way and ask him or her to disciple you in that area.
- Read books written by mature authors who demonstrate a specific gifting.
- Study the Gospels to see how Jesus exercised that gift in a healthy way.
- Practice your gift in community and ask others to give you feedback on how they experienced your use of that gift. Was it life-giving to them? Did it reflect Jesus?
- Take one gift and do something intentional in ministry this week that is an expression of that gift. Report back to another person or journal the experience.

The implications of reclaiming all five functions as a church are profound. The first-century church was a movement that participated in all five ministries as their expression of the mission of God. It went where no one else would go (A); it called out sin and injustice and introduced people to the Holy Spirit (P); it included and embraced others outside of its community (E); it cared for people (S); and it taught God's Word (T). We must reshape and reform ourselves into a visible witness of the fivefold fullness of Jesus Christ and his mission in the world.

British missiologist Lesslie Newbigin writes,

> The question which has to be put to every local congregation is the question whether it is a credible sign of God's reign in justice and mercy over the whole of life, whether it is an open fellowship whose concerns are as wide as the concerns of humanity, whether it cares for its neighbors in a way which reflects and springs out of God's care for them, whether its common life is recognizable as a foretaste of the blessing which God intends for the whole human family.[10]

Such a dynamic vision of church requires the operation of all five gifts.

Questions for Reflection

1. What examples come to mind when you think of Jesus functioning as an apostle? A prophet? A shepherd? An evangelist? A teacher? Which of these depictions does your church tend to emphasize over the others?

2. Evaluate how your church spends its resources of time, money, and leadership energy. Are they shared equally among the five functions, or do you tend to invest disproportionately in a few at the expense of others?

3. Which one or two of the five giftings given to the church resonates most with you personally in terms of how Jesus has gifted you to contribute to his mission? Which area needs the most growth for you to more fully incarnate Jesus?

Phase Four

SCALE AND SUSTAIN NEW EXPRESSIONS OF CHURCH

Every pearl is unique. No two are exactly alike. While we may think of pearls as perfect spheres, they can come in many shapes and sizes and all have some imperfections. Even the nacre surface of a pearl, which looks incredibly smooth with its shimmering luster, is not actually smooth. It is made up of millions of tiny crystals. A jeweler's test of whether a pearl is genuine is to rub it across your teeth. It should feel gritty. The roughness means it's real.

11

A Church on the Move

As we live in this "now and not yet" post-Christian culture, Ecclesia is adopting a hybrid strategy: first, to welcome Christians relocating to Hollywood to pursue their dream as artists and creatives; and second, to equip those Christians to be missionaries who embody God's kingdom and personally makes disciples among those who are not interested in pursuing faith inside a church. The Barna Group's 2019 research[1] identifies 47 percent of Los Angeles as post-Christian according to sixteen metrics,[2] and that percentage is much higher within the industry of Hollywood.

So, according to Barna's research, only 53 percent of people in Los Angeles will pursue their spirituality within the systems and structures of Christian churches. Only about half of residents in Los Angeles identify with the language, traditions, rituals, or gatherings of the Christian faith, and a much smaller fraction of those are active participants in a local church. Though many churches are not even consciously aware of what they are doing, they are essentially competing with each other for this 53 percent—targeting people who operate within Christendom but who may not be committed to a local church.

> *"96% of church growth is due to transfer growth and not churches striking into the heart of our enemy's territory. We'll consider it a win because we have the new service or program that is growing—but that growth is mainly from people coming from other churches. That's not a win! That's a staggering loss."[3]—Mike Breen*

The other 47 percent of Angelinos are on a spiritual journey and long to discover meaning and significance, but they are not interested in doing it within the constraints of traditional church activity. The best way to disciple that 47 percent will be to meet them where they already live, work, play, or create. When we lean into post-Christian culture, our churches may no longer look like neat rows of Sunday attendees, signed up to our well-organized programs. However, by engaging with people where they are, we are allowing the layers of nacre to form. Our churches may be pearls that are rough around the edges, but they're made up of new and beautifully formed disciplemaking communities.

SEVEN-DAY-A-WEEK CHURCH

Ecclesia is on a steep learning curve of discovering how we can connect with both groups of people—preserving our Sunday morning gatherings in order to resonate with notions of church from the past, while also pioneering small mission-centered communities built to be the church of the future. The hope is to change the perception that we simply "go to church on Sunday" to a realization that "we collaborate together as a church all seven days of the week." Every year we shift more time, money, and leadership resources away from ministries for our existing community and instead invest them in our mission to disciple the city; in effect replacing old cultural planks with new ones. One of the planks we are assessing is traditional small-group life.

Most local churches encourage their members to join a small group where they can come together to pray, study God's Word, and form intimate friendships. In my almost two decades of church staff experience, I have discovered that the culture of these groups tends to drift in one of two directions.

In church contexts with high residential stability and an older demographic, group members can form deep bonds that allow them to express care and love that can be transformational. The downside is that these groups can become so protective of their community experience that they are unwilling to break up to help start new groups or to open the group to church outsiders for fear of losing this intimate dynamic. They have something to offer, but can be unwilling to offer it to others.

Churches in low-stability environments, such as urban centers filled with professionals and young families, often see high turnover and low commitment to these sorts of groups. They are welcoming to new people and may even see a steady stream of fresh faces, but the people who join don't, or can't, make the commitment needed to form deep community. They are open and willing to bless others, but don't produce an experience that is transformational.

What both groups need is a catalyst; either to propel them outside of their self-preoccupation or to expedite community formation amidst transience and turnover—a slight irritant that will disrupt the status quo of the group and initiate the formation of something new.

In both cases, I believe the solution is the same: exchange the mission to *create community* for *becoming a community that pursues God's mission.* When you lead with community, you rarely get a group that engages in mission; but when you lead with mission, deep community is formed as a byproduct. After years of intermittent small-group success as a church, Ecclesia is now investing in forming teams that share a common mission field and is equipping them to bless others, trusting that deep *communitas* will form as they serve alongside each other.

ROLLING OUT A NEW EXPRESSION OF CHURCH

To help spark new missional small-group imagination in our people, Ecclesia chose another metaphor. We borrowed a contemporary feature of urban life, the food truck, to illustrate how we envision new expressions of the local church.[4]

Let me explain.

For generations the American church operated much like a restaurant. We acquired property, hung bold signage to attract customers, hired a professional to feed the people, trained a team of servers to act hospitably, and provided a menu of religious goods and services we thought would meet the appetites of a local community. We threw a launch party, and, if the quality of the food and service was good enough, we slowly took market share from other local establishments, and spiritually hungry people got fed. Some restaurant-style churches became so successful they had to increase their seating capacity or franchise into other locations. Their high-profile leaders turned into celebrities who gained a cult following.

But what happens when a restaurant-style church no longer attracts customers? Or when the community decides they don't have time for a Sunday morning sit-down meal? Or the style of cuisine you are serving falls out of favor with people? Or the high-profile leader gets caught up in a highly publicized scandal? How does a restaurant-style church stay in business when nobody is interested in coming anymore?

What if we could rethink church; not as a property with professionals and programs, but rather as Jesus' people sent out on God's mission? Imagine if the local church operated more like a fleet of food trucks.

Food trucks are small, mobile, and go to people rather than waiting for people to come to them. Each one features a specialized menu designed to connect with different tastes. Food-truck churches are operated by small teams of Jesus' followers who make disciples out among people who do not pursue spirituality in a traditional church space. They are highly contextual to their surroundings. (Remember our earlier discussion of skeleton and skin?) The food truck operators identify one geographic neighborhood, pocket of people, or third place in which to operate. Then they discern what expressions of the gospel of Jesus will resonate in that scenario and seek to embody it there.

Members of the team function in various roles and are encouraged to live out their unique APEST giftings so they help the church represent the fullness of Christ in the world. These smaller missional collaborations take fewer financial resources to launch because they utilize existing spaces and places for their activity. Since the emphasis is on making new disciples and engaging in the world, these leaders are encouraged to be not just bivocational, but "covocational,"[5]— maintaining marketplace professions that enhance and add credibility to their disciplemaking relationships. These small, nimble, decentralized forms of church are more likely to innovate, which is essential in a future where forms of church must be highly adaptable to changing cultural needs and realities.

(Ecclesia produced a short explainer video to share our vision for food truck churches. You can view it at www.churchinhollywood.com/foodtruck. Credit to artist Kenny Chapman for the image opposite.)

Rather than competing for market share, as restaurants often do, food truck operators often prefer to collaborate. In large cities, food trucks frequently belong to a commissary or central hub where they can park their trucks at night and restock on common supplies. Imagine if a local church gathered weekly, not to provide the services of a restaurant style of church, but rather as a food truck hub—where various teams came together to share stories from their mission fields, offer encouragement to other groups, get equipped for more effective service, and "refuel" from God's Word and through worship.

Commissary gatherings are intended to sustain this lifestyle of sentness and the work of the community out in the world. These weekly large-group gatherings allow for times of corporate worship, prayer, and Bible teach-

> "When the primary values are outward mission and incarnational life, the gathering becomes more about connecting people, corporate storytelling, vision casting, and celebration."[6]—Matt Smay and Hugh Halter

ing, but are defined by the shared sense of mission in the room and the commitment that gathering together is intended to propel us out to more effective scattering. This gathering does not cater to the needs of consumers who like to claim they are "not being fed"; rather it equips every disciple to know how to feast on God's presence themselves and how to feed others throughout the rest of the week.

FOOD TRUCKS IN ACTION

When restaurant-style churches try to mass-produce disciples in large gatherings, they invariably get a bland, low-bar form of discipleship. Though Jesus regularly engaged with the crowd, he made *disciples* of a much smaller number. In the same way, food truck churches aim to make small-batch, hand-crafted disciples in highly relational environments over longer periods of time. This process results in a deeper level of Christlikeness and greater participation in God's kingdom. It forms disciples who serve others as a way of modeling the life of Jesus and who look for opportunities to articulate the divine motivation behind their activity. By operating as a community that expresses all five of the APEST ministries of Jesus, they create a relational wave that often sweeps up people who are looking for loving, authentic community.

> *"I no longer believe that character formation is mostly an individual task or is achieved on a person-by-person basis. I no longer believe that character building is like going to the gym: You do your exercises and you build up your honesty, courage, integrity, and grit. I now think good character is a by-product of giving yourself away."*[7]—David Brooks

Modern evangelism strategies often draw inspiration from Jesus' first-century metaphorical command to "fish for people." Unfortunately it is usually applied through the lens of contemporary fishing—where one person with a rod and tackle uses the right bait to lure and land non-Christian fish in their local pond. The lures used in Christendom were apologetic arguments, salvation systems drawn on napkins, or rational proofs for God's existence. In our post-rational, hyper-experiential world, the metaphor of fishing for people is much more helpful if we reconsider the manner in which the disciples actually fished. They threw nets into the water, allowed the fish to get entangled in the interwoven strands, and then, alongside others, they hauled the nets into the boat. Discipling not-yet followers of Jesus is indeed like fishing for men and women, but it is rarely an individual and intellectual activity anymore; it is a communal activity in which people are swept up in a net of kingdom qualities of communal life embodied by a relatively small network of Christians.

FROM SOUR TO SWEET

One group of Ecclesians embodied a powerful example of this communal life by sharing a meal with homeless persons living in tents along U.S. Route 101. Every other Sunday afternoon, they set up a long folding table right on the sidewalk; rich and poor, successful and downtrodden, all sharing their laughter and lives together in the intimate communion of a common meal.

It all began with a man who was formerly homeless … and the hope he found in the power of grapefruit. At his lowest point, Jason was 100 pounds over-weight, unemployed, and living out of his car on the side streets of Hollywood. His first steady job in months came when a security guard company hired him to work the lobby of the historic Pacific Theater in the heart of Hollywood on Sundays while Ecclesia was meeting there. As Jason connected with Ecclesians, he began to rediscover his childhood faith—and a desire for health and trans-formation. The job led to a steady paycheck, the paycheck to a new apartment … and eventually Jason wanted to lose the weight he had gained amidst his depression and dislocation. A friend suggested he begin eating grapefruit as a healthy snack to increase his metabolism.

Within weeks Jason became known as the "Grapefruit Guy," carrying one with him wherever he went. As Jason's physical habits became healthier, he also recentered his life around Jesus, and that change bore fruit of its own. Jason wanted to find a way to offer the love and hope of Jesus to those still on the streets of Hollywood. Since Jason's radical changes were so tied to healthy eat-ing and a renewed commitment to Christ, he thought it appropriate to use food as a way to build relationships. Armed with a brown bag of grapefruit, Jason began walking the streets after his work shifts, offering the fruit and trying to make new friends. At Ecclesia, he jokingly called his crusade, "The Grapefruit Gospel." Much to his dismay, Jason learned quickly that grapefruit were not necessarily everyone's—or anyone's—favorite fruit.

Later that year, Jason was invited by another Ecclesian to a Forge Hollywood one-day training, where he was challenged to discern what is good news for the people to whom he was sent. Jason began to think through how to contextual-ize the gift of grapefruit into something that would be good news for homeless persons who were rejecting his sour offering. The next week, Jason took to the streets with his grapefruit. But rather than passing them out, he used them as a way of sharing his love for healthy comfort food and as an opening to ask the question, "What is your favorite comfort food from childhood that reminds you of home?" People lit up sharing about their mother's chicken potpie, or their grandmother's cheese enchiladas. Jason then asked if he could prepare that meal and bring it to them the following week so they might eat it together. In Jason's own words:

I seek to reconnect an identity that may have been lost through living on the streets by evoking good memories of times past and the love they received from someone they cared about via a comfort meal. We serve those on the streets for no other reason than for who they are in God's image, to remind them that they are loved, and that they are not forgotten. We turn food into love.

Jason recruited two other Ecclesians, Helen and Stephen—who were part of Forge Hollywood and possess APEST gifts that complement his—to serve as the "Grapefruit Gospel" core team. Together they led volunteers out every-other Sunday afternoon to break bread with new and old friends. Stephen, the evangelist in the group, invited the individual who suggested the menu to join the team in shopping for ingredients and serving as the "head chef" for his or her meal week. They prepared the food together as a team, adding even more relational interaction and dignity to the experience. One time, the "head chef" for the day turned to the team and said, "This is the first time in a long time I feel normal."

This Sunday meal led to new jobs, placement in housing-assistance programs, and deep discussions about how some saw God working in their lives amidst the struggles of their situations. Volunteers often stopped by the encampment on their own during the week to check in with their friends and offer tangible blessings—such as a pair of boots a young man needed for a job interview or a used bike to help another get to his new job site. As the members of the homeless community found housing, the core team coordinated a housewares and furniture donation drive within Ecclesia, and Jason continues to connect with them now that many of them are off the streets. During the 2020 coronavirus pandemic, the core team delivered groceries and supplies to members of this community when they became sick and led Ecclesia in praying for them during our daily prayer calls.

EVERYONE ON BOARD

By moving from a restaurant format of church toward a fleet of food truck churches, "we want to lower the bar of how church is done so that anyone can do it, and raise the bar of what it means to be a disciple so that they will do it."[8] Our language of food truck church is just the way we have personalized the idea of mission-centered discipleship communities. These communities are the modern expression of "a monastic missionary order, communities of encouragement, support, and training from which we emerge to live as Christians in the workplace and to which we return for reflection and renewal."[9] In these communities, "individuals are not leveraging the network for their own good, but rather have devoted themselves to the well-being of one another and the betterment of the community in which they live."[10] They are not so much church plants as gospel plants, or kingdom plants. The prayer is that, as Jesus' kingdom is planted in these places, a church will grow naturally and organically.

> "The moment you hand power over to other people, you get an explosion of curiosity, innovation, and effort."[11]
> —Joshua Cooper Ramo

FOUR FEATURES OF A FOOD TRUCK

Here's how we articulate the characteristics and principles of a Food Truck Church (FTC).

1. *Commitment of a Core*: Each FTC must have a core leadership community of at least three to five disciples of Jesus who are committed to support each other and live in a sustainable spiritual rhythm of work and rest. The leadership team members' primary or secondary giftings should cover all five APEST giftings of Ephesians 4 so that the fullness of Christ's ministry might be fulfilled. (A balanced team is essential to make sure that God's work *through* the team does not neglect or destroy God's work *in* the team.) These leaders are responsible for acquiring the resources needed to sustain the FTC, such as other members, financial assets, meeting space, etc. This discipleship core meets regularly for Bible study, to worship and pray together, and to strategize/plan larger missional events.

"If we are going to be for the world as Christ meant for us to be, we are going to have to spend more time away from the world, in deep prayer and substantial spiritual training .... We cannot give the world what we do not have."[12]—Rod Dreher

2. ***Clarity Around Context***: The core must determine a clearly defined context—such as a pocket of people, a particular neighborhood, or a regular serving project. The context cannot consist primarily of existing Christians. Third places in the community are great contexts, because they are where people already gather to form and deepen relationships, and they are neutral spaces where Christians and not-yet Christians can interact meaningfully. Within that context, the core tackles a project that allows Christians to partner with unbelievers in useful and valuable activities within the community. The important thing is to find joint projects that put Christians and not-yet Christians shoulder-to-shoulder in lengthy partnerships that allow the time for important friendships to form. Some may even wish to pioneer a business or social enterprise such as a co-working space or a day care center to bring intrinsic value to a community.

3. ***Common Practices***: An FTC clearly articulates the ways in which it will seek to be of service and blessing to others in their context. The FTC should have a clear plan for how to live out the kingdom of God and bring positive change in the context. What acts of service or hospitality, ongoing topics of conversation, or tangible acts of blessing will ensure that this group is bringing about renewal and redemption of life to the people and places around it? This is sometimes called a "rule of life" (an ancient monastic term that refers to a community's commitment to a specific practice done according to a specific schedule) or a "communal rhythm." For example, see the practice of BELLS (bless, eat, listen, learn, story) laid out in *Surprise the World*, by Michael Frost.[13]

One of the ways we train our community to discern what missional practices might be a blessing to others is by asking them these questions:

- What sucks in my/your life?
- Does it suck for anyone else?

- How could we work together for a sustained period of time to make it suck less for everyone?[14]

While some may consider this language crude, I find the irreligious language breaks down barriers and provokes good conversation that can lead to collaboration.

4. ***Intentional Community Formation***: The FTC gatherings should be open and inclusive. People must be able to belong regardless of their beliefs or moral behavior. Part of this is maintaining a wise ratio of believers to not-yet-believers. An FTC with more than 50 percent of its community as Christians will quickly become intimidating for not-yet Christians. And the primary gathering places should be neutral and natural for not-yet followers of Jesus. Remember, community is often best formed over food or fun. This group could number from fifteen to fifty—big enough to be interesting, but small enough to be intimate.

HOW TO LAUNCH A FOOD TRUCK

Brad Brisco shared these four practices of a community on mission, which we adopted as a pathway to guide the activity in our food truck workshops. (See "Sustaining Food Truck teams" on page 165.) These are adapted from his e-book, *ReThink*,[15] available online for free.

1. ***Discover***. What is God already doing? Individually and collectively we must cultivate our ability to listen well on three fronts—to God, to the local community, and to each other. It is simply impossible to ascertain the movement of God without carving out significant time to listen to his voice through prayer and Scripture reading, and we must listen to the voices of those we desire to serve.
   - Where is God actively at work in my community or context?
   - Who is the "person of peace"[16] in this community who already has influence and may be open to the values and priorities of the kingdom of God? How can we support and learn from him or her?
   - What is a repeatable prayer for this community that we can join together in praying?

- What are the contrasts in your context between the way things are and the way things will be when Jesus makes all things new?

2. ***Discern.*** Not only will we need to discern what God is already doing, but we will also need to ask a follow-up question: "In light of our collective and individual gifts and resources, how does God want us to participate in what he is doing?" The fact is that we can't do it all, which is true for both individual followers of Jesus and local congregations. But it is also true that God has gifted us all to do something! The point of discernment is to determine where and how to participate in God's mission.
   - What would sound like good news to our community?
   - What are the assets our community can offer in service?
   - What are the needs of our community that we can help meet?
   - How are we consistently listening to and learning from the people and places we are serving?
   - Who else is working in this field? What would a partnership look like?

3. ***Do.*** This may seem obvious, but the process of discernment is useless if we do not obey what God is calling us to do. When God prompts us to participate in what he is doing in the lives of others, we must respond. The FTC should gather together at least three or four times a month to fulfill the strategies of fostering faith, cultivating community, and moving each other further into mission.
   - How are our rhythms of life promoting redemption and renewal?
   - How are we intentionally discipling others by modeling the ways of Jesus and communicating the truth of Jesus to people?
   - Is what we are doing sustainable for the period of time we have agreed to collaborate?

4. ***Debrief.*** Throughout the course of engaging God's mission, we must create opportunities to process what is happening. Sometimes this simply means we need individual downtime to reflect on our activities. We may need to ask God to affirm our involvement or to ask for

clarity of direction. But it will also involve carving out time to debrief with others in our faith community. We need to know what others are seeing and sensing concerning God's activities and to hear how others are engaging God's mission.

- How do we need to adjust our meeting, activity, etc., to better meet needs?
- How will we know when we have accomplished what we've set out to do?
- If our FTC ceased to exist, how would our missional context be affected negatively?

SUSTAINING FOOD TRUCK TEAMS

Ecclesia recently began experimenting with a new format for our large-group gatherings that leverages our time together on Sunday to sustain and spark more missional engagement the other six days of the week. We call it a "missional imagination workshop," and its purpose is to train food truck church operators. The name originates from something Alan Hirsch said to me back in 2014: "The future of the church in the West will be determined by our missional imagination." These workshops are meant to stimulate creativity in God's people and deepen relationships among our missionaries, so they are more likely to collaborate during the week.

Once a month, we shorten our corporate worship to one hour. At its conclusion, we invite everyone to move into another room to participate in a workshop for a second hour. In this new setting, we gather in circles of eight to ten with others from our regions of the city. Each group engages in playful and participatory activities that allow them to begin to discern how they could come together during the week and offer a taste of the kingdom of God in a particular place or among a pocket of people.

"A creative minority is a Christian community in a web of stubbornly loyal relationships, knotted together in a living network of persons who are committed to practicing the way of Jesus together for the renewal of the world."[17]—Jon Tyson and Heather Grizzle

Gathering by region serves to connect people to neighbors from their part of the city, since they may have never met sitting in rows during worship.

We provide professional childcare during the workshop so everyone is able to join in. Not everybody chooses to participate, but the 75 percent of our community that do bring an innate desire to learn and grow, making it a rich time together.

"Find a community, a small group who can lovingly fuel your dreams and puncture your illusions .... Find some partners in the wild and wonderful world beyond church doors."[18]—Andy Crouch

As a tangible artifact that communicates and supports our new culture, one of our visual artists created a six-foot by eight-foot missional map of Los Angeles that sits in our lobby. It is printed on metal, so we can attach magnets that depict where our food trucks are operating during the week, and we also add small strips of white-board magnets so we can write prayer slogans over parts of the city.

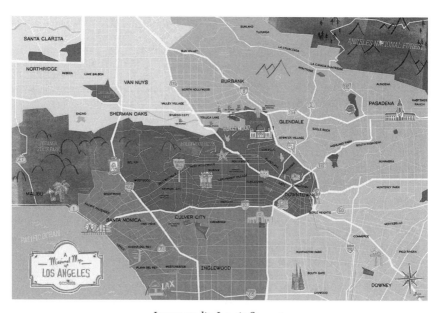

Image credit: Laurie Stewart

Our leadership evaluates these efforts regularly and adapts as we sense the need. Just as COVID-19 interrupted all of our regular rhythms, we were preparing to launch season two of the missional workshops, with an emphasis on creating groups based on professional networks, and not just neighborhood geography. Slowly, God is reshaping our hearts and minds, so we no longer imagine church as a place we go to get fed by others, but rather as a community where together we collaborate to seek the *shalom* of our city and take responsibility to make disciples.

In the appendices, I have included two examples of the sorts of participatory activities we have used in our workshops, as well as an overview of the microgrant program we formed to support our community in experimenting with new food trucks. I doubt our practices will translate directly into your context, but they are included to help you think through what could be done to help catalyze missional activity.

RETHINKING OUR ROLES

New expressions of church require that pastoral leaders identify and renounce elements of the existing culture that foster dependence on professionals, and instead encourage a culture of permission granting, power sharing, and dream awakening. We continually remind our staff that our role is not to do the ministry of the church, but to equip others to engage in God's mission in the ways he is leading them.

I suggest pastors take an inventory of their weekly schedule and work to create a balance where no more than 60 percent of their time is dedicated to overseeing internal programs, professionals, and preaching, and no less than 40 percent is spent equipping pioneering leaders, modelling missional experimentation, and deepening personal engagement with the non-church community. Tools like Younique Life Planning (www.lifeyounique.com) or The Calling Lab (www.callinglab.com) can be used to help congregants discover their unique calling and to guide them toward activating it. We are finding that, if we want others to live missionally, it is essential for the pastoral professionals to lead the way in taking risks and being willing to fail at these new forms of disciplemaking.

EXPERIMENT, FAIL, LEARN, REPEAT

Recently I pioneered a nine-month food truck experiment with my discipleship group of men in their 20s and 30s, entitled "Tavern Talks." The idea was to host a monthly public event in a local pub that would feature five-minute TED-talk-style presentations on interesting topics, followed by fifteen minutes of discussion in groups of four or five. Each night had a theme, and we curated four talks a night for the ninety-minute event. We hoped these conversations would create relationships with not-yet followers of Jesus that we could pursue throughout the next month. To be a blessing to the bar, we hosted the event on Tuesdays—bringing in business on their slowest night of the week. While I helped catalyze the idea, I played little part in the up-front leadership. Instead, the young men I disciple, along with some female Ecclesians, took turns leading the event and sharing stories. In the end, our team evaluated Tavern Talks and decided persons outside of our church community were not attending as we anticipated, so we shut it down. However, around fifty Ecclesians participated over the course of our run and were exposed to an experimental disciplemaking environment for those outside the church.

While some food truck experiments like Tavern Talks have not caught on, others have been more successful. Members of our community in Hollywood are launching missional collaborations all over Los Angeles in the places where God has sent them to embody his kingdom. They are operating in apartment complexes and neighborhoods centered around shared meals and holiday parties; in an independent film studio that recruits its staff to teach storytelling and screenwriting at a local elementary school; in pubs and bars where community forms around live music and social mixers; and in a homeless shelter that reaches out to teenagers on the street to help them escape trafficking and prostitution.

CREATING COMMUNITY FOR CREATIVES

After the financial crisis of 2008 eliminated her Wall-Street job at Lehman Brothers, Melissa Smith sensed God calling her family to relocate to Hollywood.

Her husband, Brennan, is a TV and film writer, and Melissa knows firsthand the struggles creatives face in a highly competitive and isolating marketplace. It is estimated that only 5–15 percent of screenwriters in Hollywood are currently employed in that field. Melissa wanted to create a community space where aspiring artists and creatives like Brennan could find professional support and collaboration, as well as an environment that supported them holistically—as people, not just as content producers. Her prayers led to the formation of a co-working business located just off Hollywood Boulevard, named Epiphany Space.

At its heart, Epiphany Space (www.epiphanyspace.com) is a community of artists and creative professionals who come together to create, collaborate, innovate, and ultimately be the change we all want to see in Hollywood. As Melissa says on the website, "We want you to know you matter, no matter what's going on with your career." In an industry rife with loneliness and despair, Melissa and her core team incarnate the kingdom of God by providing caring relationships that inspire hope and perseverance. Even before I arrived in Hollywood, Melissa was one of the Ecclesians who was already pioneering food-truck-style ministry in the neighborhood. While some of its members are followers of Jesus, most pursue other forms of spirituality or choose to not express any spirituality at all.

Epiphany Space operates as a daytime co-working location for individuals and small teams, but it also hosts a series of activities that support the life of these office subscribers and Hollywood residents. Each night the space is filled with life-giving activity: addiction support groups, songwriter's circles where artists can work on material in a safe and supportive environment, *The Artist's Way* book studies, write-a-thons, clothing swaps, and prayer groups. Melissa herself hosts a weekly discipleship group that is open to anyone. Other Ecclesians who work out of Epiphany Space formed an annual short film festival that hosts its opening night for the film's directors in Epiphany's outdoor courtyard. This event provides independent filmmakers with a professional and public place to showcase their films, at a rate that is more affordable than some of the larger festivals in the city.

Ecclesia's staff is one of the group members in the space. We occupy six offices on the second floor of one of the two buildings. Being members of a shared space like this keeps our pastoral team connected with the culture of Hollywood artists and the realities they face every day. We get to celebrate with them when they book a gig, sell a script, or nail an audition. Each week, Epiphany hosts a Wine Wednesday happy hour that brings many of our staff team down into the common area for drinks and conversation. Some of our staff members have taken to grabbing their laptops and working downstairs alongside other members, rather than in their own personal offices upstairs.

Epiphany Space is a great example of a food truck enterprise that makes disciples of people who are not interested in attending a church service. One member, Lisa, moved to the city to be a writer and signed up for Epiphany Space because it is more affordable than large coworking chains and has a more communal and supportive vibe. Lisa's spiritual journey had taken her through many differing forms of spirituality, including a season practicing Sufism, during which she had participated in the custom of spinning in a trance-like state as a whirling dervish. She was intrigued by the faith she sensed in many of Epiphany's staff and loved talking about her own spiritual journey with other members. Professionally, she struggled to find steady employment and was planning on cancelling her membership before Melissa offered her a free month to help her get along. Lisa was moved by the generosity.

One day a mechanic was playing hardball with repair costs on Lisa's car, and she felt they were taking advantage of her. Melissa asked me if I would walk to the shop with Lisa as an advocate. This simple but tangible act of blessing meant so much to Lisa as we faced down the repair technician together, and her car was released without her being ripped off. Over time, Lisa expressed more and more interest in Jesus and asked questions of the Epiphany and Ecclesia teams. She even invited herself to our Ecclesia gathering one week when she realized that many of us met for worship together on Sundays. On one of those mornings, she approached me after the service and said, "I want into this Jesus kingdom. How do I make Jesus my king?" A few months later, Melissa baptized Lisa in one of our gatherings, and then we commissioned her back to Epiphany as part of our team of missionaries there!

Questions for Reflection

1. What percentage of your city is post-Christian? (For reference, visit www.barna.com.) What local places or pockets of people make up that percentage, and what have you done in the past to try to engage those communities?

2. How would you describe the difference between planting a church by launching a worship service and planting the gospel through missional engagement and relational disciplemaking?

3. As you consider your own food truck church, who comes to mind as potential partners for your *core* team? What local *context* would most energize you? What *common practices* would bless people there and orient them toward God's kingdom?

12

A Church of Perpetual Innovation

We live in a globally connected world of unpredictable, non-linear, discontinuous change. In the era of the attractional-church-growth movement (1980–2000), most churches that launched or saw significant growth did so in a world that was less volatile, and where change was slower and less frequent. That predictability allowed churches to hire consultants, form committees, or put together church-planting teams to develop three-, five-, or seven-year strategic plans. Today's rate of disruption and change is rendering those notions obsolete. In prior generations, it took ten years for a new technology platform, such as radio or television, to develop and ten years for the culture to fully integrate that technology. YouTube, on the other hand, took one year to build and only one year to be embraced.[1]

For local churches, one of the most important lessons that emerged from the 2020 pandemic is the need for strategies and structures that are elastic enough to fit this ever-evolving environment. Rather than codifying long-term plans, we are wise to plot a course trajectory that is consistent with the cross-cultural, missional-incarnational approach required in a post-Christian context and then be prepared to adapt and adjust as unpredictable factors arise. More than ever, we need organizational flexibility that will allow us to form and re-form our ministry strategies in real time. Cumbersome committees and top-heavy hierarchical structures will not be nimble enough to respond when divine opportunities present themselves. The churches capable of responding in real time will be those in which every disciple feels empowered to act, knowing their kingdom efforts will be celebrated, rather than stifled, by their church's leadership.

While predicting the future is a more complicated task than ever, let's examine three evolving cultural realities facing our churches that seem to be increasing in impact.

FINANCIAL STRAIN

In the face of economic changes in society, many Western churches, in North America particularly, are feeling the need to adapt their traditional financing model of tithes and offerings. The boomer generation is the most financially committed group in many churches, but they are aging. The millennial generation behind them is simply unable to take up the slack due to the impact of two separate once-in-a-generation global economic crises. Many of them are unable to become financially independent while under the load of student loans, falling wages, rising housing costs, and a more competitive marketplace. This competition is exacerbated by the rise of automation, which economists predict will eliminate around 800 million jobs in the next decade.[2] The coronavirus has accelerated this transition to robotic automation as corporations attempt to forestall the impact of future pandemics on their manufacturing capabilities.[3]

There is also growing fear that a more secular society might eventually elect government officials who are willing to rewrite the tax codes related to charitable giving. In 2017, the Tax Cuts and Jobs Act enacted changes that mean "95 percent of taxpayers have lost their ability to receive a charitable deduction."[4] With so few people gaining a tax break from giving to a local church, it seems reasonable to assume it is now easier for the government to remove the deduction altogether. A recent financial scandal in The Church of Jesus Christ of Latter-day Saints drew national attention to $100 billion in tax-free money the church was spending on for-profit enterprise, in violation of IRS laws.[5] If public sentiment regarding religious organizations continues to skew toward skepticism and cynicism, it is conceivable that one day churches will have to pay property taxes. This would create a crippling tax burden on churches and force them to reimagine their entire way of operating.

To prepare for these possible changes, forward-thinking churches are finding ways to create multiple income streams in addition to traditional offerings. It is becoming increasingly common to see churches start businesses that leverage their property for co-working, childcare, or another seven-day-a-week use that can generate income. Mark DeYmaz's book, *The Coming Revolution in Church Economics* is a great text for churches who lack financial flexibility and have never considered notions of "social entrepreneurship," "becoming a benevolent owner," or "pioneering business as mission."

These new financial realities explain in part why so many young church planters are rejecting the traditional "large launch" Sunday-service-centric model of planting with its high demand for start-up capital. Instead, they are choosing to launch as a smaller community embedded in a local neighborhood or relational network, led by "covocational" church planters who work in the marketplace, which also becomes their mission field. Brad Brisco (who equips planters within the North American Mission Board [NAMB]) and Hugh Halter (a lifetime covocational church planter himself), are leading the charge to train these leaders and provide resources[6] to help churches prepare for a future where financial resources will be far more scarce.

Financial limitations are prompting more churches to move away from large professional staff teams and instead to catalyze everyday disciples to step into leadership. The future, then, will be less about hiring professionals and more about releasing and resourcing every follower of Jesus to step into their personal calling in God's kingdom, to recover a sense of vocation—"the place where the desires of your heart meet the longings of the world."[7] The more that leaders can empower every believer to flow with the Holy Spirit in mission, the less dependent we will become on professionals to feed them and program their ministry opportunities.

It should be readily apparent by now that the cultural context we are living in as a church will demand a much more robust and resilient disciple than the ones we produced in the churches of Christendom. Many church leaders are awakening to the reality that God's people are under-formed and unprepared to thrive in a more hostile environment. As sociologist James Davidson Hunter notes,

> Christians just aren't Christian enough. Christians don't think with an adequate enough Christian worldview, Christians are fuzzy-minded, Christians don't pray hard enough, and Christians are generally lazy toward their duties as believers.[8]

Recent books such as Mark Sayers' *Reappearing Church* and Rod Dreher's *The Benedict Option* rightly call the church to a higher standard of Christlikeness as part of our efforts to impact this new social environment.

THE DISAPPEARING MIDDLE

Another significant cultural change is the increasing polarization across sectors of society. Remember the bell curve we briefly discussed in chapter seven? In a bell curve, the majority of a specific population is concentrated near a mean, or average middle point. Bell curves are useful for plotting the height and weight of a population, scores of IQ tests, or predictable responses to change—as we saw in the Diffusions of Innovations curve. The bell curve seemed to be an accurate description of how things existed in my childhood. Most of my friends were neither rich nor poor but somewhere in the middle. A few of our school's athletes were good enough to play in college, but the majority of us were just average. And in our social circles, the last thing any of us wanted to do was stand out too much from what was considered "normal" when it came to fashion or music. In the 1980s and 90s, it seemed the good life was expected to be found somewhere in the middle of the pack.

In the last ten years, however, the bell curve has ceased to be an accurate way to represent our society. A majority of society's members are less likely to express opinions that embrace nuance and middle-of-the-road compromise and are instead more likely to speak in absolutes and extremes. While the bell curve still holds for some statistical measurements, in relation to social viewpoints and preferences, it has given way to the "well curve." In the well curve, the majority no longer clusters in the middle, but rather is divided between the two extremes.

Bell Curve   Well Curve

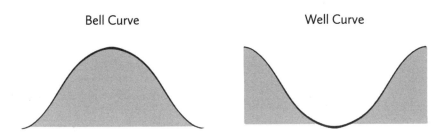

Once you have language for this phenomenon, you can begin to appreciate its ubiquity. Economically, the rich are getting richer, while the poor are getting poorer. The middle class around the world is shrinking.[9] There are far fewer moderate candidates in Western politics, as political parties in democratic nations become more extreme each election cycle. Just consider the recent election of far-right candidates in Australia, India and across Europe,[10] as well as the grassroots support among young people in the U.S. for far-left candidates, such as Bernie Sanders, a self-proclaimed Democratic socialist. In the realm of technology, consumers want the same image quality on the phone that fits in their pocket as they get from the giant seventy-five inch, 1080p, 4K television that hangs on their wall. The market capitalization of warehouse stores selling in bulk, such as Costco, are growing rapidly, while at the same time online e-commerce website Etsy—offering boutique, custom-made, artisan jewelry and apparel—gained 400 percent in value from 2017 to 2019. Traditional department stores that serve the middle price-bracket portion of the market, such as Sears, J. C. Penney, and Macy's, were already losing customers and have been further devastated by the 2020 pandemic. Urban streets are filled with both electric scooters and large sports utility vehicles, but sales of the midsize sedan are in annual decline and are increasingly being taken off the market.[11]

This penchant towards polarization is affecting local churches. Churches that were once able to navigate complex social and political issues by remaining middle of the road moderates are experiencing immense pressure from both sides to acquiesce in their direction. To stay in the middle of the stream on complex issues such as sexual orientation—valuing an orthodox biblical understanding of marriage while still affirming and embracing the LGBTQ community as made in the image of God—now seems to many like a cop out, rather than compassion. Even in the early summer months of the 2020 pandemic, as American states eased "safer at home" restrictions, conflicts arose, pitting frontline health workers against small-business advocates. While this is clearly a false dichotomy, battle lines were quickly drawn on social media, with God's name evoked by both groups. In this well-curve culture, outrage toward one's opponents is expressed so often by so many Christians, we might mistakenly believe it to be a legitimate fruit of the spirit.

The same consumer trend that rejects midsize products is now prevalent in churches as well. Megachurches (2000+ attendees) that draw commuters from all over a geographic area continue to grow numerically, while at the same time there is a proliferation of new, small, hyper-local, microchurch communities (around 25–100 attendees) that are committed to a local neighborhood and are content to gather in homes, parks, or public spaces. The church is getting larger and smaller at the same time, and this trend is likely to continue. Churches who find themselves in the middle of this numeric well curve are likely to feel the dual pinch of not offering programs and professional talent that can match their area megachurches, but also not being embedded deeply enough locally to attract members who want to "be the church" where they live and work. Ecclesia Hollywood is facing this same struggle, as Christians in their 20s moving to the city are drawn to the bright lights and celebrity of megachurches and the programs they offer, while many of our families in their 30s and 40s are looking to find a Sunday gathering in their own neighborhoods rather than in the city where we meet.

My desire is not to pass judgement on any church simply because of its size; there is only one church in a city—Jesus' church—and it needs many expressions to fulfill its purpose. I am simply identifying a trend in how people are picking churches when they relocate.

> "My guess is the biggest movement in churches of the future will be among those 30 to 300 …. That size has a lot of power especially for young adults, because they want intimacy, but they also want the energy of a larger group."[12]—Dave Gibbons

One of the benefits of the proliferation of church planting and mission-centered microchurches is a growing sense of collaboration for the sake of serving the city. Translocal networks—such as Forge, V3, Underground, Ecclesia, City to City, Communitas, Missio Alliance, and SEND, to name just a few—are connecting like-minded leaders and communities, so they can find common projects and partnerships and share best practices.

One of my favorite examples of this kind of partnership is led by Forge Colorado Springs's hub director, Rowland Smith, who started a monthly missional roundtable that he affectionately dubs "The Freaks Like Me Club." His desire is to equip and encourage leaders of smaller churches—who may feel overwhelmed, outnumbered, and under-resourced compared to those who are part of big teams working in large churches. Smaller churches tend to be more collaborative, recognizing that they cannot effect change in a city on their own. These networks are helping develop relationships that encourage leaders to share resources and work together to tackle big problems, such as chronic and situational homelessness, human trafficking, and finding homes for kids in the foster care system. Hopefully, churches will become better at celebrating city-wide kingdom wins rather than individual church success.

ONE CHURCH OF MANY COLORS

Finally, but perhaps most significantly, Western culture is becoming increasingly more ethnically diverse. In North America, it is expected that traditionally minority cultures will become the majority by 2045;[13] and "among children at every age below 10, whites are already a minority."[14] "Today, the median age of white Christians (fifty-five years old) is seven years older than the general population (forty-eight years old) and seventeen years older than the median age of religiously unaffiliated Americans (thirty-eight years old)."[15] Sadly, this "browning of America" has been met by many white Christians with suspicion, anger, and resistance.

Rather than deepening these racial and cultural divides, the church has the opportunity to celebrate God's kingdom as a place of diversity and harmony. For God to be fully glorified, his church must exist as a credible witness to his multi-ethnic kingdom and prophetically model the repentance, reconciliation, and healing necessary for that to happen. Thankfully, according to a 2018 Baylor University study, the percentage of multiracial congregations in the United

States nearly doubled from 1998 to 2012, with about one in five American congregants attending a place of worship that is racially mixed.[16] I hope this trend continues and accelerates in the years ahead.

Many denominations that have remained far too silent on the issue of race are beginning to repent and advocate for a more racially and ethnically inclusive approach to forming churches. I applaud the NAMB's

> *"Courageous Christianity embraces racial and ethnic diversity. It stands against any person, policy, or practice that would dim the glory of God reflected in the life of human beings from every tribe and tongue. These words are a call to abandon complicit Christianity and move toward courageous Christianity."[17]—Jemar Tisby*

Send Institute for publishing "A Church Planting Manifesto for 21st Century North America," which included the following statements affirming multi-ethnic churches:

- "Men and women leading in mission—from different racial, ethnic, and socioeconomic backgrounds—is a demonstration of the power of the gospel (Acts 13:1–3; James 2:1–7)."
- "We affirm that God has sovereignly allowed high levels of diversity to descend upon North America as part of his plan to raise up new disciples and new churches .... Just as the Church from around the world often understands that the Great Commission is all peoples reaching all places with all of the gospel, North America, as a microcosm of the world, requires a mission force led by diverse and culturally intelligent leaders."[18]

As diversity within the local church increases, there is a growing recognition among historically white churches that ethnicity is not something to be ignored but rather celebrated as an expression of God's creativity and design. And as we face secularism's missional challenges, multi-ethnic churches possess advantages over monocultural ones, as Dave Gibbons observes In *The Monkey and the Fish*:

It's undeniable that diversity, especially cultural and ethnic diversity, is a huge asset when it comes to innovation, creativity, and problem-solving. It stands to reason that diversity brings forth fresh viewpoints, approaches, perspectives, learnings, ideas, insights, and sensibilities, and these in turn lead to breakthroughs, whether it's an opportunity we're trying to take advantage of or a problem or crisis we're trying to address.[19]

Communities of diversity can also help expose theological misconceptions. As we explored in the gospel reductions in chapter five, much of what is expressed as the gospel in the West is cultural, not biblical, in its origin. The emphasis on victory and triumph, the prominence of the individual in God's redemptive plan, and the presentation of the gospel in terms of benefits to be gained are all examples of Western values that distort biblical truth when they become the *only* way of reading Scripture.

As Darrell Guder put it, "Every particular culture's translation of the gospel contributes to a witness that corrects, expands, and challenges all other forms of witness in the worldwide church."[20] Those who have been mired in a purely Western church need these perspectives to de-colonize our theology. For my white brothers and sisters, I highly recommend reading Soong-Chan Rah's book, *The Next Evangelicalism: Freeing the Church from Western Cultural Captivity*.[21]

"Contrary to popular opinion, the church is not dying in America; it is alive and well, but it is alive and well among the immigrants and ethnic minority communities and not among the majority white churches in the United States."[22]—Soong-Chan Rah

The marginalization of Christianity is a new experience for most white Western-European Christians who have traditionally enjoyed a place of prominence in society. But this sense of displacement and dislocation is an all-too-familiar experience for our brothers and sisters of color. As the church is pushed into a state of exile, we would be wise to learn from each other and give special attention to the collective wisdom of ethnic and racial groups with more experience in lamenting and trusting God in times of suffering and disorientation.[23]

Ideally, this unique situation for white Christians will create empathy and appreciation for the continued marginalization of people of color and lead to more action to end the inherent systems of racism that remain in Western culture.

An often-overlooked benefit of the rise in global immigration to the West is that many of these immigrants arrive with faith in Jesus that has been forged in suffering, and is more robust than the faith they find in the Western church. The traditional notion of missions— "from the West to the rest"—may be inverted in the next century as God brings his people from around the globe into Western lands mired in secularism. As the West increasingly grows into a mission field, the church should celebrate and embrace the presence of gospel workers who come seeking to join God's kingdom work here.

> *"It is good for those who have had the dominant cultural position to learn with an attitude of humility, and to acknowledge that our dominant posture has often made us arrogant, complacent, entitled and proud."[24]—Jon Tyson and Heather Grizzle*

Personally, I am finding it incredibly difficult to transition a dominant-culture church into a more multi-ethnic community. I've lost count of the number of people who've left Ecclesia, accusing our leadership of drifting toward Marxism, adopting "critical race theory," or becoming "Social Justice Warrior Christians" because we promote the value of racial and ethnic diversity and seek to expose racial inequalities as gospel issues. I am learning so much by leading alongside black and brown brothers and sisters, and I know that many in our community remain because they appreciate a church that is willing to tackle these issues.

I will forever treasure the morning we witnessed an incredible move of the Spirit that prompted spontaneous expressions of racial reconciliation. During a shared worship service with Hope in the Hills Church—a predominantly African American community in Beverly Hills pastored by a dear friend, Dr. Naima Lett—the Holy Spirit began to convict white members of our community to come forward and seek forgiveness for attitudes and acts of racism for which they wanted to publicly repent and receive forgiveness. Dr. Lett and other members of her community graciously pastored and prayed with our community and assured people of their forgiveness in Christ. It was a holy moment.

I am thankful for a few resources that have guided me along this path, specifically *Divided by Faith* by Michael Emerson and Christian Smith, *White Awake* by Daniel Hill, *The Color of Compromise* by Jemar Tisby, and the work of Mosaix Global Network.[25]

EMBRACE THE ANOMALY

I recently shared with the Ecclesia staff and elders a quote from an e-mail I received from Alan Hirsch, summarizing Thomas Kuhn's work on paradigm shifts in science and society:

> All paradigm shifts start with a sense of anomaly, that sense that something is wrong in the system—there are flaws in its knowledge. This leads to what he calls a "roaming of the mind" in search for alternative answers. Strangely, it is always the people who have really mastered the prevailing paradigm, its very best thinkers, who, sensing the anomaly, begin to seek out others who likewise are recognizing the bugs in the system. They begin to compare notes together, discern commonalities, and eventually form a "school of thought" within the prevailing paradigm, one that begins to address the problems in the parent paradigm. This process of highlighting problems in the system is often experienced as critical and therefore encounters some resistance from the insiders of the prevailing paradigm, but eventually the new paradigm—if it offers a truer way of understanding the problem—goes on to win the day.

I share it here as a hopeful reminder that all organizations possess the potential to move from the resistant posture of the human eye to the embracing posture of an oyster. As we are all acutely aware, established practices and paradigms can become extinct almost overnight. When the coronavirus first hit the U.S. in March of 2020, a storm of irritating new realities swept in, creating an eye-or-oyster-moment for local churches. Many churches saw the inability to meet for in-person worship as a threat to their existence and sought to replicate their existing programs and services across new technology. In many cases, leaders attempted to maintain all of the formality of their existing worship services without acknowledging that it was being viewed by families in pajamas or couples in their bedrooms. They set up "drop boxes" in the parking lot for offering checks, removed Communion from their church service, and rushed to return to "normal" as soon as possible, with the reopening of in-person services, regardless of the numerous limitations, such as mask wearing, restrictions on singing, and a lack of personal contact; many churches even violated legal guidelines to do so.

Other churches, however, embraced the new contextual challenge and leveraged the disruption to introduce adaptive strategies and pioneered beautiful new expressions of mission, community, and worship. They supplied under-resourced students with laptops, so they could continue their education online, created food distribution centers, and gave generously to fund Covid-19 benevolence accounts used to assist those who were suddenly without employment. They launched virtual community groups to support people with addictions who were struggling in isolation, and to help others facing the mental health challenges of anxiety and depression. Their adaptive response led to experimentation with more interactive teaching, crowdsourced worship compilations, and new worship practices, such as contemplative prayer times. Churches expanded their ecclesiology to allow members to receive in-home Communion as families, and intergenerational elements were added to their online worship services to celebrate the participation of children and youth. These sorts of adaptive and innovative changes were made by communities with the courage to see the possibilities an irritant can bring when a posture of positivity and creativity is adopted.

I hope this book sparks a desire to view the constant changes we face, and the swirling storms of secularism, not as a threat to our cause as Jesus' church, but as an opportunity for a more creative and faithful interaction with the culture around us. Similar to the pearl-making process, learning how to re-form a local church will take time and will require layer upon layer of innovation. We must also remember that the oyster that makes the pearl is not the one who is most blessed by its beauty. Whilst we might be the ones who do the hard work of creating, innovating, and allowing the layers to build and shape this new thing of beauty, it may be the next generation that actually harvests the final product.

I pray God works through your local church with courage, creativity, and perseverance to form some pearls for the world to behold!

Questions for Reflection

1. Imagine this potential cultural shift: after years of technological obsession that borders on addiction, the tide shifts and people reject their device dependence. They now long for authentic face-to-face engagement and places free from technology. How could your local church adapt and view this change as a disciplemaking opportunity? Are your current leadership and financial structures and systems nimble enough to respond, or would innovators feel burdened by bureaucracy?

2. What resources do you have as a church that you could leverage to create a business for the common good that would also generate income to sustain your church? Think in terms of facility space, skills, knowledge, and experiences.

3. How can your church serve as a peacemaker and bridgebuilder in a culture that is increasingly polarized and divided? How might you address complex social issues in the community while still reflecting the values of the kingdom of God, such as unity and empathy?

Appendix 1
Asking Great Questions

As missionaries seeking to make disciples in our everyday lives, it's important to understand the power of questions.

Questions demonstrate that we are interested in learning about other people and entering into deeper relationships.
Christians are infamous for making absolute statements of truth, and for thinking we have all the answers. But asking questions is much more effective—and more subversive—than making statements. When we ask questions, we demonstrate humility and mutuality. Notice how, when God pursues a relationship with someone who is already predisposed to be defensive or hesitant, he often leads with a question.

- To Adam and Eve: Where are you? Who told you that you were naked? Have you eaten from the tree that I commanded you not to eat from? (Genesis 3:9,11.)
- To Cain: What have you done? (Genesis 4:10.)
- To Hagar: Where have you come from, and where are you going? (Genesis 16:8.)
- To Elijah: What are you doing here? (1 Kings 19:13.)

Questions direct conversations in a natural way.
My friend Mike Morrison, the former dean of the University of Toyota, often reminds me, "Organizations evolve in the direction of their most frequently asked questions." Conversations often go in the direction of the most profound questions, and people often grow toward the questions they are asked.

Questions often get reciprocated in conversations.

If you ask good questions, the person you're talking to will often ask you questions in return, giving you a chance to share your faith in a natural way. You can also respond to a question someone asks you by asking the same question back. This models vulnerability. For example, you might say:

- "That's a hard question; how would you answer it?"
- "Wow, that's a good question; what about you?"
- "I'm not sure. Do you have an answer to that?"

Questions help us discern people's longings.

Through our questions and prayerful discernment, we are hoping to discover the kingdom longings that exist inside people so that we can pray for them, speak God's truth to these longings, and tangibly bless them in ways that relate to these desires. We are praying that, as we engage with people, God would reveal answers to questions such as:

- Where is their past or present pain?
- What are their core fears in life?
- What is the prize they are striving for in life? How do they measure personal success?
- What is broken in their life, and how do they identify that brokenness within them?
- Where do they find strength and power to press on when life is hard?
- What are the idols they worship to find value, identity, and purpose in life?
- What do they think about God? What do they think God thinks about them?
- What is their familiarity with the life, mission, and teachings of Jesus?

Know when questions should be asked indirectly.

Asking questions directly can come across as intrusive and even offensive in some cultures. It is often wiser to uncover heart issues in a less direct way, similar to the way Jesus used parables. A parable is an illustrative story that delivers truth in an indirect, roundabout way. Indirect questions can have a similar effect of uncovering the truth in a person's life.

Here are some more indirect ("parabolic") questions you might naturally raise in a conversation with someone who is not yet a follower of Jesus.

- What are you celebrating as a success in life right now?
- What do you value most in life?
- What are your biggest challenges, and what is life teaching you through them?
- What was the best thing/worst thing to happen to you this week?
- What do you want most out of life?
- If you were to receive a text that made you say, "Wow, that is great news!" what might it say?
- What fears or anxieties tend to consume your thoughts most often?
- If God appeared to us, what would you ask him or her?
- Why do you think God seems so real to some people and so unreal to others?
- Did you grow up in a family that talked about Jesus?

Tips to remember when using questions in your own disciplemaking:

- ***Be Courageous:*** The thing keeping you from a deep and insightful conversation with someone may just be the courage to ask one meaningful question.
- ***Be Curious:*** People like talking about themselves to people who listen well. Ask God to give you genuine concern for others and the ability to hear their hearts. Ask God to reveal to you how *he* sees them.
- ***Be Compassionate:*** Express empathy; make good listening sounds to show you are mirroring their experiences of sharing, and refrain from making judgments about what they share.

A good question is not concerned with a correct answer. A good question cannot be answered immediately. A good question challenges existing answers. A good question is one you badly want answered once you hear it, but had no inkling you cared before it was asked. A good question creates new territory of thinking. A good question reframes its own answers. A good question is the seed of innovation in science, technology, art, politics, and business. A good question is a probe, a what-if scenario. A good question skirts on the edge of what is known and not known, neither silly nor obvious. A good question cannot be predicted. A good question will be the sign of an educated mind. A good question is one that generates many other good questions. A good question may be the last job a machine will learn to do. A good question is what humans are for.[1]

Appendix 2
Missional Imagination
Workshop Examples

ECCLESIA WORKSHOP 1: BIOCHURCH

[Adapt this example to fit your congregation and your circumstances.]

Supplies needed: Pens, Post-it notes, timer (or phone).
Set-up: Have people seated around the room, at tables, in groups of 8–10.

The scenario:
Imagine you and your spouse/roommate/family are about to move into a biodome—an enclosed structure that allows for self-sustained living. You will live there for five years alongside 5,000 strangers. On the first day you enter, you meet a few other followers of Jesus and decide that it would be good to form a church together.

What communal practices and rhythms of life would you form as a local expression of church? To put it another way, how do you plan to grow as disciples of Jesus and make disciples over the next five years?

Instructions:

1. Invite participants to take five minutes and brainstorm alone. Using the pens and Post-it notes on the table, write each unique idea on a separate Post-it.
2. After five minutes, invite participants to turn to a partner and share their ideas. Combine points where ideas overlap by sticking those Post-it notes together. Let this happen for another five minutes.

3. Ask the group to share aloud some of their ideas and place the Post-it notes on the table in front of the group as they do. You won't have time for each group to report all of their ideas individually, so if other groups share similar ideas, they can add their Post-it notes to that string as the sharing is happening.

4. After ten minutes of sharing, ask the group, "What common themes are emerging? What categories do these activities fall into?"

5. Continue this discussion until the facilitator calls the room to attention (after about 50 minutes, total). He will draw a triangle with the UP/IN/OUT discipleship priorities, aka FAITH/COMMUNITY/MISSION, with Jesus at the center (a basic picture of Jesus' church).

6. The group will finish by sharing with each other responses to these questions: "How do you feel as you imagine forming a church in a biodome compared to the reality of making disciples as a church in the city of Los Angeles? What are the biggest differences between those two realities that affect your attitudes toward them?"

Facilitate the discussion, drawing out observations such as:

- The limits of the biodome led to feelings of empowerment and creativity, while the expanse of L.A. leads to feelings of being overwhelmed and discouraged.

- The commitment of five years led us to think we could really make a difference, whereas L.A. living can feel transient and unpredictable.

- The limitation of 5,000 people in an enclosed space meant that we would live in proximity to the same people and see them more frequently.

- The idea of a blank slate and starting fresh as a church without preexisting baggage excited us, whereas in L.A./Hollywood, church can have such a negative connotation.

- Doing this as a group activity made me excited about doing these activities with others, whereas often in L.A., we feel alone and too far from others who want to live God's mission every day.

Possible take-aways:

The hope is that Ecclesia begins to think and imagine ways that we could create these sorts of limits in our lives that would inspire missional living. How could we create a "biodome atmosphere" in our lives? e.g.,

- Limit ourselves to one specific "third place" in our local proximity that we could frequent regularly.
- Recruit a small community of people who would imagine how to be the church in a specific neighborhood or among a specific pocket of people and commit to living that way over a long period of time.

ECCLESIA WORKSHOP 2: SEEK THE SHALOM OF THE CITY

[Adapt this example to fit your congregation and your circumstances.]

Supplies needed: Snap bracelets (or other grouping method), prepared group notebooks, access to "shalom" video.

Set-up: Tables or chairs for groups of 8–10 people.

Gathering: [10:55 a.m.]
Jon will dismiss the leaders early from the main service. Please head into the café, take a snap bracelet, and gather with the other leaders from your region in one of the seating circles in the room. As Ecclesia comes into the room and individuals find their color bracelet/region, they will join your circle. When you get to eight people and the circle is full, send the other leaders off into new circles to do the same. This helps fill groups and gets them started more quickly.

Opening:
As soon as you have a full group, sit down, and begin. Go around the circle, say your name and use three words to describe the area of L.A. in which you live. As everyone shares, have someone write all the words on a blank sheet of paper in your group notebook. After everyone has shared, hold up the list. Ask, "What makes your area unique in L.A.?" (It is okay to acknowledge that these are large regions, so not everyone's experience will be the same.) Please put this sheet back in the notebook so we can keep it.

Video: [11:20 a.m.]
Introduce today's topic: Seeking God's *shalom* in our region of L.A. Show this four-minute video on the concept to set up the discussion: Bible Project, "Word Study: *Shalom*—'Peace'" [https://www.youtube.com/watch?v=oLYORLZOaZE]

(Leader's Note: The Hebrew word *shalom* means "peace, prosperity, and communal flourishing." *Shalom* is not just the absence of conflict, but also the presence of wholeness and righteousness in a place. The word is also used to describe a place where *shalom* is functioning as it will one day when the kingdom of God comes in its fullness.)

Discussion: [11:25 a.m.]
Each of the following questions is written on one single sheet of paper in the notebook on your table. As you ask each question, pull that page out. After someone answers aloud, give the sheet of paper to him or her to write that answer on the sheet. You can use the cover of the notebook as a surface to write on. *In effect you are beginning to create a missional handbook for your region. These notebooks will be kept as resources for your area going forward.*

For example:
- The leader asks, "What do you love about our region that makes it positively unique among other parts of L.A.?"
- Mary replies, "I love the cultural diversity and how most people seem to celebrate each other's differences."
- The leader says, "Great, Mary. Write that down on this sheet and we will keep adding to it as we go. Who else has an answer?"
- After a while move on to the next question, taking that page out of the book and answering it together, aloud, and recording your answers.

Here are the questions that are found in the notebooks (you will likely not get through them all, but we gave you enough to keep discussion going):

- What do you love about our region that makes it positively unique among other parts of L.A.?
- Where are the places of pain in our region that are worthy of lament?
- What groups of people seem to be struggling in our community?
- What about our region sucks for a whole lot of its residents? How do people account for or explain the causes behind what's wrong?
- In our region, what are the specific idols that people worship to give their lives meaning and value? How does their worship of these idols negatively affect the community?

- What do you sense God is already doing to create *shalom* in our region? Are there ways that we could join him in that activity?
- What existing organizations might be potential partners for seeking the *shalom* of our region? Who might be the "experts" in our area from whom we could learn?
- What types of "third spaces" are popular in our region, and do you have a favorite one to frequent? In your experience, do these spaces actually serve to build new relationships and deepen community?
- Where do you see people or places of unrealized potential in our region?

Closing: [11:50]

Close the time by spending ten minutes in prayer for the *shalom* of the people and places in your area. Thank God for the beauty and goodness of your region and offer supplication to him for some of its brokenness and injustice. Pray for God to open your eyes to ways you can express care individually and as a group in the coming month.

Appendix 3
Microgrants for Missional
Collaborations (Food Trucks)

To help catalyze missional collaborations, Ecclesia has established a microgrant program. Individuals or small teams from among the Ecclesia family can apply for up to $500 of funding to assist in pioneering new missional initiatives in their neighborhood or among a pocket of people in Los Angeles. The projects must be consistent with Ecclesia's values and mission, and must serve the purpose of building disciplemaking relationships and embodying the values of the kingdom of God. The project should bless a community of people and not simply meet the needs of an individual.

Microgrants are designed to support innovation and encourage groups with limited resources. The funds might help buy products or materials, rent space for a gathering, or create promotional materials for a project, but they are not to be used to compensate leaders for their time. Ideally the funds will be distributed directly to a vendor or as reimbursement for expenses.

Some examples of projects that would align with Ecclesia's mission are:

- Keeping a local neighborhood's parks clean, safe, and exhibiting God's beauty.
- Bringing new businesses and employment into under-resourced neighborhoods.
- Community development—cultivating active participation and contribution among local members of a community to promote its flourishing.

- Promoting/facilitating sustainable urban farming that provides food to local families.
- Creating a community garden that unites residents of a local neighborhood.
- Pioneering a program to provide safe rides home from local bars.
- Developing businesses that promote and sell fair and ethical fashion.
- Establishing a tutoring program for GED, literacy classes, or ESL classes.

We do not fund:

- Events that are exclusively intended to gather or support those who are already followers of Jesus.
- Fundraisers for, or ongoing organizational support of, 501(c)3 non-profit organizations.
- Production costs for art such as films, studio music, or publishing.
- Personal salaries or expense funds of individuals.
- Campaigns for political candidates.

Grant Amount: Up to $500

Simple Microgrant Application

Project leader(s) and contact information:
How long have you been active among Ecclesia?
What is your primary context (neighborhood, third place, pocket of people, etc.)?
Briefly describe your project idea:
How would the funds be used?
How will you measure the success of the project?
How much money are you applying for?
How might this project lead to a long-term sustainable Food Truck?
Date submitted:

Acknowledgments

I remain forever thankful for the original eight "Bible thumpers" in Sigma Chi back at The College of William and Mary: Gaskins, Gates, Bauer, Krewatch, Brantley, Barclay, Beege, and Redd. When I decided I was never going back to church, Jesus sent his church to me.

Kristyn and I are so thankful to the three generous and inspiring church communities that we are privileged to still call family: Williamsburg Community Chapel, The Well, and Ecclesia Hollywood. The greatest part of serving has been doing the work alongside the members, leaders, staff, and elders of these churches. Our family cherishes the friendships and memories from each community, and a name or face from our past will often come to mind and spark deep joy in our hearts.

Thank you to the 250 individuals and families from the Chapel who faithfully supported our family both financially and in prayer while we were living in Brussels, including more than fifty who actually came to visit us in person! You provided the scholarship for this incredible education. I pray we are good stewards of it.

Thank you to the ministry mentors along the way: Bill and Lindy Warrick; Dick and Ginny Woodward; Carlton and Shannon Deal; and Al and Deb Hirsch for your transparency, accessibility, and wisdom. Special thanks to marriage mentors and friends, Emerson and Sarah Eggerichs, who first exposed me to the eye and oyster analogy during their *Love and Respect* conference we hosted in Williamsburg in 2011.

Thank you to my family for patiently and graciously loving me and praying for me at every stage of my spiritual journey, even the more arrogant and self-righteous moments, and always embracing me as a work in progress.

Thank you to the faithful few men who have been with me for over twenty-five years of my Jesus journey and who call forth the best in me while knowing the worst of me.

Finally, I want to thank the courageous liminal leaders from Forge International, Communitas International, and Movement Leaders Collective who welcomed us into their respective tribes and who challenge us to keep following Jesus into the unknown. Special thanks to my editor, Anna Robinson, for all your hard work in making me sound more clear and concise than I actually am.

> "by the grace of God I am what I am, and
> his grace toward me was not in vain."
> —1 Corinthians 15:10 ESV

Notes

Foreword

1. Karl Marx, *Critique of Hegel's Philosophy of Right* (Cambridge: Cambridge University Press, 1970).

Introduction

1. Deuteronomy 7:7.
2. Matthew 13:31–32.
3. Darrell L. Guder, *The Continuing Conversion of the Church* (Grand Rapids, Michigan: Eerdmans, 2000), 90.

1: Sunday's Always Coming

1. The pearl-making process, drawn from the following sources: "Formation of a Pearl: Secret Life of Pearls," YouTube, uploaded by Nat Geo WILD, April 23, 2016, https://www.youtube.com/watch?v=m07OvPEoR6g; "Pearl," *Wikipedia*, https://en.wikipedia.org/wiki/Pearl#Natural_pearls; "How Do Oysters Make Pearls?" *How Stuff Works*, https://animals.howstuffworks.com/marine-life/question630.htm.
2. Lausanne Committee for World Evangelization, *The Pasadena Consultation: Homogeneous Unit Principle* (Lausanne Occasional Paper 1, 1978).
3. Many thanks to my friend Brad Brisco for giving me the language to describe these three crises.
4. Robert Chao Romero, *Jesus for Revolutionaries: An Introduction to Race, Social Justice, and Christianity* (Christian Ethnic Studies Press, 2013), 238.
5. Greg L. Hawkins and Cally Parkinson, *Reveal: Where are You?* (Illinois: Willow Creek Association, 2007).
6. Bob Burney, "A Shocking 'Confession' from Willow Creek Community Church," *Crosswalk.com*, October 30, 2007, www.crosswalk.com/pastors/11558438.

7. David Platt, *Radical: Taking Back Your Faith from the American Dream* (Random House, 2010).

8. Dave Gibbons, *Small Cloud Rising: How Creatives, Dreamers, Poets, and Misfits Are Awakening the Ancient Future Church* (California: Xealots, 2015), Kindle edition, Kindle location 243.

9. Brian Sanders, *Underground Church: A Living Example of the Church in its Most Potent Form* (Exponential Series) (Grand Rapids: Zondervan, 2018).

10. Brenda Salter McNeil, *Roadmap to Reconciliation 2.0: Moving Communities into Unity, Wholeness and Justice* (Downers Grove, IVP, 2020), Kindle edition, Kindle location 857.

11. Brian Sanders used this phrase in a breakout at the Tampa Underground's 'Underground Open' conference in 2018.

2: From Hero to Zero

1. Eric Hoffer, *Reflections on the Human Condition* (New Jersey: Hopewell Publications, 2006), 22.

2. See updated version of this book, Clare De Graaf, *The 10-Second Rule: Following Jesus Made Simple* (Brentwood, Tennessee: Howard Books, 2013).

3. Martin Robinson, *The Faith of the Unbeliever* (Oxford, UK: Monarch Books, 2001), 33.

4. George G. Hunter III, *The Celtic Way of Evangelism, Tenth Anniversary Edition: How Christianity Can Reach the West ... Again* (Tennessee: Abingdon Press, 2010), 108.

5. Alan Hirsch, *The Forgotten Ways: Reactivating Apostolic Movements* (Grand Rapids: Baker, 2016), 4.

6. "In Hoc Signo Vinces [In this sign conquer]," Christian History Institute, https://christianhistoryinstitute.org/incontext/article/constantines-cross. Ironically, *In hoc signo vinces* is engrained in my memory, as it is the motto of my college fraternity, Sigma Chi.

7. John Ortberg, *Who Is This Man? The Unpredictable Impact of the Inescapable Jesus* (Michigan: Zondervan, 2014), Kindle edition, Kindle location 959.

8. For an excellent one-chapter summary of these philosophical changes, see chapter two of Rod Dreher, *The Benedict Option: A Strategy for Christians in a Post-Christian Nation* (New York: Sentinel, 2017). For an extensive read, see Stanley J. Grenz, *A Primer on Postmodernism* (Grand Rapids: Eerdmans, 1996).

9. Robinson, *The Faith of the Unbeliever*, 20.

10. This sentiment is repeated often by Mark Sayers on his podcast with John Mark Comer, *This Cultural Moment*, produced by Bridgetown Church and Red Church, MP3 audio, https://thisculturalmoment.com. Many thanks to Sayers and Comer for their excellent podcast upon which much of this chapter's observations are based.

11. N. T. Wright, *The Challenge of Jesus: Rediscovering Who Jesus Was and Is* (Downers Grove: Intervarsity Press, 1999), 203.

12. James K. A. Smith, *How (Not) to Be Secular: Reading Charles Taylor* (Grand Rapids: Eerdmans, 2014), Kindle edition, Kindle location 44.

13. Charles Taylor, *A Secular Age*, (Cambridge: Harvard University Press, 2007), 18.

14. Robinson, *The Faith of the Unbeliever*, xi.

15. Quoted in Alan Hirsch and Mark Nelson, *Reframation: Seeing God, People, and Mission Through Reenchanted Frames* (Georgia: 100 Movements Publishing, 2019), 123.

16. William Defebaugh, "Oprah: 'Speaking Your Truth Is the Most Powerful Tool We All Have,'" *L'Officiel*, January 1, 2018, https://www.lofficielusa.com/film-tv/oprah-speaking-your-truth-is-the-most-powerful-tool-we-all-have.

17. Olivia Goldhill, "Polyamory is a quietly revolutionary political movement," *Quartz*, December 20, 2018, https://qz.com/1501725/polyamorous-sex-is-the-most-quietly-revolutionary-political-weapon-in-the-united-states.

18. Mark Sayers, *Disappearing Church: From Cultural Relevance to Gospel Resilience* (Chicago: Moody Publishers, 2016), 60.

19. Ibid, 79.

20. Laura Santhanam, "Youth suicide rates are on the rise in the U.S.," *PBS News Hour*, October 8, 2019, https://www.pbs.org/newshour/health/youth-suicide-rates-are-on-the-rise-in-the-u-s; and Press Association, "Antidepressant prescriptions in England double in a decade," *The Guardian*, March 29, 2019, https://www.theguardian.com/society/2019/mar/29/antidepressant-prescriptions-in-england-double-in-a-decade.

21. "Europe and right-wing nationalism: A country-by-country guide," *BBC News*, November 13, 2019, https://www.bbc.com/news/world-europe-36130006.

22. Romans 1:25.

23. Julian Barnes, *Nothing to Be Frightened Of* (New York: Knopf, 2008), 1.

24. Tod Bolsinger, *Canoeing the Mountains: Christian Leadership in Uncharted Territory* (Westmont: IVP Books, 2018), 193.

25. Robinson, *The Faith of the Unbeliever*, 12.

26. Megan Brenan, "Nurses Again Outpace Other Professions for Honesty, Ethics," *Gallup*, December 20, 2018, https://news.gallup.com/poll/245597/nurses-again-outpace-professions-honesty-ethics.aspx.

27. David Kinnaman and Gabe Lyons, *unChristian: What a New Generation Really Thinks About Christianity... and Why It Matters* (Michigan: Baker Books, 2007), 29–30.

28. For more see, George Barna and David Kinnaman, *Churchless: Understanding Today's Unchurched and How to Connect with Them* (Texas: Barna Group, 2014) and David Kinnaman, *You Lost Me: Why Young Christians Are Leaving Church ... and Rethinking Faith* (Michigan: Baker Books, 2011).

3: The End of Industrialized Disciplemaking

1. This was one of my many liminal experiences overseas that made me increasingly aware that my race, ethnicity, and gender as a white, European-American male granted me the privilege of rarely having to feel this sense of disorientation—of being an outsider. This book does not afford me the space to dive into that separate journey, but I am conscious—even as I write this hypothetical situation—of how often this is a day-to-day reality for many people of color and for women in American who are forced to navigate predominantly white male spaces.

2. Kinnaman and Lyons, *unChristian*, 226.

3. Kim Hammond and Darren Cronshaw, *Sentness: Six Postures of Missional Christians* (Illinois: IVP Books, 2014), Kindle edition, Kindle location 626.

4. Os Guinness, *Fool's Talk: Recovering the Art of Christian Persuasion* (Illinois: IVP Books, 2015), Kindle edition, Kindle location 631.

5. Michael Frost, *Surprise the World: The Five Habits of Highly Missional People* (Colorado: NavPress, 2015), 22.

6. "What does this mean?" Acts 2:12; "Are these charges true?" Acts 7:1; "May we know what this new teaching is that you are presenting?" Acts 17:19.

7. Lesslie Newbigin, *The Gospel in a Pluralist Society* (Michigan: Eerdmans, 1989), Kindle edition, Kindle location 2506.

4: Reversing Our Disciplemaking Pathways

1. Reggie McNeal, *Missional Renaissance: Changing the Scorecard for the Church* (San Francisco: Jossey-Bass, 2009), 21.

2. @bradleybrisco (July 8, 2018), [Tweet]. Retrieved from https://twitter.com/bradleybrisco/status/1015954600770273281.

3. Kirsteen Kim, "Rethinking Mission: Fuller's School of Intercultural Studies on the most common misunderstandings of mission today," https://www.fuller.edu/wp-content/uploads/2019/06/RethinkingMission_FullerSeminary.pdf.

4. Brad Brisco, "A God Who Sends," *Facts & Trends*, September 26, 2013, https://factsandtrends.net/2013/09/26/a-god-who-sends.

5. McNeal, *Missional Renaissance:* 46.

6. John 2:1–12.

7. Neil Cole, *Church 3.0: Upgrades for the Future of the Church* (San Francisco: Jossey-Bass, 2010), Kindle edition, Kindle location 1381.

8. For more information on the "one another" commands see Jeffrey Kranz, "All the 'one another' commands in the NT [infographic]," March 9, 2014, https://overviewbible.com/one-another-infographic/.

9. Bolsinger, *Canoeing the Mountains*, 42.

10. Bill Gardner with Richard Gretsky, "Bible Translation Through the Ages," *Wycliffe,* January 28, 2015, https://www.wycliffe.org/blog/posts/bible-translation-through-the-ages.

11. Newbigin, *The Gospel in a Pluralist Society*, Kindle location 4366.

5: The Good News Gone Bad

1. Guinness, *Fool's Talk*, Kindle location 383.

2. I was first introduced to this idea of the reductionism of the gospel in Guder's *The Continuing Conversion of the Church*. The idea is developed further in Hirsch and Nelson's *Reframation*.

3. I am grateful for the contributions on this topic by my new friend Jeff Vanderstelt in his book *Gospel Fluency: Speaking the Truths of Jesus into the Everyday Stuff of Life* (Wheaton, IL: Crossway, 2017). I tend to define the term a little differently than he does, but I find his work very helpful in reclaiming a fuller understanding and application of the gospel in our lives.

4. Walter Brueggemann, *Finally Comes the Poet: Daring Speech for Proclamation* (Minneapolis: Fortress Press, 1989), 23.

5. Lisa Sharon Harper, *The Very Good Gospel: How Everything Wrong Can Be Made Right* (New York: WaterBrook, 2016), 6.

6. James Davison Hunter, *To Change the World: The Irony, Tragedy, and Possibility of Christianity in the Late Modern World* (New York: Oxford University Press, 2010), 236.

7. Debra Hirsch, *Redeeming Sex: Naked Conversations About Sexuality and Spirituality* (Illinois: IVP Books, 2015), Kindle edition, Kindle location 2695.

8. Jon Tyson and Heather Grizzle, *A Creative Minority: Influencing Culture Through Redemptive Participation* (Heather Grizzle, 2016), 28.

9. Luke 19:1–10.

10. John 8:1–11.

11. Luke 23:34.

12. Matthew 16:18.

13. 1 Corinthians 1:2 NASB.

14. Leonard Sweet, *Nudge: Awakening Each Other to the God Who's Already There* (Colorado Springs: David C. Cook, 2010), Kindle edition, Kindle location 422.

15. Romans 2:4 NASB.

16. Hirsch, *Redeeming Sex*, Kindle location 2694.

17. Jayson Georges, *The 3D Gospel: Ministry in Guilt, Shame, and Fear Cultures* (Timē Press, 2017), Kindle edition, Kindle locations 124–474.

18. Lesslie Newbigin, *Foolishness to the Greeks: The Gospel and Western Culture* (Grand Rapids: Eerdmans, 1988), 4.

19. Hirsch and Nelson, *Reframation*, 102–103.

20. Sweet, *Nudge*, Kindle location 1657.

21. Guinness, *Fool's Talk*, 125.

22. David W. Augsburger, *Caring Enough to Hear and Be Heard* (Michigan: Baker, 1982), 12.

23. Andre Henry, "Culture Care and Music," YouTube, uploaded by Fuller Studios, https://www.youtube.com/watch?v=rcVxnHrkXMI.

24. N. T. Wright, *Surprised by Hope: Rethinking Heaven, the Resurrection, and the Mission of the Church* (San Francisco: Harper One, 2008), Kindle Edition, Kindle Location 4604.

25. Hunter, *The Celtic Way*, Kindle location 1542.

26. Matthew 3:2, 4:17, 10:7 NASB.

27. Revelation 21:5 NASB.

28. N. T. Wright often quotes this, alluding to a book title by David Lawrence, *Heaven: It's Not the End of the World! The Biblical Promise of a New Earth* (Scripture Union UK, 1995).

29. 2 Peter 3:10–13 reveals that when Jesus returns, he will judge the whole earth and everything that is not part of God's purposes or intentions will perish in a purifying fire, but 1 Corinthians 3:10–15 promises that the work built on the foundation of Jesus will remain.

30. Wright, *Surprised by Hope*, Kindle location 3085.

31. Dallas Willard, "*Your Place in This World*," *The Graduate's Bible* (Holman Christian Standard Bible) (Nashville: Holman Bible Publishers, 2004), 1120.

6: Mobilizing Disciplemaking People

1. Joshua Cooper Ramo, *The Age of the Unthinkable: Why the New World Disorder Constantly Surprises Us And What We Can Do About It* (New York: Little, Brown and Company 2009), Kindle edition, Kindle location 24.

2. Ibid, Kindle location 620.

3. Ibid, Kindle location 1308.

4. Susan Beaumont, *Inside the Large Congregation* (Maryland: Rowman & Littlefield Publishers, 2011), Kindle edition, Kindle location 510.

5. I'm borrowing from JR Woodward and Dan White, Jr., *The Church as Movement: Starting and Sustaining Missional-Incarnational Communities* (Illinois: IVP Books, 2016), 156–157; they draw from Joseph R. Myers, *The Search to Belong: Rethinking Intimacy, Community, and Small Groups* (Grand Rapids: Zondervan, 2003), 22–24. Edward T. Hall first developed the concept and coined the language of these groupings. See Edward T. Hall, *The Hidden Dimension* (New York: Anchor Books, 1990).

6. Raymond J. Bakke and Jim Hart, *The Urban Christian* (Illinois: IVP Academic, 1987), Kindle edition, Kindle location 603.

7. I've used this term already in this book by necessity because my missions sending organization, Christian Associates International, recently renamed itself Communitas International—to champion this powerful connection that comes when a faith community engages deeply in mission together.

8. Tom Rath, *StrengthsFinder 2.0* (Washington D.C.: Gallup Press, 2007).

9. Brian Sanders, *Underground Church*, Kindle location 1875.

7: The Power of Starting Small

1. George Leonard, *Mastery: The Keys to Success and Long-Term Fulfillment* (New York: Plume, 1992), Kindle edition, Kindle location 953.

2. Everett Rogers, *Diffusion of Innovations* (New York: Free Press, 2003).

3. Seth Godin, *Unleashing the Ideavirus* (Do You Zoom, 2000), 37. This book is available for free at https://seths.blog/wp-content/uploads/2008/12/2000Ideavirus.pdf.

4. Idea taken from Samuel Chand's book, *Cracking Your Church's Culture Code: Seven Keys to Unleashing Vision and Inspiration* (San Francisco: Jossey-Bass, 2010), where he argues that people respond to change, not based on the change, but based on how it is presented, who presents it, the clarity of the change, the rate of change, and how the change will affect them.

5. Alan Hirsch and Dave Ferguson, *On the Verge: A Journey Into the Apostolic Future of the Church* (Exponential Series) (Grand Rapids: Zondervan, 2011), Kindle edition, Kindle location 4698.

6. Rogers, *Diffusion of Innovations*, 205.

7. Eugene Peterson, *The Pastor: A Memoir* (San Francisco: HarperOne, 2012), 16.

8. "Minority rules: Scientists discover tipping point for the spread of ideas," *Science Daily*, July 26, 2011, https://www.sciencedaily.com/releases/2011/07/110725190044.htm.

9. Hugh Halter and Matt Smay, *The Tangible Kingdom: Creating Incarnational Community* (San Francisco: Jossey-Bass, 2008), Kindle edition, Kindle location 2504.

10. The term "third place" was coined by sociologist Ray Oldenburg to describe neutral places of common ground where people often develop friendships—such as pubs, gyms, salons, parks, schools, cafés, co-working spaces, art studios, etc. Sadly, for many Christians, church has become their third place, taking up every bit of their spare time and keeping them from missional engagement in the world around them. See Ray Oldenburg, *The Great Good Place* (Cambridge: DaCapo Press, 1989).

11. Michael Frost, *Exiles: Living Missionally in a Post-Christian Culture* (Michigan: Baker Books, 2006), Kindle edition, Kindle location 1131.

12. This concept of "just in time" learning is taken from the Japanese "Kanban" management system. See Hisham Sabry, "Six Rules For An Effective Kanban System," *Process*

Excellence Network, September 21, 2010, https://www.processexcellencenetwork. com/lean-six-sigma-business-performance/articles/what-is-kanban.

13. McNeal, *Missional Renaissance*, 10.

14. Rogers, *Diffusion of Innovations*, 434.

15. Dave Gibbons, *The Monkey and the Fish* (Grand Rapids: Zondervan, 2009), Kindle edition, Kindle location 690.

16. Halter and Smay, *The Tangible Kingdom*, Kindle location 3188.

17. For more information, or to purchase materials, go to www.thedynamicadventure. com.

8: Disruptive Disciplemaking

1. Robinson, *The Faith of the Unbeliever*, 27.

2. Halter and Smay, *The Tangible Kingdom*, Kindle location 2541.

3. Guinness, *Fool's Talk*, Kindle location 320.

4. Viktor Shklovsky, "Art as Technique," in *Russian Formalist Criticism: Four Essays*, ed. And trans. L. T. Lemon and M. J. Ries (Lincoln, NE: University of Nebraska Press, 1965), 3.

5. Scott Redd, "Saying it Anew: Strange-Making as a Pedagogical Device," in *For the World*, edited by J. S. Holcomb and G. Lucke (Phillipsburg, N.J.: Presbyterian and Reformed, 2015), 24.

6. Ibid, 26.

7. See, for example, Matthew 11:19, Luke 11:15, Mark 3:21, Mark 2:21–22.

8. Matthew 22:23–46.

9. I tend to believe she was infertile and that her husbands divorced her for not providing offspring.

10. Tara Beth Leach, *Emboldened: A Vision for Empowering Women in Ministry* (Downers Grove, IL: InterVarsity Press, 2017), 185.

11. See Genesis 28, Exodus 3, Numbers 22.

12. Gabe Lyons, *The Next Christians: Seven Ways You Can Live the Gospel and Restore the World* (New York: Doubleday, 2010), 214.

13. Chip Heath and Dan Heath, *Made to Stick: Why Some Ideas Survive and Others Die* (New York: Random House, 2007), Kindle edition, Kindle location, 249.

14. I recognize there are many perspectives on whether it is worth reclaiming and redeeming the term "Christian" in culture. Some may disagree with my choice to shun that

word publicly, and I respect your decision to try to reclaim it. We each have to contextualize our disciplemaking to the local setting we find ourselves in, and I think it's best to refrain from condemning others who operate in another one. Please know that by sharing my language choices I do not intend to minimize the convictions of others.

15. Matthew 10:16 (ESV).

16. Mark 12:16–17.

17. Alan Hirsch loves to use this phrase borrowed from the character Morpheus in the film, *The Matrix*.

18. John 13:1–17.

19. Robinson, *The Faith of the Unbeliever*, 137.

20. Lyons, *The Next Christians*, 67.

21. Michael Frost, *Keep Christianity Weird: Embracing the Discipline of Being Different* (Colorado Springs: NavPress, 2018), 47.

22. Victor Hugo, *Les Misérables*, English version, trans. Isabel F. Hapgood (Public Domain Books), Kindle edition, Kindle location 2222.

9: Enough of the Same Old Ship

1. James K. A. Smith (@james_ka_smith), Twitter, June 6, 2016; cited in Hirsch and Nelson, *Reframation*, Kindle location 95.

2. JR Rozko, "Transitioning from Traditional to Missional," *Fresh Expressions*, October 19, 2011, http://freshexpressionsus.org/2011/10/jr-rozko-transitioning-from-traditional-to-missional.

3. Andy Crouch, *Culture Making: Recovering Our Creative Calling* (Downers Grove, Illinois: InterVarsity Press, 2013), Kindle edition, Kindle location 312.

4. Ibid, Kindle location 944.

5. Danielle Strickland, *A Beautiful Mess: How God Re-Creates Our Lives* (Grand Rapids: Monarch Books, 2014), 15.

6. Rikke Friis Dam, "The MAYA Principle: Design for the Future, but Balance it with Your Users' Present," *Interaction Design Foundation*, March 2020, https://www.interaction-design.org/literature/article/design-for-the-future-but-balance-it-with-your-users-present.

7. Derek Thompson, "The Four-Letter Code to Selling Just About Anything," *The Atlantic*, January/February 2017, https://www.theatlantic.com/magazine/archive/2017/01/what-makes-things-cool/508772/.

8. Alan Hirsch and Michael Frost, *The Faith of Leap: Embracing a Theology of Risk, Adventure & Courage* (Michigan: Baker Books, 2011), Kindle edition, Kindle location 174.

9. See their journeys discussed in Francis Chan, *Letters to the Church* (Colorado Springs: David C. Cook, 2018); Gibbons, *The Monkey and the Fish*; Sanders, *Underground Church*; Daniel Mark Epstein, *Sister Aimee: The Life of Aimee Semple McPherson* (Boston: Mariner Book, 1994); Kate Hennessy, *Dorothy Day: The World Will Be Saved by Beauty: An Intimate Portrait of My Grandmother* (New York: Scribner, 2017).

10. Rozko, "Transitioning from Traditional to Missional".

11. Judges 7, Deuteronomy 7:6–7, Luke 6:12–16.

12. See, for example, "The Learning Pyramid," *Wikipedia*, https://en.wikipedia.org/wiki/Learning_pyramid.

13. For more see "Flipped Classroom," *Wikipedia*, https://en.wikipedia.org/wiki/Flipped_classroom.

14. Peterson, *The Pastor*, 22.

10: Getting the Body in Shape

1. Alan Hirsch, *5Q: Reactivating the Original Intelligence and Capacity of the Body of Christ* (Atlanta: 100 Movements Publishing, 2017).

2. Some argue there are only twelve apostles—or as many as fourteen if you include Paul and/or Matthias. But remember the New Testament refers to many other members of the early church as apostles, such as Barnabas (Acts 14:14), and Andronicus and Junia (Romans 16:7). The fact that twelve men were initially designated as apostles, or disciples, does not imply there are no more apostles in the church, any more than it implies there are no more disciples in the church.

3. Neil Cole, *Primal Fire: Reigniting the Church with the Five Gifts of Jesus* (Carol Stream: Tyndale Momentum, 2014), Kindle edition, Kindle location 325.

4. JR Woodward, *Creating a Missional Culture: Equipping the Church for the Sake of the World* (Downers Grove, IL: InterVarsity Press, 2012), Kindle edition, Kindle location 3589.

5. Hunter, *The Celtic Way of Evangelism*, Kindle location 317.

6. The MeToo Movement began in 2006 by Tarana Burke against sexual harassment and sexual abuse. In 2017, after the highly publicized sexual abuse allegations

against Harvey Weinstein, American actress Alyssa Milano posted on Twitter, "If all the women who have been sexually harassed or assaulted wrote 'Me too' as a status, we might give people a sense of the magnitude of the problem"—leading to an explosion of the hashtag #MeToo as women shared their own stories. Later, Emily Joy and Hannah Paasch began using the hashtag #ChurchToo to encourage women to share stories of sexual abuse in the church. The emphasis on sharing these personal stories publicly led to the removal of several prominent men from leadership positions.

7. Alan Hirsch and Tim Catchim, *The Permanent Revolution: Apostolic Imagination and Practice for the 21ˢᵗ Century Church* (San Francisco: Jossey-Bass, 2012), Kindle edition, Kindle location 2531.

8. I highly recommend 5Qcentral.com as a great resource where you can find diagnostic tests you can administer to leaders, as well as blogs and podcasts from other church leaders, and even coaching cohorts to help raise your APEST intelligence quotient, or "5Q."

9. This list is derived in part from Tim Catchim's work in *The Permanent Revolution* (co-authored with Alan Hirsch), as well as from content he delivered in a 5Q leadership cohort we co-coached.

10. Lesslie Newbigin, *Sign of the Kingdom* (Grand Rapids: Eerdmans, 1980) cited in Woodward, *Creating a Missional Culture*, 22.

11: A Church on the Move

1. "The Most Post-Christian Cities in America: 2019," *Barna Group*, 2019, https://www.barna.com/research/post-christian-cities-2019.

2. Ibid. To qualify as "post-Christian," individuals had to meet nine or more of the following sixteen criteria; "highly post-Christian" individuals meet thirteen or more of the factors: Do not believe in God; identify as atheist or agnostic; disagree that faith is important in their lives; have not prayed to God (in the last week); have never made a commitment to Jesus; disagree the Bible is accurate; have not donated money to a church (in the last year); have not attended a Christian church (in the last 6 months); agree that Jesus committed sins; do not feel a responsibility to "share their faith"; have not read the Bible (in the last week); have not volunteered at church (in the last week); have not attended Sunday school (in the last week); have not attended religious small group (in the last week); Bible engagement scale:

Low (have not read the Bible in the past week and disagree strongly or somewhat that the Bible is accurate); not born again.

3. Mike Breen, "How Celebrity, Consumerism, and Competition Are Killing the Church," *Verge*, www.vergenetwork.org/2013/09/03/how-celebrity-consumerism-competition-are-killing-the-church.

4. Great thanks to my friend, Jack Wolfe, for permitting me to borrow this metaphor of his and pass it off as my own so often!

5. Brad Brisco coined this term in his e-book, *Covocational Church Planting*, which can be downloaded from the North American Mission Board at https://www.namb.net/send-network-blog/ebook-covocational-church-planting.

6. Halter and Smay, *The Tangible Kingdom*, Kindle location 3207.

7. David Brooks, *The Second Mountain: The Quest for a Moral Life* (Random House, 2019), Kindle edition, Kindle location 202.

8. Neil Cole, "From Seating Capacity to Sending Capacity," *CMA Resources*, September 16, 2008, https://www.cmaresources.org/article/from-seating-capacity-to-sending-capacity.

9. Stuart Murray, *Post-Christendom: Church and Mission in a Strange New World*, 2nd ed. (Oregon: Cascade Books, 2018), 280.

10. Tyson and Grizzle, *A Creative Minority*, 20.

11. Ramo, *The Age of the Unthinkable*, Kindle location 2944.

12. Dreher, *The Benedict Option*, Kindle location 290.

13. Frost, *Surprise the World*, 22.

14. I first came across these questions in an article about twin sisters, Miki and Radha Agrawal—entrepreneurs who have started everything from a gluten-free, farm-to-table pizza restaurant to an underwear line. Read it at https://consciouscompanymedia.com/social-entrepreneurship/what-do-millennials-want-these-next-gen-capitalists-know.

15. Brad Brisco, *ReThink: 9 Paradigm Shifts for Activating the Church* (SEND Network, 2019), https://churchplantingatcbwc.files.wordpress.com/2018/10/rethink.pdf.

16. In Matthew 10:11 and Luke 10:6, Jesus sends his disciples into new cities with instructions to seek hospitality from a person of peace who will welcome and host them in his or her home. This initial contact person will facilitate their mission in the city. For more on the strategic benefits of this idea, check out the resource, "Person of Peace Tool" from 100 Movements, https://images.outreachapps.com/

wp-content/uploads/sites/528/2019/04/02105025/Person-of-Peace-tool-100M-1.pdf.

17. Tyson and Grizzle, *A Creative Minority*, 12.

18. Crouch, *Culture Making*, Kindle location 4165.

12: A Church of Perpetual Innovation

1. Steven Johnson, *Where Good Ideas Come From: The Natural History of Innovation* (New York: Riverhead Books, reprint edition, 2011), 22.

2. James Manyika, et. al, "Jobs lost, jobs gained: What the future of work will mean for jobs, skills, and wages," *McKinsey & Company*, November 28, 2017, https://www.mckinsey.com/featured-insights/future-of-work/jobs-lost-jobs-gained-what-the-future-of-work-will-mean-for-jobs-skills-and-wages.

3. Johannes Moenius, "One nasty side effect of coronavirus: Robots will take our jobs at an even faster rate," *Marketwatch.com*, April 13, 2020, https://www.marketwatch.com/story/one-side-effect-of-coronavirus-robots-will-take-our-jobs-at-an-even-faster-rate-2020-04-13.

4. Mark DeYmaz, *The Coming Revolution in Church Economics: Why Tithes and Offerings Are No Longer Enough, and What You Can Do about It* (Michigan: Baker Books, 2019), 60.

5. Jon Swaine, Douglas MacMillan, Michelle Boorstein, "Mormon Church has misled members on $100 billion tax-exempt investment fund, whistleblower alleges," *The Washington Post*, December 17, 2019, https://www.washingtonpost.com/investigations/mormon-church-has-misled-members-on-100-billion-tax-exempt-investment-fund-whistleblower-alleges/2019/12/16/e3619bd2-2004-11ea-86f3-3b5019d451db_story.html?arc404=true.

6. See for example Brad Brisco's free e-book, *Covocational Church Planting*, referenced in chapter eleven.

7. Frederick Buechner, *Wishful Thinking: A Seeker's ABC* (San Francisco: Harper One, 1973), 118.

8. James Davison Hunter, *To Change the World: The Irony, Tragedy, and Possibility of Christianity in the Late Modern World* (New York: Oxford, 2010), 24.

9. Hillary Hoffower, "The middle class is disappearing in countries around the world, and it means millennials won't have the same opportunities their

parents did," *Business Insider,* April, 12 2019, https://www.businessinsider.com/middle-class-disappearing-among-millennials-oecd-2019-4.

10. Ishaan Tharoor, "The Global Far Right is Here to Stay," *The Washington Post,* May 29, 2019, https://www.washingtonpost.com/world/2019/05/29/global-far-right-is-here-stay.

11. Daniel Pund, "I've Come to See the Conventional Sedan as an Anachronism," *Car and Driver,* January 26, 2019, https://www.caranddriver.com/features/columns/a26036377/sedans-out-of-style-column.

12. Gibbons and Brazil, *The Monkey and the Fish,* Kindle location 2426.

13. William H. Frey, "The US will become 'minority white' in 2045, US Census projects," January 1, 2019, https://www.brookings.edu/blog/the-avenue/2018/03/14/the-us-will-become-minority-white-in-2045-census-project/.

14. Robert Jones, "White Christian America ended in the 2010s," January 1, 2020, https://www.nbcnews.com/think/opinion/2010s-spelled-end-white-christian-america-ncna1106936.

15. Ibid.

16. Unknown, "Multiracial Congregations Have Nearly Doubled, But They Still Lag Behind the Makeup of Neighborhoods," June 20, 2018, https://www.baylor.edu/mediacommunications/news.php?action=story&story=199850.

17. Jemar Tisby, *The Color of Compromise: The Truth about the American Church's Complicity in Racism* (Grand Rapids: Zondervan, 2019), 24.

18. sendinstitute.org/manifesto.

19. Gibbons, *The Monkey and the Fish,* Kindle location 1697.

20. Guder, *Continuing Conversion of the Church,* 90.

21. Soong-Chan Rah, *The Next Evangelicalism: Freeing the Church from Western Cultural Captivity* (Illinois: Intervarsity Press, 2009).

22. Ibid, 14.

23. For great resources on this concept of modern-day exile I recommend: Walter Brueggemann, *Cadences of Home: Preaching Among Exiles* (Louisville: Westminster John Knox Press, 1997); Lee Beach, *The Church in Exile: Living in Hope After Christendom* (Illinois: IVP Academic, 2015); Michael Frost, *Exiles*; and Brian Zahnd, *Postcards from Babylon: The Church In American Exile* (Spello Press, 2019).

24. Tyson and Grizzle, *A Creative Minority,* Kindle location 156.

25. Michael Emerson and Christian Smith, *Divided by Faith: Evangelical Religion and the Problem of Race in America* (New York: Oxford University Press, 2000); Daniel Hill, *White Awake: An Honest Look at What It Means to Be White* (Downers Grove: InterVarsity Press, 2017); Jemar Tisby, *The Color of Compromise: The Truth About the American Church's Complicity in Racism* (Grand Rapids: Zondervan, 2019); Mosaix Global Network (www.mosaix.info).

Appendix 1: Asking Great Questions

1. Kevin Kelly, *The Inevitable: Understanding the 12 Technological Forces That Will Shape Our Future* (New York: Viking, 2016).

Reframation

Seeing God, People, and Mission Through Reenchanted Frames
Alan Hirsch & Mark Nelson

Reframation is a passionate manifesto, calling followers of Jesus to reframe and reenchant our worldview, enlarging our perception of God and gospel. It's an invitation to stretch our minds, expand our hearts, and awaken ourselves and those around us to the grand story of God.

Rooted in Scripture and drawing on poetry, literature, the arts, philosophy, and pop culture, *Reframation* refuses to settle for pious platitudes, and appeals to each and every one of us to experience and articulate the good news narrative in ways that resonate with the spiritual hunger and longings of those in our contemporary culture.

"A timely book for the current flattened, frightened world in which we live."
—WALTER BRUEGGEMANN

"Whimsically beautiful and stunningly thoughtful."**—LINDA BERGQUIST**

"Packed with eye-opening and potentially life-transforming insights."**—GREGORY A. BOYD**

"In a time when more people are turning away from the church, *Reframation* helps us rediscover the beauty of the gospel and artfully extend it to those who need it the most."**—GABE LYONS**

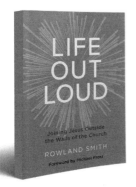

Life Out Loud

Joining Jesus Outside the Walls of the Church
Rowland Smith

As pastor and worship leader Rowland Smith started to join Jesus outside the walls of the church—in everyday places with everyday people—he discovered an exciting and dynamic faith.

Soundly framed by practical theology, personal reflection, and experiential knowledge, Rowland charts a course we can all walk, and invites you to discover an adventurous life with Jesus—your own life out loud.

"Read this if you want to better understand what it looks like to engage God's redemptive mission in the places you live, work, and play."**—BRAD BRISCO**

"Full of practical wisdom and missional insights." **—ALAN AND DEBRA HIRSCH**

"An invitation that reminded me of Jesus on every page."**—BRIAN SANDERS**

"A refreshing read that lightens the religious load."**—HUGH HALTER**

---

info@100Mpublishing.com I www.100Mpublishing.com

Ready or Not

Kingdom Innovation for a Brave New World
Doug Paul

There was a time when Christians pioneered the future—from business to church, mathematics to justice reform. Along the way, that redemptive, adaptive movement became change averse and frozen in time. But ready or not, the invitation is for kingdom leaders to reclaim their calling to innovate

Weaving together stories with surprising twists, studies with striking conclusions, and spellbinding cultural analysis, Doug Paul unlocks the five phases of kingdom innovation and reveals that whenever God's people have leaned into innovation, the world has shifted on its axis.

"Prepare to be surprised and delighted, and ultimately, roused to action." **—MARK BATTERSON**

"Provocative and compelling, this is an essential book to help us meet the moment."
—WILL MANCINI

"*Ready or Not* teaches us how to rediscover Christianity's core DNA of innovative creativity—and at just the right time." **—TOD BOLSINGER**

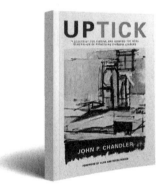

Uptick

A Blueprint for Finding and Forming the Next Generation of Pioneering Kingdom Leaders
John P. Chandler

In our rapidly changing world, churches need to shape people for adaptive leadership, and we especially need this formation to impact young leaders, who may go on to influence both church and society for decades to come.

Packed with insights and ideas, *Uptick* will enable you to become more effective in developing missionally minded, kingdom leaders, whatever your context.

"Essential reading for anyone seeking to invest in a fresh generation of leaders, and a valuable resource." **—JO SAXTON**

If you want to help the church live the future in the present, pick up this book."**—JR WOODWARD**

"Anyone looking to develop mature, kingdom-focused disciples needs to read this guide."
—DR. AMY L. SHERMAN

"*Uptick* is a veritable treasure trove, a manifesto of movemental wisdom and ought to become a classic, definitive text." **—ALAN AND DEBRA HIRSCH**

---

info@100Mpublishing.com | www.100Mpublishing.com